# Lawn Care

A Wiley Brand

# Lawn Care

2nd Edition

## by Suzanne DeJohn and National Gardening Association

## Lawn Care For Dummies®, 2nd Edition

Published by: **John Wiley & Sons, Inc.**, 111 River Street, Hoboken, NJ 07030-5774, www.wiley.com

For general information on our other products and services, please contact our Customer Care Department within the U.S. at 877-762-2974, outside the U.S. at 317-572-3993, or fax 317-572-4002. For technical support, please visit https://hub.wiley.com/community/support/dummies.

Wiley publishes in a variety of print and electronic formats and by print-on-demand. Some material included with standard print versions of this book may not be included in e-books or in print-on-demand. If this book refers to media that is not included in the version you purchased, you may download this material at http://booksupport.wiley.com. For more information about Wiley products, visit www.wiley.com.

Library of Congress Control Number is available from the publisher.

ISBN 978-1-394-36237-0 (pbk); ISBN 978-1-394-36239-4 (ebk); ISBN 978-1-394-36238-7 (ebk)

Printed and bound by CPI Group (UK) Ltd, Croydon, CR0 4YY

C9781394362370_101225

# Contents at a Glance

# Table of Contents

# Introduction

A lawn is so much more than just a patch of grass; it's the soft spot in your yard where you play with your kids, entertain friends and family, spread out the picnic blanket, and settle in for an evening of stargazing. For many of us, a well-kept lawn is a thing of beauty, a bright and healthy expanse that creates a welcoming stage for our homes and gardens. Grass lawns also buffer some of the harsher edges of the world we live in, trapping the dust kicked up by traffic, cooling the air, and cutting down on glare and reflected heat.

However, there's another reality to lawns. They can take a lot of work to maintain properly. How much time do you want to spend mowing, fertilizing, and watering your lawn? Time, after all, is a precious resource for many of us. Also, water — which most lawn grasses need in abundance — is also a precious resource. Gardeners who live in arid regions are rethinking the role of lawns in their landscapes. Should they reduce the size, or do they need a lawn at all? Increasingly, prolonged droughts, water shortages, and irrigation restrictions are becoming a way of life in many places. And even where rainfall is plentiful, conserving water and other natural resources are critical endeavors for those of us striving for more sustainable lifestyles.

The good news is that you can have a lush and healthy lawn while reducing your maintenance chores and minimizing its environmental impact.

## About This Book

What's the ideal lawn? It depends. You may want a smooth carpet for lawn games and backyard parties. The people next door may want just enough grass to keep the dust down when the kids play. The neighbor across the street may dream of a lawn filled with pollinator-friendly clover and wildflowers.

Because there's no universal ideal when it comes to lawns, you get to decide what you want. This book will help you figure that out. Once you do, you'll also find information on how to get your version of the ideal lawn and then determine how you can maintain it with a minimum amount of effort and resources. Growing a lawn is not about doing one big thing right. Rather, it's about doing many small things right.

You don't need to read this book from cover to cover — although you might find it a fascinating read and a good way to dig deeply into the subject. For most read-ers, it's helpful to seek out the information you need, right when you need it. That's why the book is organized into logical, self-contained chapters. You can jump to a section and get the necessary information without having read all the previous chapters. The very detailed index also lets you navigate to specific information.

# Foolish Assumptions

In writing this book, I assume a few things about you and your experience with lawns:

>> At some point in your life you've played on a lawn or walked barefoot on one and know firsthand the joy that brings.

>> You've noticed how a well-kept lawn, no matter the size, complements a house and other structures and creates an anchor in a landscape.

>> You likely fall into one of the following categories. You don't have a lawn, but you'd like to start one. You have a lawn and want to know how to make it look better. You have a lawn, and you'd like to streamline maintenance chores. You're curious about how you can make your lawn and landscape more eco-friendly.

>> You're looking for practical, easy-to-understand information that helps you accomplish your lawn goals.

# Icons Used in This Book

As you read through this book, you'll come across icons in the margin that point out particularly useful or important information:

**WARNING**

This icon alerts you to actions that may be dangerous to you, your plants, or the environment. Proceed with caution.

**TIP**

If there's a tidbit of particularly useful information or helpful advice, it's flagged with this icon.

**TECHNICAL STUFF**

This icon marks more in-depth information for readers who want to dig deeper into the subject matter.

**REMEMBER**

Remember icons call out information that is especially important to keep in mind.

## Beyond the Book

Proper watering is one of the most important aspects of caring for your lawn. Find step-by-step instructions for installing an automated, underground irrigation system that makes watering easy and helps conserve this precious resource in the bonus chapter at www.dummies.com/go/lawncarefd2e.

You can also check out the Cheat Sheet, which includes suggestions for creating a healthy and sustainable lawn and tips for calculating the approximate square footage of your lawn, as well as sources for lawn-related information and products. To find the Cheat Sheet for this book, visit www.dummies.com and type **Lawn Care For Dummies Cheat Sheet** in the Search field.

## Where to Go from Here

The information in this book is designed for easy access, so you can start about anywhere you want. If you're looking for inspiration on integrating a lawn into your landscape or are new to lawns and aren't sure what type of grass will grow best for you, head to Part 1. Go to Part 2 for the scoop on preparing your yard for planting and learning how to plant a new lawn. If you already have a lawn and need the lowdown on maintenance best practices, jump to Part 3. Part 4 is your go-to for help with tackling lawn problems. And if you're curious about specific ways to make your lawn and landscape more sustainable, head over to Part 5.

# 1
# Designing Your Perfect Lawn

Find out how to design a lawn to fit your needs by answering some important questions, such as how big a lawn do you need and want? How much time are you willing to spend caring for it? How can you plan a lawn so that it complements your home and landscape? Would lawn alternatives fit the bill for some areas?

Get the scoop on the grasses that make up lawns, including the types of turfgrasses that are the most suitable for your region.

Find out all about the nine lawn climates in the U.S., which one you live in, and the grasses that grow well in each one.

Get an in-depth look at soil, including how to determine what kind of soil you have and techniques for building healthy soil that will support a thriving lawn.

Chapter **1**

# Thinking about Design

Whether you're starting out with a new lawn installation, considering renovating an existing lawn, or pondering how a lawn fits into your landscape as a whole, you'll soon be making some important decisions.

Start by asking yourself, "What do I want my lawn to do for me?" You might, for example, want your lawn to be a welcoming place where you and your family can spend time outdoors, relaxing in the hammock, playing croquet, and firing up the grill for weekend barbeques. Perhaps you envision your lawn as an attractive setting for perennial gardens and other ornamental plantings. Or maybe your homeowners association has specific rules about the lawn on your property. (It's best to check with them first before you make major changes.)

The information in this chapter will help you understand your options so you can design the lawn that's right for you.

## Lawns, Defined

Simply put, a lawn is garden of grasses and other durable plants that together form a ground cover. This carpet of green offers an inviting, resilient surface that can withstand people walking and kids playing. That said, not everyone's interpretation of a lawn is the same. To some people, a lawn should be neatly manicured. To others, a lawn can be wilder and a little rougher around the edges.

Wherever you fit on that spectrum, a healthy, thriving lawn provides you with a host of benefits.

## Lawns: A look back

Grasses are some of the few plants that can withstand the repeated cutting back to near ground level (more on that in Chapter 3). The concept of lawns dates back centuries — even millennia — when grazing livestock kept land open by nibbling vegetation and prevented shrubs and other woody plants from taking over.

In medieval Europe, maintaining a perimeter of low-growing plants offered guards at castles and estates an unobstructed view of their surroundings so they could easily scan for threats. Later, settlers in North America cultivated open, treeless spaces around their houses as way to tame the wildness surrounding them.

It wasn't until the 1700s that landscape designers in England and France began promoting the idea that a well-kept lawn was a symbol of high social status and evidence that the property owners were of sufficient means to have time for recreational activities. Commoners, in contrast, had to use their land for sustenance — for growing vegetables, fruits, and herbs and for grazing their animals. Only the wealthy had the resources needed to maintain unproductive "lawns" (a term that originally referred to a natural open area in the woods), as well as the leisure time to enjoy them. Today, well-maintained, grass-covered yards are the norm, so much so that municipalities and homeowners associations — and sometimes neighbors — demand them. As you read on, keep in mind that highly manicured lawns are a relatively recent phenomenon!

## What lawns do for you

There are good reasons that most landscapes incorporate areas of mown grass around the house. Here are some of the benefits of lawns.

>> **Aesthetic:** A well-kept lawn acts as an inviting bridge between your home and landscape elements like patios and ornamental plantings. Green grass offers a backdrop for creative expression, such as flower beds and yard décor. Lawns help trap the road dust kicked up by vehicles, as well as wind-borne debris and pollen.

>> **Recreational:** Where but on a lawn can you play catch with your kids, set up a badminton game, or kick around a soccer ball? Grass is the perfect play surface — it's soft and forgiving, yet tough and durable. Family get-togethers, summer picnics, and neighborhood gatherings would be much less enjoyable if the yard was just a patch of dirt or filled with prickly weeds.

» **Environmental:** Like all green plants, lawn grasses absorb carbon dioxide from the air and give back fresh oxygen. In contrast to bare soil and paved surfaces, lawns slow the movement of water and allow rainwater to permeate the soil rather than running off into storm drains and overwhelming sewer systems. Grass plants have deep, fibrous root systems that help hold soil in place, decreasing the erosion of precious topsoil. A lawn maintained using sustainable, environmentally friendly techniques promotes a healthy soil ecosystem that, in turn, supports healthy plants. Replacing heat-absorbing pavement with lawns and landscape plants helps cool the air around your home, reducing the need for air conditioning.

» **Financial:** "Curb appeal" adds real value to your home. A well-maintained lawn and landscape can increase a property's value by 15 percent or more, while a bedraggled one may turn away potential buyers before they even get to the front door.

# Considering Sustainability

Now that we've sung the praises of lawns, let's look at the other side of the coin. Lawns that are manicured to perfection are significant consumers of limited resources, such as fertilizers and water. In addition, improper application and overuse of the insecticides, herbicides, and fungicides employed by many home-owners and lawn care companies can cause significant harm to the environment. Lawns will always have their place, but it's important to be practical about them and keep in mind the cost of the "perfect" lawn.

According to the National Wildlife Federation, lawns cover over 40 million acres of land in the United States, and they consume immense resources, including a mindboggling 9 billion gallons of water per day. In return, most lawns offer little in the way of food or habitat for birds, pollinators, and other wildlife. Creating a landscape that serves all life forms — human and wild — starts by envisioning your yard as part of the larger ecosystem. It doesn't require sacrificing your patch of green lawn! Instead, it invites you to consider how you define your ideal landscape.

TIP

As you design your lawn and landscape, consider including features that help counter the environmental challenges posed by expansive, manicured lawns. Learn more about these in Chapter 19, Chapter 22, and Chapter 23.

Here are some landscape options that support wildlife, conserve and protect water supplies, and/or require less maintenance than traditional lawns.

>> **Pollinator gardens:** The plight of pollinators continues to make headlines, with good reason. About one out of every three bites of the food we eat depends on pollinators, so protecting them is of utmost importance. Replacing some of your lawn with wildflowers, incorporating native plants in your landscape, and reducing your use of lawn chemicals are good places to start.

>> **Xeriscaping:** First coined in 1981 by the Denver Water Department, the term xeriscaping (pronounced ZARE-eh-scape-ing or ZEER-eh-scape-ing) refers to a style of landscaping that is focused on water conservation and reducing the need for irrigation while still maintaining an attractive landscape. Denver, Colorado, like many arid and semiarid areas of the western United States, doesn't receive enough natural rainfall to support lush lawns. Xeriscaping (also known as water-wise or dry landscape gardening) offers alternatives, such as replacing thirsty turfgrass and gardens with drought-tolerant plants — especially native plants that are well-adapted to the climate and support local wildlife. Some municipalities even offer rebates and other incentives for replacing lawns with less water-intensive landscape options.

>> **Rain gardens:** Located in naturally occurring or human-made low spots in your landscape, rain gardens collect water runoff so the soil can slowly absorb it and recharge the groundwater. As a bonus, you can plant your rain garden with water-tolerant native plants to provide food and habitat for pollinators and other wildlife.

>> **Low-mow and no-mow lawns:** Planting slow-growing dwarf grasses allows you to mow less often compared to traditional turfgrasses. The nonprofit Pollinator Partnership (https://pollinator.org) advocates for the planting of "bee lawns" made up of low-growing flowering ground covers, such as creeping thyme, that don't need mowing. Although many pollinating insects don't sting, if you're hesitant to plant bee-friendly plants in areas that get lots of foot traffic, choose out-of-the-way spots for this alternative.

>> **No Mow May:** The goal of this initiative, originally launched in the United Kingdom but now gaining traction in North America, is to pause mowing in May. This allows any flowers in your lawn to bloom so they can provide nectar to pollinators at a time when there may be few other plants in bloom.

>> **Meadowscaping, wildscaping, and "lazy lawns":** Transforming some of your lawn into a meadow, choosing plants to support wildlife, and allowing some of your lawn to go without regular fertilizing and irrigation are ways to reduce the resources needed to maintain a manicured lawn. Learn more about planting a wildflower meadow in Chapter 21.

# Deciding on Design

Although most yards share a few common elements, such as walkways and areas of lawn, your landscape is as unique as you are. You get to decide what features you want to incorporate and what atmosphere you want to create. It's time to look at how and where a lawn fits into your overall landscape plan.

## Determining the size

Lawns are usually one of the most labor-intensive parts of a landscape. You need to mow, water, fertilize, and more. It just makes sense to consider how much time you want to spend on your lawn — and what else you might want to do with some of that time, even if it's lounging in a hammock!

What activities do you realistically need lawn space for? By looking carefully at how people use lawns, water agencies in the West determine that many people only need about 600 to 800 square feet of grass. This is about the size of a standard three-car garage or pickleball court, and it's enough for a small play area and some lawn chairs. Now, if you want to play volleyball, badminton, or croquet, you need a little more lawn. A rectangle measuring 45 × 80 feet (3,600 square feet) is plenty.

The average size lot in the United States is about 14,000 square feet, or ⅓ acre. Subtracting the size of the average house (2,500 square feet) plus extra for driveway and paths, that leaves about 10,000 square feet of yard space. That's far more lawn than the average family will use! Knowing this opens the door to more interesting, environmentally friendly, and time-saving choices. Leaving an area of the yard in its natural state, if you're lucky to have such a spot, is the simplest place to start. For example, if part of your yard is naturally wooded, consider leaving it that way. Allowing an out-of-the-way section of your yard to become overgrown (as long as it's not with invasive plants) provides habitat for birds, pollinators, and other wildlife.

## Integrating lawns into your landscape plans

Even if your lot is a square or rectangle, your lawn doesn't have to be. Circular lawns, kidney-shaped lawns, and undulating swathes of lawn are usually more visually interesting. In addition, an irregularly shaped lawn can soften the effects of a square yard surrounded by a tall fence. Start by pondering these questions:

>> **Where will you put your lawn?** A backyard lawn makes sense because that's where the kids can play safely and where you can relax, and it offers refuge from street noise and neighbors. A well-maintained front lawn makes the face

of the house more pleasing and inviting, and it might even be mandated by your homeowners association or municipality. Whether you want lawn on the sides of your house depends on how you use those spaces and how accessible they are for mowing.

>> **What other plantings will you include?** The soft formality of a lawn offers an appealing contrast to areas planted with trees, shrubs, and flowers. Planting a vegetable garden? Choosing the sunniest spot for the best yields. What about some berry bushes to provide fruit for you or for wildlife? Consider some of the other landscape options mentioned earlier in this chapter, such as a wildflower planting or rain garden.

>> **Are you renovating or starting from scratch?** If you're starting with a well-established landscape that you're happy with, you may want to keep existing features in place and focus your efforts on renovating existing lawn areas. If you're starting from scratch, the sky's the limit!

Make a list of all the existing features in your landscape, such as patios, fences, arbors, walkways, and sheds. Then make a wish list of features you hope to add in the future. You'll want to keep all these in mind as you begin designing your lawn.

# Putting Pencil to Paper

Now it's time to put your ideas down on paper. This book doesn't have room for a complete lesson in landscaping, but sometimes simply putting some rough shapes on paper can really help you visualize what your lawn may look like.

## Drawing a landscape map

Here are the steps to drawing a landscape map.

1.  **Take a piece of graph paper and rough out a sketch of the house and yard, trying to keep it to scale (1 inch to 10 or 20 feet usually works).**

    You'll probably have to take a few measurements outdoors to get the dimensions of your house right. Mark the directions (north, south, east, west) on the map.

2.  **Sketch in the driveway as well as your garage, shed, patio, and so on.**

3.  **Add circles to note the locations of large trees and shrubs.**

4.  **Add the approximate locations of any flower beds and vegetable gardens, either existing ones or those you plan to install.**

    You don't need to get these exact; this sketch is just a starting point.

5. **Note where shade from buildings and large trees falls at different times of day and sketch this on the map.**

   Lawn grasses grow best in full sun to part shade. Areas in deep shade are best planted with shade-loving plants or used for other purposes.

6. **Mark any low-lying areas that stay wet for more than 24 hours after a heavy rain.**

   These would be good spots for a rain garden. If needed, you may be able to install drainage or regrade the slope to direct water away from areas you hope to plant in lawn. Learn more about drainage in Chapter 7.

7. **Note possible locations for the landscape features from your wish list.**

The open areas remaining in your sketch are likely spots for your lawn. Figure 1-1 shows a sample landscape map.

TIP

As you design the shape of your lawn, keep in mind all the maintenance chores. Awkward spaces and narrow strips, for example, can be difficult to mow and water properly.

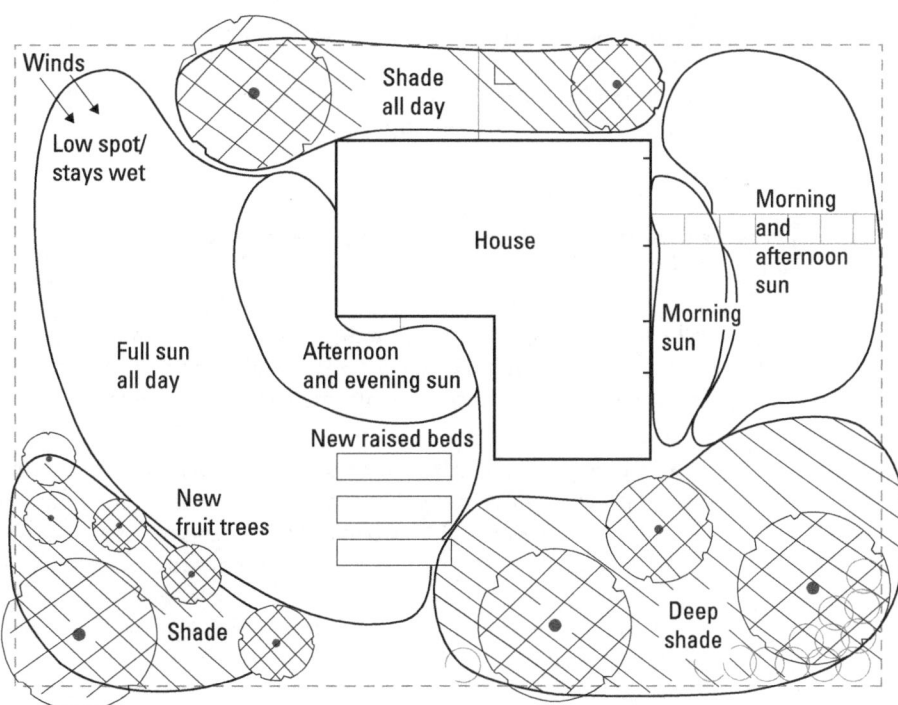

**FIGURE 1-1:** Example of a rough landscape map.

# Working with professional designers

If your landscape is large or has lots of elements, or if you're just unsure of where to start, you may want to get help from a professional. Although there's an upfront cost, getting professional advice can save you time, money, and aggravation in the long run, and, best of all, it can help ensure you get the lawn and landscape of your dreams.

A *landscape designer* can help you figure out the best layout for the various features in your yard. They can recommend the best spot for new gardens and other elements, offer plant suggestions, and generally help you envision how you to make the most of your yard. You can hire them simply to offer suggestions or to draw up as detailed a plan as you'd like. They may be able to offer recommendations for landscape contractors that build or install the landscape elements you decide on. Landscape designers aren't required to have any professional degree or license.

A *landscape architect* may be the right professional for you if you hope to install extensive hardscape elements, like patios and stone walls, and/or water features like ponds. A landscape architect has a university degree and a license from the state you live in. They generally work on large-scale residential, commercial, and municipal projects. If your yard poses big challenges, such as rocky outcrops or dramatically steep slopes, they have the know-how to help. You can meet with them for a simple consultation or hire them to draw up a complete landscape plan. Some landscape architects will also arrange for subcontractors to do landscape installations under their supervision.

# Designing a Low-Maintenance Lawn

One of the simplest ways to reduce the time and money needed to maintain your lawn is to make it smaller! In addition, you can incorporate some of the following design techniques to make your lawn easier to care for:

>> **Put in mowing strips.** These strips are usually several inches wide and encircle all or part of your lawn. Usually made of cement or wood, they sit at ground level and allow you to run the wheels of your lawn mower right up to the edge of the grass so that you don't have to come back and trim by hand later. Mowing strips also can prevent aggressive lawn grasses from growing out of bounds and becoming weeds in nearby planting areas.

>> **Use edgings.** Edgings are usually thinner and often less permanent than mowing strips. They are also less expensive and easier to install. Even though you can't run your mower wheels on top of them, edgings can help keep grasses in bounds and give your lawn a nice clean edge. They also can make the lawn easier to trim. Learn more about edgings in Chapter 8.

>> **Don't plant lawns in narrow or awkwardly shaped areas.** Narrow strips of grass like you usually see between street and sidewalks are hard to mow and almost impossible to water properly. Go with a ground cover or other lawn alternative (see Chapter 19) — that is, if your city or homeowners association lets you. Some cities and associations require grass in these narrow strips.

>> **Don't plant lawns on steep slopes.** Grass growing on a steep incline is dangerous to mow. Slopes are also hard to water; the water quickly runs off before the soil can absorb any of it.

>> **Don't plant lawns in heavily shaded areas.** Some grasses can grow in light shade, but most prefer full sun and will struggle in deep shade. Don't bother trying to grow grass under trees with dense foliage. In addition to the deep shade they cast, the trees' roots battle with the lawn for water and nutrients. And the trees almost always win.

>> **Keep a grass-free zone around trees and shrubs.** Remove grass and weeds in a 2- to 3-foot diameter circle at the base of trees and shrubs and apply a thin layer of organic mulch, such as bark chips, to help keep weeds at bay. (Keep the mulch a few inches away from the trunks to prevent rot, and never pile mulch against the trunks.) You'll reduce the time needed for string trimming and also reduce the chance of damaging the trunks with the mower or trimmer. Learn more about lawn trees in Chapter 20.

# Chapter **2**

# Lawn Climates, Big and Small

The climate in the area where you live determines which grasses are best adapted to making a lawn. Differences in how hot the weather gets in summer, how cold it gets in winter, and how much rain you get (and when you get it) not only determine which grasses will grow but also how you care for them.

This chapter describes factors that influence a region's climate and describes the nine lawn climates of the United States. Within each of these regions, it gets more localized, so this chapter also examines the small differences in climate that can occur in your neighborhood or even your yard. These small differences can change how you grow a lawn.

## Lawn Climates: The Big Picture

Since the mid-1800s, scientists around the world have been collecting and logging weather data, such as the averages and extremes of temperature and precipitation as well as other variables. They've also logged the intensity, frequency, and duration of weather events like hurricanes and droughts.

In contrast to *weather*, which describes current conditions or those that happen over a relatively short time (days or weeks), *climate* takes the long view. It takes the weather statistics collected over 30 years or more and uses them to describe the average conditions in a place. Scientists can also gather climate information by looking at ice cores, tree rings, and ocean sediments to get a sense of a region's climate long before there were instruments to measure it.

TECHNICAL
STUFF

Most areas of the United States and southern Canada fall into a climate category called *temperate*, where summers are warm and winters are cool to cold. Parts of Alaska, Canada, and high-elevation regions in the continental United States have *subarctic* climates, with short, mild summers and long, cold winters. Much of the southern third of the United States has a *subtropical* climate, with long, hot summers and mild winters. The southern tip of Florida and most of Hawaii have *tropical* climates, though there are mountaintops in Hawaii that are surprisingly cold and snowy.

Many factors influence climate, and knowing your climate's characteristics will help you determine what types of grasses will grow best and how to care for them. Factors that influence climate include the following:

>> Heat — intensity and duration

>> Light — intensity and duration

>> Humidity — a measure of the quantity of water vapor that is suspended within the air

>> Wind

>> Lowest winter temperatures

>> Rainfall — when and how much

>> Proximity to large bodies of water

>> Elevation

In general, cool-season grasses are best adapted to temperate and subarctic climates, while warm-season grasses grow best in subtropical and tropical climates. However, because of the variability in the climates across the United States, turf experts have divided the country into nine *lawn climates.*

# Lawn Climates of the United States

Figure 2-1 shows the nine lawn regions in United States. In the regional break-downs that follow, you'll see mention of the types of lawn grasses that do particularly well in each region. This information is meant as a general guide. Keep in mind that variations within a region may make one lawn grass a better choice than another.

**TIP**

It's wise to get more specific information from local experts or your local cooperative extension office. You can find a link to your state extension office at `https://extension.org/find-cooperative-extension-in-your-state`.

In some regions, the climate simply isn't conducive to growing lawn grasses. In hot, dry climates, for example, lawns require frequent irrigation just to stay alive, much less thrive, so consider waterwise alternatives to lawns, such as xeriscaping (landscaping that uses drought-resistant plants). Find more information on lawn alternatives in Chapter 19.

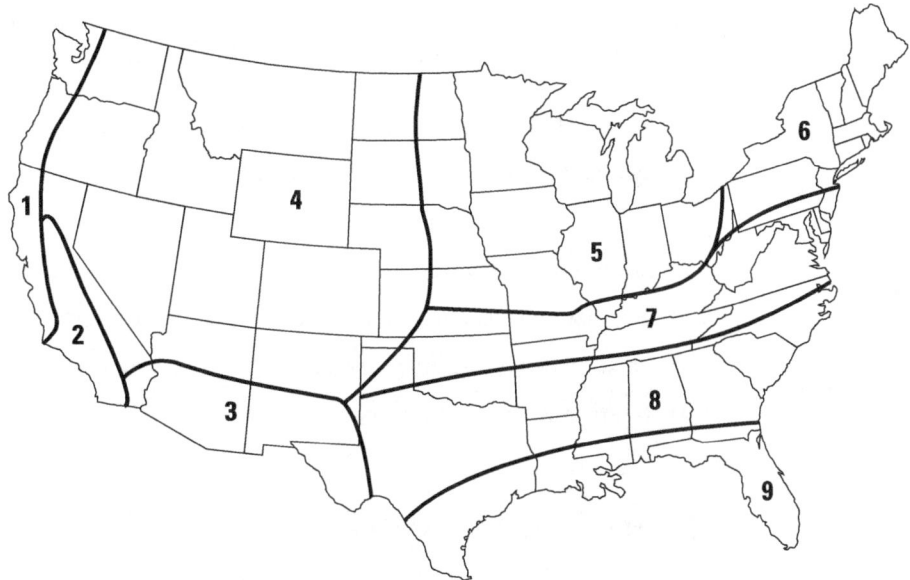

**FIGURE 2-1:**
Lawn climates of the United States.

The following sections are descriptions of each region, the types of grasses that grow best, and a summary of the best times to plant and fertilize in that region. (Find details on grass types in Chapters 4 and 5 and on planting grasses in Chapters 8 through 10; see Chapter 12 for fertilizing information.)

# Zone 1: Coastal West

Rain is generally plentiful in the Coastal West, although in the southern parts of the area it rains mostly in winter. The summers are dry. Cool-season grasses are best adapted to this region. Soils are often acidic.

> » **Sow cool-season grasses:** March to April and September to October
>
> » **Lay cool-season sod:** March to October
>
> » **Fertilize:** April to June and September to November or December

# Zone 2: Western transitional zone

Summers are generally long, dry, and warm in the Western transitional zone, which includes central and southern California. The winters are mild. You can grow either warm-season or cool-season grasses in this zone.

Warm-season grasses, such as bermudagrass, are preferable where water supplies are short. You can overseed warm-season grasses with cool-season grasses like tall fescue or ryegrass to keep lawns green in winter.

> » **Sow cool-season grasses:** March to April and September to October
>
> » **Lay cool-season sod:** February to November
>
> » **Plant warm-season grasses:** May to September
>
> » **Lay warm-season sod:** March to October (year-round in some areas)
>
> » **Fertilize cool-season grasses:** February to May and September to November
>
> » **Fertilize warm-season grasses:** Late March to September
>
> » **Overseed:** October to November

# Zone 3: Arid Southwest

The Arid Southwest zone boasts long, hot summers and relatively dry weather year-round. It includes the low-elevation desert climates of California, Arizona, and New Mexico. Warm-season grasses, such as hybrid bermudagrass and zoysiagrass, are your best choices. You can overseed warm-season grasses with annual or perennial ryegrass to keep them green year-round. Plant tall fescue, as well as natives like buffalograss, in higher elevation areas. Soils are generally alkaline.

>> **Sow cool-season grasses (higher elevations only):** April to May and September to October

>> **Plant cool-season sod (higher elevations only):** April to October

>> **Sow warm-season seed:** April to May

>> **Plant warm-season sod:** March to October (year-round in some areas)

>> **Fertilize cool-season grasses:** September to March for overseeded lawns

>> **Fertilize warm-season lawns:** March to November

>> **Overseed:** October to November

# Zone 4: Cold and dry areas of the West

Zone 4 encompasses the cold and dry areas of the West, including high-elevation areas and the Great Plains. These climates are particularly tough, with wide fluctuations in temperature and rainfall and frequent high winds. Tough, native grasses such as buffalograss, crested wheatgrass, and blue grama are often ideal choices. You can grow warm-season grasses in some southern areas. Otherwise, cool-season grasses such as tall fescue and Kentucky bluegrass are preferable.

>> **Sow cool-season seed:** March to April and August to September

>> **Plant cool-season sod:** March to October (year-round in some southern areas)

>> **Seed and sod warm-season grasses:** May to July

>> **Fertilize cool-season grasses:** April to June and September to November

>> **Fertilize warm-season grasses:** May to August

# Zone 5: Midwest

The Midwest has cold, snowy winters and warm, humid summers with frequent rainfall. Cool-season grasses are widely planted, although you can find some hardier zoysiagrass lawns in southern areas.

>> **Sow cool-season grasses:** April to May and August to September

>> **Plant cool-season sod:** April to October

- **Seed and sod warm-season grasses:** May to July
- **Fertilize cool-season grasses:** April to June and September to November
- **Fertilize warm-season grasses:** May to August

# Zone 6: Northeast

Cold, snowy winters; warm, humid summers with frequent rain; and acidic soils are the norm in the Northeast. Cool-season grasses predominate. You can grow some hardier warm-season grasses in southern coastal areas.

- **Sow cool-season grasses:** April to May and August to September
- **Plant cool-season sod:** April to October
- **Seed and sod warm-season grasses:** May to July
- **Fertilize cool-season grasses:** April to June and September to October
- **Fertilize warm-season grasses:** May to August

# Zone 7: Eastern transitional zone

Summers are generally warm and humid in the Eastern transitional zone. The winters are mild but can be cold, especially at higher elevations. You can grow either warm-season or cool-season grasses, but local adaptation is very important because neither is perfectly suited. Overseeding warm-season grasses with cool-season grasses in fall keeps lawns green year-round.

- **Sow cool-season grasses:** March to May and September to October
- **Plant cool-season sod:** March to October
- **Seed and sod warm-season grasses:** April to August
- **Fertilize cool-season grasses:** March to June and September to November
- **Fertilize warm-season grasses:** April to August

# Zone 8: Central Southeast

The Central Southeast zone is warm and humid, and most of the zone gets plenty of rain. (The middle to western part of Texas tends to be drier.) Soils are often acidic. Warm-season grasses such as bermudagrass, zoysiagrass, St. Augustinegrass, and centipedegrass are well-suited. Plant tall fescue in cooler, high-elevation areas. You also can use cool-season grasses to overseed warm-season grasses to keep lawns green throughout winter.

>> **Sow cool-season grasses:** September to October

>> **Plant cool-season sod:** Year-round

>> **Seed warm-season grasses:** April to August

>> **Plant warm-season sod:** April to September

>> **Fertilize cool-season grasses:** March to May and September to November

>> **Fertilize warm-season grasses:** March to late September

## Zone 9: Gulf Coast, Florida, and Hawaii

Warm, humid, and wet best describes Zone 9. You get rain, rain, and more rain — diseases can run wild. Warm-season grasses are the only grasses suited for this area. Good choices include bermudagrass, bahiagrass, centipedegrass, zoysiagrass, and St. Augustinegrass.

>> **Sow warm-season seed:** April to August

>> **Plant warm-season sod:** Year-round

>> **Fertilize warm-season grasses:** March to November and year-round in Hawaii and southern Florida

# Zeroing in on Microclimates

There may be small areas around your landscape that experience different conditions — warmer, cooler, drier, shadier — than the rest of your yard, and these differences can influence the type of grass you choose to grow and how you care for it. These small variations from the overall climates of your yard are called *microclimates.* Microclimates usually occur because of the presence of some large object — your house, an expanse of pavement, or a body of water.

TIP

Take a walk around your house at various times of the day and you'll understand the concept. For example, in the morning, the east side of your house might be sunny and warm. After noon, the east side probably gets shadier and the west side gets sunnier and hotter. The north side of your house may be shady and cool all day, while the south side may stay sunny and warm from dawn to dusk. Each area has its own little microclimate that changes, not only as the sun moves from east to west during the day, but also as the sun moves from south to north from winter to summer.

Large expanses of asphalt soak up heat during the day and release it at night. Large bodies of water, such as lakes, heat up and cool down more slowly than surrounding air, keeping temperatures more moderate than areas further away. A light-colored, south-facing wall or fence reflects sunlight back onto the plants in front of it.

TIP

These variations in microclimates explain why it's usually a good idea to use a mixture or blend of different grasses when you plant a lawn with cool-season grasses. You can find out more about mixtures and blends in Chapter 3. For example, if your yard has some sunny spots and some shady spots, you may choose to plant a mixture of Kentucky bluegrasses and fescues. The Kentucky bluegrasses do great in the sunnier areas but can thin out in the shade. The more shade-tolerant fescues can fill in the thin spots. (Warm-season grasses vary so much in appearance, such as color and width of leaf blade, that they are rarely planted as mixes.)

Here are some microclimates you might find around your home and how they can affect the grass you plant and how you care for it.

WARNING

>> **Shade:** Not getting enough sunlight (less than four hours a day) really wreaks havoc on turfgrasses. The lawn starts to thin out, is prone to insects and disease, and just doesn't grow well. Your house, other buildings, and some types of fences can create shade. Trees can be densely shaded underneath; in some cases, you can prune lower branches or thin the crown to let more sunlight reach the ground. Certain grasses, including fine fescue and St. Augustinegrass, are more tolerant of shade than others. You can even find some varieties of specific grasses that are somewhat more tolerant of shade. (Find out more in Chapters 4 and 5.) Cultural techniques that minimize stress on the plants can help grass grow in shade, such as mowing higher, fertilizing less, and keeping people from walking on it. Better yet, rather than trying to force grass to grow in the shade, consider alternatives, such as planting shade-loving ground covers or applying mulch. Find more ideas for lawn alternatives in Chapter 19.

>> **Sun:** Intense sunlight reflected from the side of your house or a light-colored wall can cause a nearby lawn to dry out faster. If you don't compensate and apply more water to those areas, the grass gradually declines and is vulnerable to weeds and insect invasion.

>> **Heat:** Warmth stored in pavement, such as driveways, patios, and walkways, radiates out into nearby lawn areas. These parts of the lawn are quick to dry out and may be more subject to certain pest problems.

>> **Slope:** Slopes — especially south-facing ones — dry out faster than other areas of a lawn. The water drains away faster and so these areas need more frequent watering than flat spots. Another option is to replant with rugged perennials that will prevent erosion and don't require mowing.

>> **Soil:** Soil type also may vary around the house and landscape. For example, sandy soils drain water quickly and need more frequent irrigation than clay soils. Sandy soils also don't retain nutrients as well as clay soils. See Chapter 6 for more help understanding soils.

# Chapter **3**

# Discovering Lawn Grasses

There are about a dozen species of grass commonly used for lawns, and this represents just a tiny fraction of the more than 12,000 species that make up this diverse group of plants. In addition to making yards beautiful, grasses also feed us. Three species of grasses (wheat, corn, and rice) provide more than half of the total plant calories consumed by humans across the globe.

In the United States, vast swaths of the country's midsection were once covered with prairie grasses. These remarkable plants thrived in part because they were able to withstand repeatedly munching by buffalo and other grazing herbivores. This offers a clue as to why grasses can tolerate the "grazing" people do by mowing the lawn every week.

This chapter explains how grasses grow and uncovers the characteristics of different types of grasses.

# How Grasses Grow

Imagine if you took a mower to your perennial gardens or vegetable beds every week and repeatedly chopped down the plants to a few inches above the soil. The plants would certainly struggle, and they might not survive at all. Yet this is what we do to our lawns!

Grasses are unusual among plants because their growth points (see Figure 3-1) are located at the base of the leaf blades (intercalary meristems) rather than at the top of the plant (apical meristems). That's why they can tolerate repeated mowing and continue to produce new growth.

Apical meristem

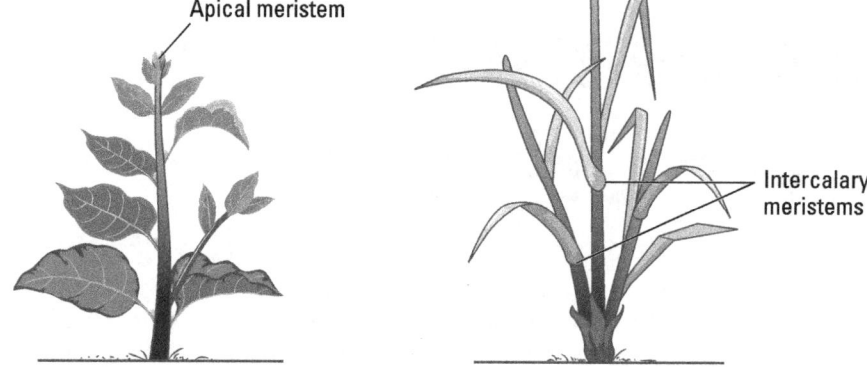

Intercalary meristems

**FIGURE 3-1:**
Most plants produce new growth at their tops; grasses produce new growth at nodes along their stems.

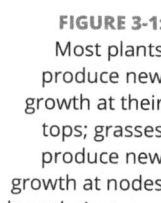

There are both annual and perennial types of grasses. An annual plant completes its life cycle, from germination to the production of seeds, within one growing season, and then dies. A perennial plant lives for more than two years. (A biennial plant completes its life cycle in two years; there are no biennial grass species.)

# Grasses Used in Lawns

Few plants other than grasses can grow so close together and create what you want for a lawn. Even grasses require intense care in order to become a primo lawn. You need to mow, water, and fertilize, at the very least.

The dozen or so grass species commonly used in lawns vary in several important ways, including the following:

>> Tolerance to cold and heat

>> Pattern of growth

>> Adaptability to differing light levels (sun, shade)

>> Amount and frequency of watering they need

>> Optimal mowing height

>> Fertilizer requirements

>> Tolerance to foot traffic

## Cool-season versus warm-season grasses

**TIP**

One of the biggest factors in choosing a type of grass for your lawn is its adaptability to cold and heat. Lawn grasses can be divided into two types: cool-season and warm-season. Plant the wrong kind, and your lawn will struggle, if it survives at all.

Generally, cool-season grasses are best suited for moist, northern climates, where summers, although warm, are relatively short, and winters are cold. Warm-season grasses are the grasses of southern climates, where summers are long and hot (consistently warmer than 85 degrees Fahrenheit), and winters are relatively mild. Learn more about lawn climates in Chapter 2. Cool-season grasses are covered in Chapter 4, and warm-season grasses are covered in Chapter 5.

## Patterns of growth

There are two basic growth patterns of lawn grasses: bunching and spreading (see Figure 3-2). The growth pattern affects grasses' appearance and how quickly they spread into bare areas.

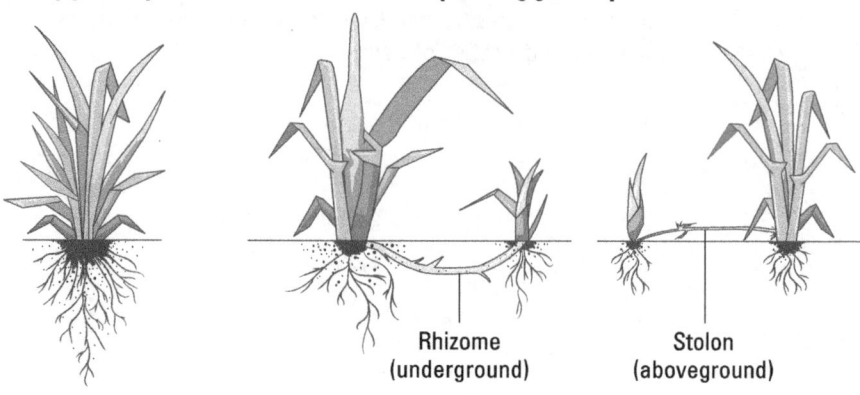

**Bunching growth pattern**  **Spreading growth patterns**

Rhizome
(underground)

Stolon
(aboveground)

FIGURE 3-2:
Bunching grasses
form clumps.
Spreading
grasses creep
along the ground
via horizontal
stems called
rhizomes
(underground)
or stolons
(aboveground).

## Bunching grasses

Bunching grasses grow in clumps and spread very slowly by tillers, which are stems that grow vertically from the base of the plant. Common bunch-type grasses include perennial ryegrass and tall fescue. Lawns planted solely with bunching grasses can look patchy over time because the plants are slow to fill in bare spots.

If you've ever admired ornamental grasses in a perennial bed, chances are good that you were looking at a bunching grass. Fountain grasses, for example, produce tall clumps with gracefully arching stems. Blue fescue forms tidy mounds of silvery blue foliage. Feather reed grass grows in narrow, upright clumps.

## Spreading grasses

Spreading type grasses produce stems that grow horizontally either underground (called rhizomes) or aboveground (called stolons). At varying intervals along these horizontal stems, the plants send out new shoots and roots. This means that spreading grasses can fill in bare or damaged areas much more quickly than bunching grasses. Spreading grasses include bermudagrass, buffalograss, Kentucky bluegrass, St. Augustinegrass, and zoysiagrass.

# Grass seed mixes

Grass seed is often sold as a combination of different types of grass to take advantage of each one's strengths and minimize its drawbacks. When choosing mixes, be sure they are well-suited to your region and climate (see Chapter 2 to determine your lawn climate).

# WHAT'S IN A NAME?

Common names can be confusing. For example, the name loosestrife might be interpreted to mean yellow loosestrife (*Lysimachia punctata*), a popular garden perennial, or purple loosestrife (*Lythrum salicaria*), a noxious, invasive weed. Botanists have a two-part system of plant naming — genus and species — which helps eliminate confusion. The first part of the plant name is the genus, and it represents a group of closely related plants. The next name identifies the species; it refers to a specific plant within the genus.

Sometimes you see a third name, which identifies a variety or *cultivar* (short for *cultivated variety*). Varieties are plants that have unique features that make them slightly different from the species. Some of them are naturally occurring, but often they have been developed by plant breeders to have certain desirable characteristics. For example, "Bonsai" is a dwarf cultivar of tall fescue. Turf specialists are continually working to develop cultivars that offer improvements over existing ones through plant breeding and field trials.

TECHNICAL
STUFF

Grass seed (and sometimes grass sold as sod) is described using these terms:

>> **Straights** are made up of just one type of grass or just one variety (or cultivar). Warm-season grasses, such as bermudagrass and St. Augustinegrass, are usually sold this way.

>> **Blends** are combinations of several (usually two to four) different varieties of one type of grass. Cool-season grasses, especially tall fescues, are often sold this way. An example of a blend is a package of seed or sod that contains 30 percent 'Virtue' tall fescue, 30 percent 'Monarch' tall fescue, and 40 percent 'Duster' tall fescue.

>> **Mixtures** are combinations of different types of grasses. For example, Kentucky bluegrass commonly gets mixed with some fine fescue and perennial ryegrass.

Usually, a mixture or blend of grasses results in a stronger, more versatile lawn. That's because different areas of your yard likely vary from other areas, sometimes in small ways, sometimes in big ways. For example, some areas are sunny, some are shady. You probably have some wet spots and some dry spots. By planting a mix or blend of grasses, you ensure that the lawn grows well under all the different conditions and looks good over your entire yard.

For example, Kentucky bluegrass creates a beautiful carpet of green in full-sun areas but struggles in shade. Fine fescues do better in shade but don't stand up well to foot traffic. Tall fescue stands up better to foot traffic but has a relatively coarse texture. A mixture of these will provide their combined benefits. When you look at the lawn, you can't tell what's growing where; you just see uniform turf.

TIP

Improved disease resistance is another good reason to plant mixtures or blends. If a disease wipes out one variety in a blend of tall fescues, another resistant variety picks up the slack and takes over — and you probably won't even notice. If the lawn had been made up of just the one variety, you might have lost the whole lawn.

There are general grass seed mixes as well as those labeled for specific lawn conditions. The label on the box or bag will give you the percentages of each type of seed in the mixture. (See Chapter 8 for more information on grass seed labels.)

## Conservation mixes

Conservation mixes, which are affordable mixtures that include a variety of grass types, are designed to suit a wide range of soil types and environmental conditions. They grow quickly and reliably and are valued for their ability to rapidly cover bare soil. Some conservation mixes include wildflowers or clover and are specifically designed for erosion control, soil stabilization, and wildlife habitat creation.

## Green-up mixes

WARNING

These blends promise a fast green-up, and they deliver! The problem is that they usually contain lots of annual ryegrass, which only lasts for one growing season. Annual ryegrass is often included in seed blends because it germinates quickly and acts as a nurse crop to help the perennial grasses take hold. However, if there's too much annual ryegrass in the mix, you'll get a brown lawn at the end of the year. (Annual ryegrass is also used to overseed lawns in the south to keep them green all winter.)

## Contractor's and landscaper's mixes

These affordable blends usually contain lots of annual ryegrass (see the preceding section). They establish quickly to transform bare soil into green lawn after new construction or landscaping renovations, but they don't always contain the best seed choices for a high-quality, long-lasting lawn.

## Shade mixes

Try to grow a sun-loving grass in a shady spot and you'll get weak growth that is prone to disease problems. Although no grass varieties will thrive in deep shade, some tolerate light to medium shade. Shade mixes contain a blend of these relatively shade-tolerant species, usually including fine fescues.

## Drought-resistant mixes

Some grasses, such as buffalograss, are native to regions that regularly experience dry spells and are therefore naturally better adapted to drought. In addition, plant breeders continually introduce new, more drought-tolerant varieties of turfgrass. Look for mixes that include varieties approved by the Turfgrass Water Conservation Alliance (www.tgwca.org). TWCA-qualified varieties meet or exceed the standard for drought tolerance at all locations across at least two years of trialing.

## Single-species grass blends

Most lawns in regions that favor warm-season grasses are planted with a single species; however, seed blends may contain multiple varieties of that species. For example, a bermudagrass mix might contain multiple varieties of bermudagrass that have different strengths — some that are slightly more cold hardy, for example, and others that recover more quickly from wear and tear.

## Erosion control mixes

Often suggested for hillsides that are prone to erosion as well as other hard-to-mow areas, these may include a variety of grasses, clover, and low-growing flowers that establish quickly. They can be left unmowed and allowed to go to seed for a natural appearance, or they can be mowed occasionally for a tidier appearance.

## The benefits of clover in seed mixes

TIP

Including clovers in your lawn confers several benefits — and not just the luck you'll get from finding a four-leaf one. Clovers are hardy and resistant to pests and diseases, and they thrive in full sun to medium shade. Best of all, they also reduce the need for synthetic nitrogen fertilizers. Like all legumes, clovers form a mutually beneficial relationship with soil bacteria, allowing them to "fix" nitrogen — that is, to convert nitrogen in the air into a form that plants can use. That nitrogen helps feed nearby grasses.

Clovers' nectar-rich blooms attract pollinators like butterflies and bees, adding biodiversity to your landscape. That said, if imagining your backyard barbecue or picnic area abuzz with honeybees feels less than ideal, you have a few options. There are new varieties of white clover (sometimes called mini or micro clovers) that are lower growing, with smaller leaves and fewer flowers, making them particularly well-suited for lawns. Another option is to relegate clover to less-used areas of your lawn.

If you decide that a lawn isn't the best choice for your yard, or if you'd like to convert part of your lawn to something other than grass, then you have plenty of alternatives. Check out some of them in Chapter 19.

# Chapter **4**

# Cool-Season Grasses

L awn grasses are broken into two categories: cool-season and warm-season. If you plant the wrong kind, your lawn will struggle, if it survives at all. This chapter is all about cool-season grasses. (For information about warm-season grasses, read Chapter 5. If you're unsure of the type of grass for your region, Chapter 2 covers lawn climates of the United States and which category of grasses grow best in each.)

## Where the Cool Grasses Grow

Generally, cool-season grasses are best suited for moist, northern climates, where summers, although warm, are relatively short, and winters are cold. Such grasses also do well in high elevations with adequate rainfall and coastal areas where temperatures are moderate — that is, temperatures don't stay above 90 degrees for long periods.

Cool-season grasses grow actively in the cool weather of spring and fall at temperatures averaging 60 degrees Fahrenheit to 75 degrees Fahrenheit. As summers get warmer, cool-season grasses grow slower and are subject to more disease problems. They may turn brownish and go completely dormant when the weather is dry and hot for extended periods. Proper watering helps keep cool-season grasses green throughout the summer season. (See Chapter 11 for information on watering lawns.)

**WARNING**

In hot-summer areas where water restrictions are common, you may have to get used to a brown lawn for a month or two. Usually, fall rains will bring the dormant grasses back to lush, green life again. However, if a brown summer lawn is not your idea of a good lawn, then warm-season grasses might be a better choice. Note that cool-season grasses won't survive extended periods of extreme heat and drought; warm-season grasses are a better choice for regions that experience these conditions. (See Chapter 5 for details on warm-season grasses.)

If you live in a transitional zone between cool- and warm-season climates (where the ground doesn't freeze in winter), cool-season grasses stay green all winter and might be a good choice. But, in such areas, you should talk to knowledgeable staff at your neighborhood nursery or contact your local cooperative extension office about the most appropriate grasses. You can find a link to your state cooperative extension office at `https://extension.org/find-cooperative-extension-in-your-state`.

**TIP**

In southern climates, you can use cool-season grasses to green up winter lawns by overseeding. In the fall, evenly spread cool-season grass seed, such as annual or perennial ryegrass, over the lawn. When the grass germinates and grows, you get a temporary green cover throughout the winter. For instructions on how to overseed warm-season grasses with cool-season grasses, see Chapter 14.

## Discovering the Cool-Season Grasses

Common cool-season grasses include Kentucky bluegrass, fescues, and ryegrass. Of those, Kentucky bluegrass has been the most-planted lawn for years. However, newer varieties of tall fescue are gaining ground; they offer improvements like finer texture compared to older varieties while maintaining the benefits tall fescue is known for, such as excellent vigor and resistance to harsh conditions, including drought and heat.

The following sections describe the most common cool-season grasses. Each entry includes some of the grasses' attributes. Keep the following in mind:

>> Some of the drawbacks listed, such as tendency to develop thatch, can be addressed by maintaining healthy soil, aerating, and other maintenance techniques (see Chapters 6 and 11 through 14).

>> Most cool-season grasses are sold in mixtures or blends (see Chapter 3) to take advantage of the different grasses' benefits and minimize their drawbacks.

**TECHNICAL STUFF**

>> Varieties differ in how well-suited they are to different regions, and new varieties are continuously being introduced. Check with your cooperative extension office to find the best varieties for your area.

>> Some grass varieties are described as containing *endophytes*. The seed is "infected" with these beneficial fungi that help the grass repel pests and diseases. For best results, plant when the seed is fresh.

## Kentucky bluegrass

Kentucky bluegrass (*Poa pratensis*), by far the most popular type of bluegrass for lawns, gets its name from its rich, blue-green color and from the origin of some of the early commercial grass seed. The grass is medium- to fine-textured with canoe-shaped blade tips. You can find many varieties of Kentucky bluegrass available in seed or sod, and most types have been hybridized to optimize hardiness. As a standalone lawn, however, Kentucky bluegrass rates at moderate wear only — that is, it can be slow to recover from the wear-and-tear of a heavily used lawn.

Kentucky bluegrass mixes well with fescues and perennial ryegrasses, which provide better diversity and help to offset the bluegrass's weaknesses in shade, drought tolerance, and wearability. Kentucky bluegrass does well in all but the hot-summer climates of the South and Southwest and the extreme climate of the Plains. The northeastern and northwestern United States, Canada, and the mountain and cool areas of the South are fine for it. Kentucky bluegrass generally has high tolerance to cold temperatures, and many varieties resist diseases such as leaf spot, striped smut, rust, red thread, and, to a lesser degree, the patch diseases. (See Chapter 17 for more information on lawn diseases.)

Kentucky bluegrass has a relatively shallow root system and needs ample water, or it'll go dormant in dry, warm weather. Where dry summers are the rule (as in most of California), Kentucky bluegrass is losing favor to tall fescues, which respond better after periods of drought.

Always go for named varieties when selecting Kentucky bluegrass. The myriad choices include varieties with improved disease resistance, better shade tolerance, greater hardiness, and local adaptation. Annual bluegrass (*Poa annua*) is a weed in many lawns. For information on this grass, see Chapter 15. Rough-stalked bluegrass (*Poa trivialis*) is sometimes used in grass mixtures for very shady, moist areas.

## The fine fescues

The fine-fescue family — chewings fescue, creeping red fescue, and hard fescue — are fine-textured, bristle-leafed plants with medium green color and deep roots. Though they do have adaptive differences, the different fescues are pretty much indistinguishable to the untrained eye.

Fine fescues are seldom grown alone and are often combined with Kentucky bluegrass to create mixes that offer better diversity and disease resistance, as well as tolerance to shade and drought. Fine fescues are best suited for the northern United States and Canada, at cooler elevations in the mid regions, and in cool coastal areas of the Northeast and Pacific Northwest.

## Chewings fescue

Chewings fescue (*Festuca rubra commutata*) grows in medium- to light-green bunches. As a deep-rooted bunching grass, it doesn't produce creeping stolons or rhizomes, so it can be slow to recover from damage or heavy traffic. (Learn how different grasses grow in Chapter 3.) For this reason, chewings fescue is rated at moderate wearability. Chewings fescue has excellent shade and cold tolerance and decent drought tolerance, making it a good choice to mix with Kentucky bluegrass. Like bluegrass, chewings fescue can go dormant in very hot summers. It's susceptible to fungal diseases in hot, wet weather and may develop thatch (especially in acid soils), which puts it into a high-maintenance bracket among the fescues. Many varieties have been bred for better disease resistance, shade tolerance, durability, and local adaptation.

## Creeping red fescue

Creeping red fescue (*Festuca rubra*), also known as red fescue, has fine-textured, narrow, deep-green leaves. This grass has deep roots, but recovers slowly from damage or traffic, placing it in the moderate-wear category. Planted alone, creeping red fescue forms a uniform turf, but it mixes well with other grasses and frequently gets combined with Kentucky bluegrass to increase diversity and general hardiness. Creeping red fescues are less susceptible to drought and heat than the chewings fescues, and they tolerate shade and cold better than the other fescues, making them a good choice to mix with Kentucky bluegrass. Creeping red fescues don't tolerate wet soils, clay, or excess nitrogen feeding. They're susceptible to fungal diseases, especially in the South or in lawns where the soil is kept too wet. Diseases include dollar spot, leaf spot, powdery mildew, red thread, and gray snow mold. (See Chapter 17 for more information on lawn diseases.) You can leave creeping red fescue unmowed to create a lush groundcover effect.

## Hard fescue

Hard fescue (*Festuca longifolia*) is a fine-bladed, slow-growing grass that doesn't root as deeply as the other fescues. Hard fescue forms clumps that have only moderate wearability, recovering slowly from damage.

Hard fescue mixes well with bluegrasses and ryegrasses. This highly drought- and shade-tolerant grass can establish itself well on infertile soil. Hard fescue is the best of the fescues when it comes to heat tolerance; it stays greener over the summer season. Some varieties of hard fescue have been bred to contain endophytes to improve resistance to pests and diseases; seed packages clearly mark the presence of these endophytes.

## Tall fescue

Tall fescue (*Festuca arundinacea*) is a dense grass that grows roots up to 3 feet deep. Once a coarse pasture grass, the new, turf-type varieties have softer, finer-textured leaves. The workhorse of the fescues, tall fescue tolerates high traffic and often gets planted on sports fields. Tall fescues are often mixed with Kentucky bluegrasses, and they're also often planted as a blend of several fescue varieties. This grass is ideal for transitional zones — where it's too hot for other cool-season grasses and too cool for warm-season grasses. Some varieties, usually sold as dwarf tall fescues, have been bred for slow, low growth. You don't need to mow dwarf tall fescues as often as standard varieties.

Tall fescue is heat-, shade-, and drought-tolerant and stays green year-round except during very hot, dry summers. Many of the newer varieties resist diseases and pests (some contain endophytes); however, in hot, wet conditions, tall fescues can become infected with brown patch. (See Chapter 17 for more information on lawn diseases.)

## Ryegrasses

There are two types of ryegrasses: annual and perennial. Although both are quick to germinate and grow, the annual ryegrass is a low-cost utility grass used primarily for winter lawns in the South. Perennial ryegrass is a premium-type lawn grass.

### Annual ryegrass

Annual ryegrass (*Lolium multiflorum*) lives for only one season, and I mention it in this chapter for three reasons:

>> You can plant it as a temporary lawn where you've prepared the site, but the season is wrong to plant a more permanent grass.

>> You can overseed warm-season lawns in fall to keep them green throughout the winter. For more information on overseeding, see Chapter 14.

>> You can use annual ryegrass at low rates as a *nurse grass* (to shade young seedlings and hold the soil) for Kentucky bluegrass. As the bluegrass becomes established, the annual ryegrass eventually dies out.

Annual ryegrasses are medium green, fast-growing plants with medium coarse blades and shallow roots. The blades grow in an upright, bunching pattern and can take moderate traffic. Annual ryegrasses aren't usually used in high-quality seed mixes (or if they are, then only in small amounts), as they grow too quickly, pushing out the perennial grasses only to die at the end of the year. Annual ryegrasses are not heat-, drought-, shade-, or cold-tolerant.

### Perennial ryegrass

Perennial ryegrass (*Lolium perenne*) has fine-textured, deep-green, glossy blades and shallow root systems. These grasses mix very well with Kentucky bluegrass and fescues, adding a needed toughness in disease resistance and wearability to their less-durable counterparts. Perennial ryegrasses are often used on high-traffic lawns and do well in all cool-season areas. Perennial ryegrass can also be used to overseed warm-season grasses to provide color throughout the winter. (For more information on overseeding, see Chapter 14.) Some varieties of perennial ryegrass contain endophytes.

## Bentgrasses

Creeping bentgrass (*Agrostis stolonifera*) is a fine-textured perennial that forms a tightly knit turf. This grass is often used for putting greens, lawn-bowling greens, and grass tennis courts. Creeping bentgrass has its place for these special purposes, but from a home gardener's point of view, that's about all I can say about it that's positive.

Bentgrasses are very shallow rooted, and they need frequent watering and fertilizing. The shallow roots and the requirement for constantly moist soil can lead to a host of diseases and pest problems. They also produce wiry stolons on the surface of your lawn and form thick mats of thatch, thus requiring frequent aerating and dethatching (see Chapter 14 for the hows and whys). If allowed to grow more than 1 inch tall, bentgrass also tends to bend in a sideways growth pattern (thus its name), forming a mat of blades that are often discolored except at the very tips.

Colonial bentgrass (*Agrostis tenuis*) doesn't require the same extreme level of maintenance, and it isn't as suitable for low mowing. Colonial bentgrass grows well in cool, high-rainfall areas, such as the Pacific Northwest.

Even when cultivated with care, bentgrasses are susceptible to a wide range of diseases that can break your heart — not to mention your back and bank account. It's best to avoid these grasses!

# Comparing Cool-Season Grasses

Sometimes it's helpful to see at a glance how different grasses compare. This section examines how the most common cool-season grasses measure up in specific categories.

## Grass texture

A lawn's texture generally depends on the width of the grass blade. The thinner the blade, the finer the texture. Here's a chart of grasses according to texture:

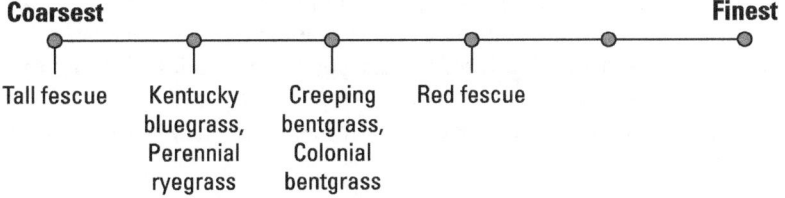

## Heat tolerance

The ability to withstand heat can vary depending on whether the weather is hot and humid or hot and dry. In general, cool-season grasses grow slowly or go dormant in very warm weather. Here's a scale of heat tolerance:

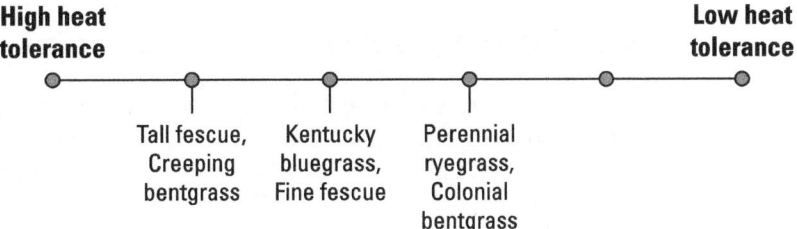

# Cold tolerance

Cold tolerance can vary depending on local conditions, such as windiness or persistent snow cover. Cultural practices, such as how you time fertilizer applications, also can affect hardiness. This scale shows the relative cold tolerance of cool-season grasses:

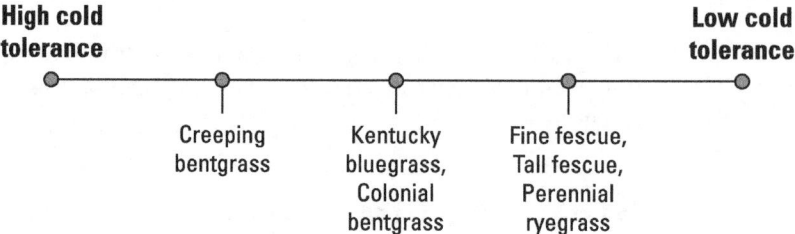

# Drought tolerance

How well a grass responds to drought depends on a number of factors, including cultural practices prior to the drought — for example, how high you mow the grass and how effectively you nurture soil health. Warm-season grasses are generally more drought-tolerant than cool-season grasses. The following chart shows the relative drought tolerance of cool-season grasses:

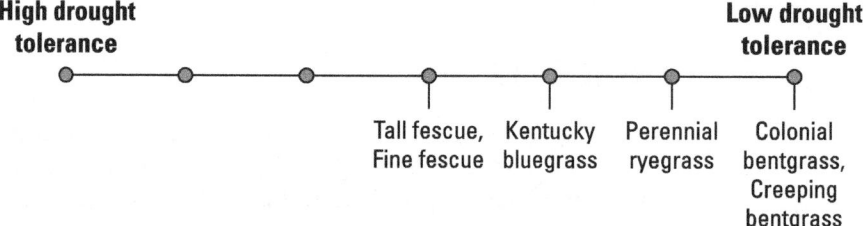

# Shade tolerance

Most grasses grow best in direct sunlight, but some can take varying degrees of shade better than others. Even within grass types, some varieties are better adapted to shade than others. When grasses get too much shade, they thin out, grow poorly, and are subject to disease. Here's a chart of grasses according to shade tolerance:

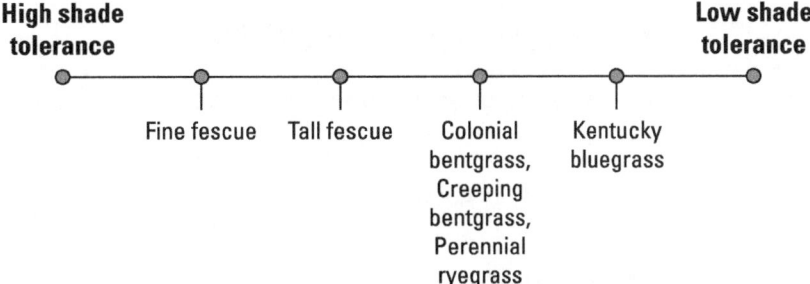

## Mowing-height adaptation

Most cool-season grasses are best mowed higher than their warm-season coun-terparts. For more on mowing, see Chapter 13. Here's a breakdown of individual grasses' mowing height preference:

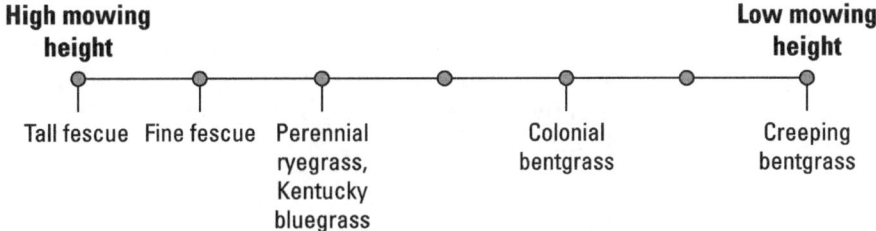

## Nitrogen requirements

Grasses vary in their need for fertilizer to promote healthy growth. Nitrogen is just one nutrient, but it's one that helps grass stay green and growing vigorously. For more information on fertilizing, see Chapter 12. Here's a chart showing differ-ent grasses' nitrogen requirements:

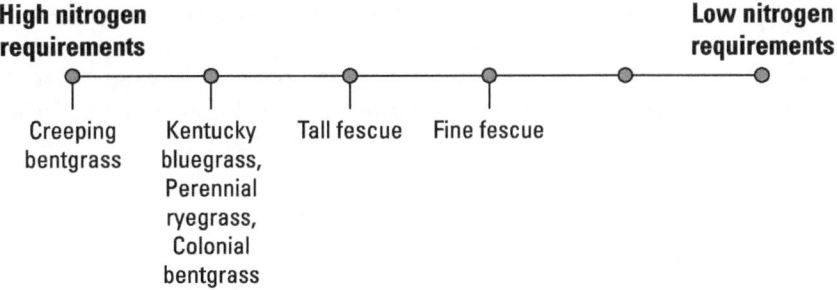

# Disease susceptibility

Disease problems vary from region to region, so it's best to consult a knowledge-able neighborhood nursery or your local cooperative extension service for information specific to your area. Here's a comparison of grasses from high to low susceptibility to disease:

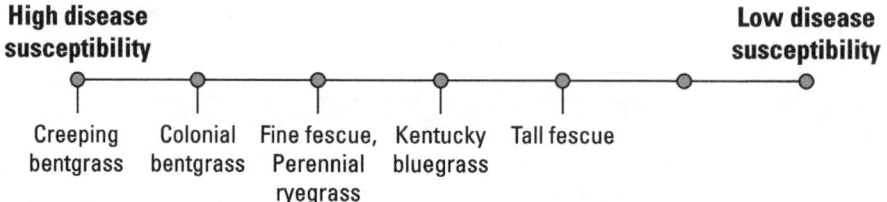

**High disease susceptibility** — **Low disease susceptibility**

Creeping bentgrass · Colonial bentgrass · Fine fescue, Perennial ryegrass · Kentucky bluegrass · Tall fescue

# Tolerance to salty soils

Some grasses are better than others when it comes to withstanding soils with high salt content. If you live in a coastal or desert area or where road crews use salts to melt ice in the winter, then take a look at the following list that shows grasses' relative tolerance to salt:

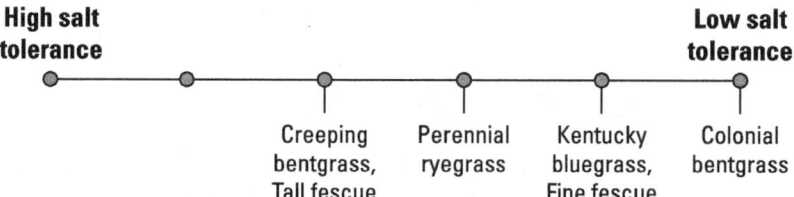

**High salt tolerance** — **Low salt tolerance**

Creeping bentgrass, Tall fescue · Perennial ryegrass · Kentucky bluegrass, Fine fescue · Colonial bentgrass

# Wear resistance

Which grasses can take the most traffic? The most rugged types have a high wear resistance and are ideal for sports fields or lawns that really get a lot of use. Try a softer, less wear-resistant grass in areas like a quiet reading spot or a low-traffic side yard. The following chart shows different grasses' wear resistance:

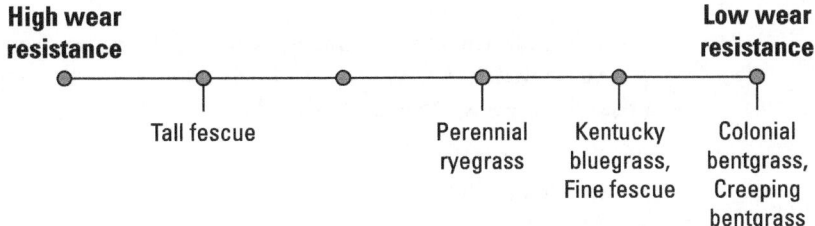

## Recuperative powers

What if the lawn gets too much traffic or gets damaged some other way? Here are the grasses listed according to rate of recovery:

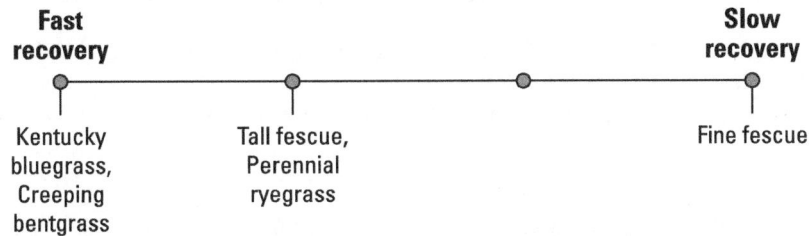

## Establishment rate

Here's a look at which grasses fill in the quickest after planting:

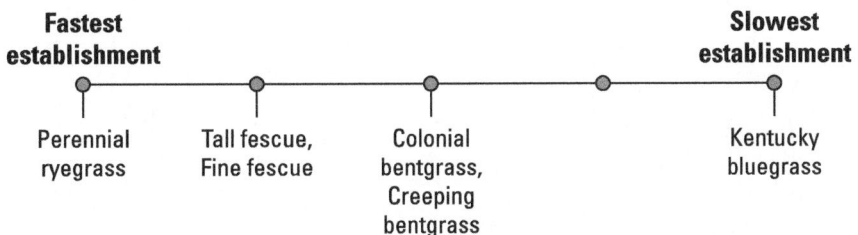

## Tendency to produce thatch

Thatch is a layer of organic matter that forms between the grass blades and the soil line and consists of tightly woven, living and dead grass stems, roots, and crowns. Thatch makes almost every step of lawn care more difficult, from watering to fertilizing to mowing. In general, cool-season grasses are less likely to develop thatch than warm-season grasses. Here's a comparison of cool-season grasses' tendency to generate thatch:

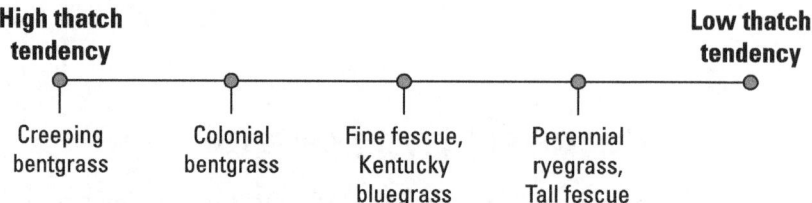

## Total maintenance, cost, and effort

Throw all the factors together for a comparison of how hard you have to work, how much time you have to spend, and how much it costs to maintain a lawn of each type of grass. Here's how cool-season grasses rate in total maintenance needs:

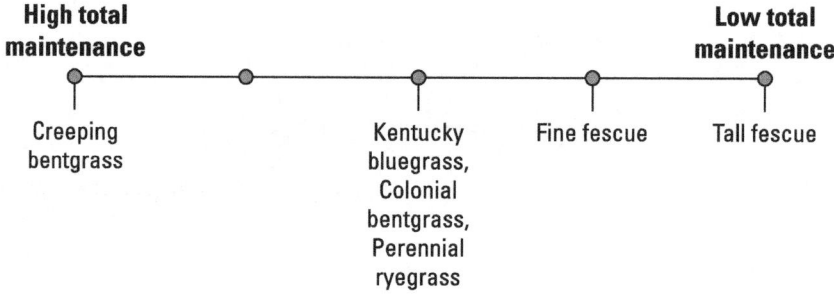

# Chapter **5**

# Warm-Season Grasses

As the name suggests, warm-season grasses grow best where it's warm. They're tough grasses and adapt well to a variety of conditions, but most don't like it where the ground freezes in winter. So, pour yourself a cool glass of iced tea and take a look at the warm-season grasses.

## Where the Warm Grasses Grow

Warm-season grasses are the grasses of southern climates, where summers are long and hot (consistently over 85°F), and winters are relatively mild. These grasses aren't as cold-hardy as the cool-season grasses. Zoysiagrass, one of the more common warm-season lawn types, is the hardiest and grows farthest north into the eastern transition zones where temperatures don't fall much below -10°F. Still, zoysiagrass grows slowly and turns brown when daytime high temperatures drop below 60°F.

TIP

The American native grasses, buffalograss and blue grama, which this chapter also covers, are very hardy and have a place in areas where droughts are common and low maintenance is desired. (See Chapter 2 to find out what kind of climate you live in, if you're not sure.)

Warm-season grasses grow most vigorously during the warm months of summer and turn brown in winter. These grasses are sometimes overseeded with mixes of annual and perennial ryegrass, to get a green lawn year-round. Plant warm-season grasses after the weather warms in mid-to-late spring through early-to-mid fall.

As a group, the warm-season grasses are mostly vigorous, spreading plants, and left unchecked, they can invade garden beds and become weedy. (Learn more about how grasses spread in Chapter 3.) They also have the propensity to develop thatch (see Chapter 14), especially when overfertilized and overwatered. The finer textured species look best when mowed low with a reel mower, especially when mowed at 2" or less, because a rotary mower is less effective at providing a uniform cut, notably on uneven turf areas (for more on mowing, see Chapter 13).

# The Warm-Season Grasses

Commonly used warm-season grasses include bahiagrass, common and hybrid bermudagrass, centipedegrass, St. Augustinegrass, and zoysiagrass. If you live in a hot-summer climate, chances are that your lawn has one of these grasses growing in it.

Plant breeders continuously work to improve the appearance, pest resistance, drought resilience, and other features of lawn grasses, so consult with knowledgeable staff at your neighborhood nursery or contact your local extension office about new and improved varieties. You can find a link to your local cooperative extension office at `https://extension.org/find-cooperative-extension-in-your-state/`.

## Bahiagrass

Bahiagrass (*Paspalum notatum*) is a tough, coarse grass that roots deeply and extensively. This grass spreads by short horizontal stems (stolons) that root at close intervals, making it effective at stabilizing erosion-prone soil. Bahiagrass is low-growing and forms an open turf with less density and less tendency to form thatch than other warm-season species. Because its blades are so tough, bahiagrass has excellent wearability.

Bahiagrass is shade-tolerant, moderately drought-tolerant, and does well in acidic, sandy, or infertile soils of the Southern Coastal Plains of the United States. The grass stays green longer than most of the warm-season grasses over the winter months. You can overseed bahiagrass with a mix of annual and perennial ryegrasses for a green winter lawn.

Bahiagrass tends to send up tall seedheads soon after mowing, which can be unsightly. Both its leaf blades and seed stems are very tough, so mower blade should be kept sharp. Seedhead production and lack of density are the reasons why bahiagrass is less popular than other warm-season grasses. Low water and fertilizer requirements and resiliency to infertile, sandy soil make it a popular choice where irrigation is not available and a manicured lawn is not required.

Occasionally, mole crickets and dollar spot are problems for bahiagrass. (See Chapters 16 and 17 for more information on insects and lawn diseases.)

A relative of bahiagrass, seashore paspalum (*Paspalum vaginatum*) is sometimes grown in coastal regions along the Gulf of Mexico and southern Atlantic Ocean where soils are very salty. Seashore paspalum is more finely textured and a darker green than bahiagrass, and it's very prone to disease problems. It's usually sold as sod.

# Bermudagrass

A medium green, medium- to fine-textured turf, bermudagrass spreads quickly by both aboveground stems (stolons) and belowground stems (rhizomes). This rapid spreading can cause it to become an invasive weed if it's not kept in check. You can choose from two bermudagrasses: common bermudagrass (*Cynodon dactylon*) and hybrid bermudagrass (*Cynodon dactylon* crossed with *C. transvaalensis*). Of the two, hybrid bermudagrass is preferred because it forms a denser lawn and doesn't produce viable seed. Therefore, it spreads a bit less vigorously as a weed.

Heat-loving and fast-growing, bermudagrass has deep roots and subsurface rhizomes that make it relatively drought-tolerant. It has excellent wearability, so it's a good choice for high-traffic lawns. Bermudagrass doesn't do well in shade and turns brown in winter until daytime temperatures reach a consistent 60°F. You can overseed it with a ryegrass to have a greener lawn in the winter. (For directions on how to overseed, see Chapter 14.)

Bermudagrass is a popular choice for lawns in the southwestern, southeastern, and mild-winter areas along the western United States and in similar climates. It grows well in most soils, from sand to clay. (For more on soil types, see Chapter 6.) The turf's fast growth means it requires frequent feeding and mowing, and it tends to produce thatch.

### Common bermudagrass

**WARNING**

Native to Africa and possibly to Europe, Australia, and parts of Asia, common bermudagrass has become established throughout the warmer regions of the United States, into the lower Midwest and coastal New England. It's considered a noxious weed in some areas.

In humid climates, common bermudagrass is susceptible to a range of diseases, including large (brown) patch, dollar spot, and pythium blight, as well as pests such as armyworms, sod webworms, and others. (See Chapters 16 and 17 for more information on insects and lawn diseases.)

### Hybrid bermudagrass

The hybrid bermudagrasses are softer, denser, greener, and more finely textured than the common bermudagrass. These improved versions root as deeply and are just as aggressive, so you must take steps to prevent them from invading flower gardens and other places you don't want them. Hybrid bermudagrasses are generally susceptible to the pest and diseases that attack common bermudagrass, but there are varieties available that were bred for resistance to some diseases and pests.

Of the warm-season turf species, bermudagrass is the tolerant of wear and tear. To keep it looking its best, you should mow it frequently. Infrequent mowing removes much of the green, which is at the top portion of the bermudagrass stems. Avoid excessive fertilizing and watering to minimize thatch buildup.

## Centipedegrass

Centipedegrass (*Eremochloa ophiuroides*) is a medium- to fine-textured, yellow-green grass that spreads by creeping stems, giving the grass its name. This grass has shallow roots, making it only moderately tolerant to drought, slow to fill in as a lawn, and slow to recover from wear and tear. Centipedegrass is not a good choice for high-traffic areas.

This grass's slow growth, low fertilizer needs, and good resistance to some diseases and pests make it a good, low-maintenance lawn grass. However, it's one of the first of the warm-season grasses to turn brown in hot, dry weather and to go completely dormant with the arrival of winter.

Centipedegrass does well in the poor, acidic soils of Hawaii and the southeastern United States. This grass tolerates moderate shade but doesn't tolerate the salt from sea spray. Centipedegrass can turn yellow in alkaline soils, but greens up with applications of iron sulfate or iron chelate. This yellowing condition is *chlorosis.* (Learn more about plant nutrients in Chapter 12.)

Centipedegrass is susceptible to large (brown) patch, gray leaf spot, and dollar spot. (See Chapters 16 and 17 for more information on insects and lawn diseases.)

## St. Augustinegrass

St. Augustinegrass (*Stenotaphrum secundatum*) is a fast-growing, deep-rooted, coarse- to medium-textured grass with broad, dark green leaves. The grass spreads rapidly by horizontal stems that root at close intervals to form a thick, dense turf. St. Augustine is the most shade tolerant of the warm-season grasses but isn't as drought tolerant as bermudagrass or zoysiagrass.

This grass is quite popular in southern climates, from Florida to California, because of its tolerance to heat, sun, shade, and salt. St. Augustinegrass can grow in most soils but prefers nutrient-rich, well-drained, soil.

WARNING

Because it spreads by surface runners, thatch buildup and resultant diseases and pests can become a problem. St. Augustinegrass is susceptible to large (brown) patch, gray leaf spot, mole crickets, sod webworm, chinch bugs, white grubs, and a virus called St. Augustine Decline (SAD, for short). Most new varieties specifically resist this viral disease. The grass has relatively high watering needs and poor cold tolerance; prolonged temperatures much below 25°F can kill the grass.

## Zoysiagrass

Zoysiagrasses (*Zoysia* species) are fine- to medium-textured, dark green, and moderately deep rooted. The two primary types of zoysiagrass are *Zoysia japonica*, which is somewhat coarse textured (wider leaf blades), and *Zoysia matrella*, which is fine textured, as well as hybrids of the two. Wide-bladed types have moderate shade tolerance, but newer fine-bladed types have even better shade tolerance. Zoysiagrass may be planted by sod or plugs. (Learn more about planting plugs in Chapter 10.) Newer varieties spread and fill in faster.

Like centipedegrasses, old varieties of zoysias turn brown early in the winter and are slow to green up in the spring. However, newer varieties grow much faster and green up more quickly due to their short winter dormancy requirements. They thrive on almost all soils and perform well in the shade and near salt spray. Zoysias have excellent drought tolerance. When soil gets really dry, they just go into a kind of suspended animation (technically, physiological processes shut down). They also have good wear tolerance. Zoysiagrasses do well in the Upper South, Coastal South, and Southern California.

When properly cared for, zoysias are fairly pest- and disease-resistant when compared to other warm-season grasses. However, armyworms, billbugs, sod webworms, large (brown) patch, and dollar spot can occasionally create problems (see Chapters 16 and 17). Overfertilizing and overwatering can promote buildup of thatch in zoysiagrass (see Chapter 14).

# The Native Grasses

North America's native grasses are growing in popularity because of their relatively low demand for precious resources and labor. For the most part, native grasses need little water once established, very little fertilizer, and a haircut only a few times a year.

Native grasses are very tough once established, and although they turn brown during dormancy, they tolerate wide temperature fluctuations. Because native grasses haven't been bred for uniformity, they provide a more informal-looking lawn cover. The two most popular warm-season native grasses are blue grama and buffalograss. Keep an eye out for other native grasses that are becoming readily available for planting as lawn.

## Blue grama

Blue grama (*Bouteloua gracilis*) is a hardy, grayish-green, fine-textured pasture grass with slightly fuzzy blades. Although this grass goes dormant, it tolerates extreme heat and cold fluctuations (down to -40°F!) and does well in the arid regions of the north central Great Plains to the arid Southwest.

Blue grama is very drought-tolerant and offers moderate wearability but is slow to recover from wear damage. Blue grama seed is often mixed with buffalograss seed for a better-looking ground cover.

## Buffalograss

Buffalograss (*Buchloe dactyloides*) is fine-textured, low-growing, and grayish green. Where it's well adapted, it can tolerate minimal maintenance.

Buffalograss is drought-tolerant once established and becomes even more so if mowed infrequently and high. This grass thrives in areas that receive only 10" to 15" of rain a year, but it will go brown if allowed to go completely dry. It's more lawn-like in appearance than other native grasses and has a softer, more fine-bladed texture than most other warm-season species. Buffalograss is more expensive to plant, whether by seed, sod, or plug than most other warm-season turf species.

Heat- and sun-loving, buffalograss tolerates dry, compacted, clay soils but doesn't do well in shade or sandy or poorly drained soils. Buffalograss goes brown with the first frost of winter and is slow to green up in spring. Buffalograss is fairly disease- and pest-resistant, as long as watering or rainfall is infrequent. Weeds can become a problem if the grass gets overfed, overcut, or overwatered either by irrigation or in areas with more than 30" of annual rainfall.

Despite the limitations of buffalograss, it's a good option in drought-prone regions and when kept as a "mini meadow" by mowing only a few times per year at a taller height.

# How the Grasses Compare

Sometimes it's helpful to see at a glance how different grasses compare. In this section, you'll see how the most common warm-season grasses measure up in specific categories.

## Grass texture

A lawn's texture mostly depends on the width of the grass blade. The thinner the blade, the finer the texture. Most lawns have a relatively fine texture, but some are finer than others. This chart rates warm-season grasses according to texture:

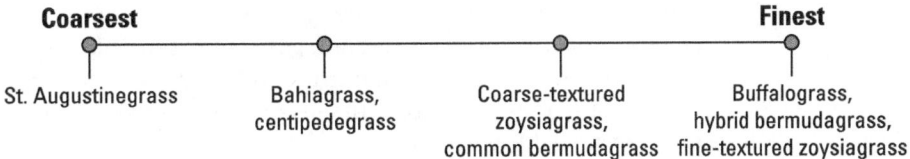

**Coarsest** — St. Augustinegrass — Bahiagrass, centipedegrass — Coarse-textured zoysiagrass, common bermudagrass — **Finest** Buffalograss, hybrid bermudagrass, fine-textured zoysiagrass

## Heat tolerance

The ability to withstand heat can vary depending on whether the weather is hot and humid or hot and dry, so local adaptation of the following grasses may vary because of differences in humidity. In general, warm-season grasses tolerate heat better than cool-season grasses, which go dormant or grow slowly in very warm weather. The following grasses have a similar high heat tolerance, with zoysiagrass being the most heat tolerant and bahiagrass the least tolerant:

High heat tolerance ——— Low heat tolerance

Zoysiagrass, hybrid bermudagrass, common bermudagrass, buffalograss, centipedegrass, St. Augustinegrass, bahiagrass

## Cold tolerance

Cold tolerance can vary depending on local conditions such as windiness or persistent snow cover. Cultural practices, such as how you time fertilizer applications, also can affect hardiness. Warm-season grasses are generally not as hardy as cool-season grasses. Here's how they measure up:

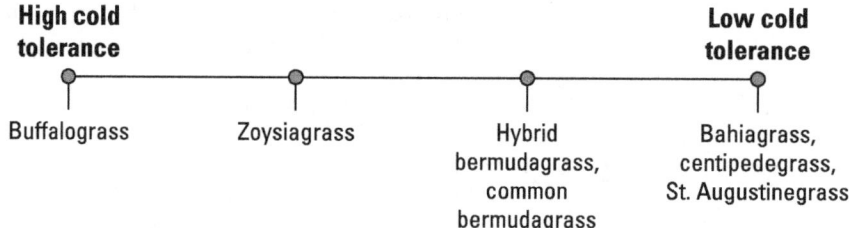

High cold tolerance ——— Low cold tolerance

Buffalograss | Zoysiagrass | Hybrid bermudagrass, common bermudagrass | Bahiagrass, centipedegrass, St. Augustinegrass

## Drought tolerance

How well a grass responds to drought depends on a number of factors, including cultural practices prior to the drought — for example, how high you mow the grass and how effectively you nurture soil health. Warm-season grasses are generally more drought-tolerant than cool-season grasses. Here's how they rate in terms of drought tolerance:

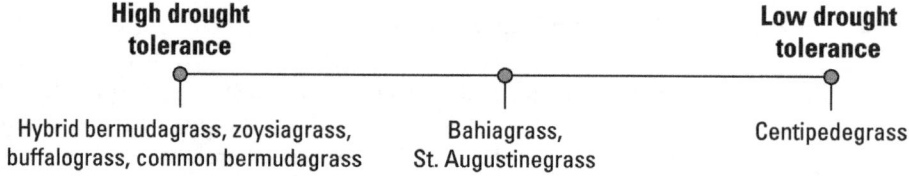

High drought tolerance ——— Low drought tolerance

Hybrid bermudagrass, zoysiagrass, buffalograss, common bermudagrass | Bahiagrass, St. Augustinegrass | Centipedegrass

# Shade tolerance

Most grasses grow best in direct sunlight, but some can take varying degrees of shade better than others. Even within grass types, some varieties are better adapted to shade than others. When grasses get too much shade, they thin out, grow poorly, and are subject to disease. Here's how the warm-season grasses compare:

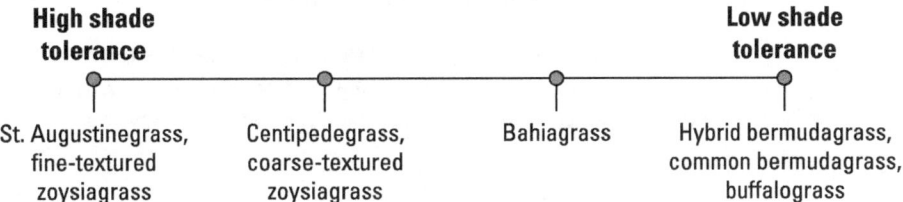

**High shade tolerance** — St. Augustinegrass, fine-textured zoysiagrass | Centipedegrass, coarse-textured zoysiagrass | Bahiagrass | Hybrid bermudagrass, common bermudagrass, buffalograss — **Low shade tolerance**

# Mowing-height adaptation

Some grasses grow better at taller heights; others prefer to be mowed shorter. In general, you need to mow warm-season grasses lower than cool-season grasses. For more on mowing, see Chapter 13. Here's how warm-season grasses compare:

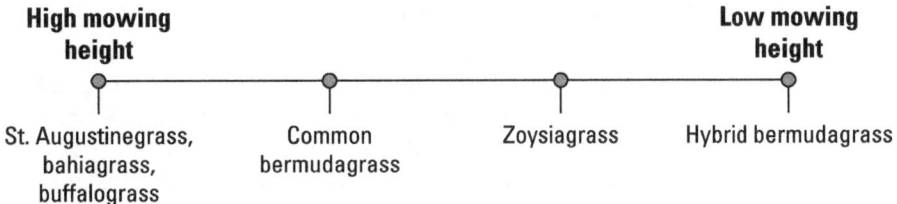

**High mowing height** — St. Augustinegrass, bahiagrass, buffalograss | Common bermudagrass | Zoysiagrass | Hybrid bermudagrass — **Low mowing height**

# Nitrogen requirements

Grasses vary in their need for fertilizer to promote healthy growth. Nitrogen is just one nutrient, but it's one that helps grass stay green and growing vigorously. For more information on fertilizing, see Chapter 12. Here's a chart showing different grasses' nitrogen requirements:

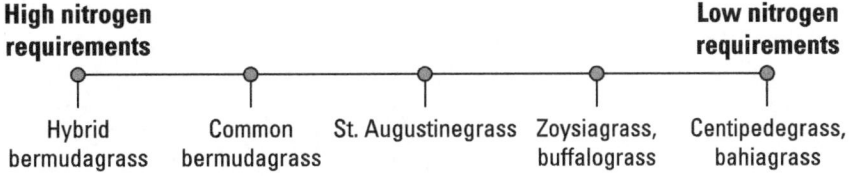

**High nitrogen requirements** — Hybrid bermudagrass | Common bermudagrass | St. Augustinegrass | Zoysiagrass, buffalograss | Centipedegrass, bahiagrass — **Low nitrogen requirements**

## Disease susceptibility

Disease problems vary from region to region, so it's best to consult a knowledgeable neighborhood nursery or your local cooperative extension service for information specific to your area. Here's a comparison of warm-season grasses' susceptibility to disease:

## Tolerance to salty soils

Some grasses are better than others when it comes to withstanding soils with high salt content. If you live in a coastal or desert area or where road crews use salts to melt ice in the winter, then take a look at the following comparison:

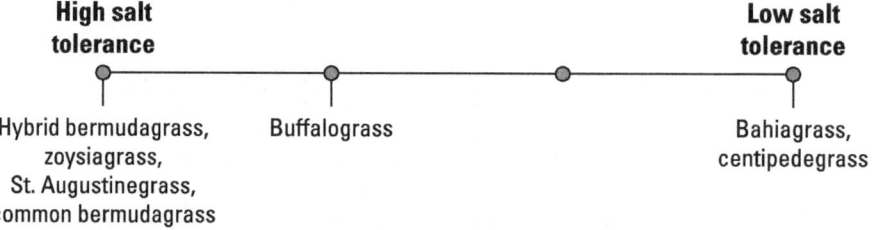

## Wear resistance

Which grasses can take the most traffic? The most rugged types have a high wear resistance and are ideal for sports fields or lawns that really get a lot of use. Try a softer, less wear-resistant grass in areas like a quiet reading spot or a low-traffic side yard. The following chart shows different grasses' wear resistance:

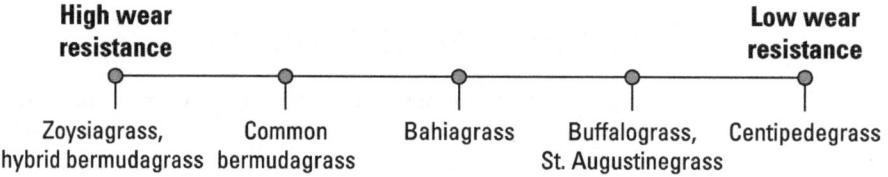

# Recuperative powers

What if the lawn gets too much traffic or gets damaged some other way? Here are the grasses listed according to rate of recovery:

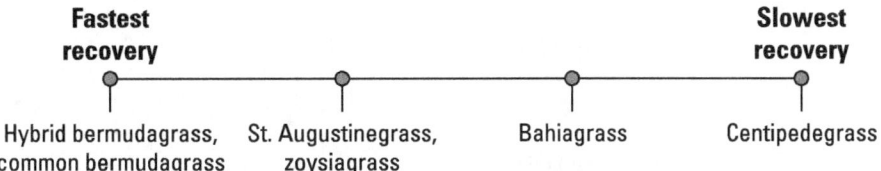

| Fastest recovery | | | Slowest recovery |
|---|---|---|---|
| Hybrid bermudagrass, common bermudagrass | St. Augustinegrass, zoysiagrass | Bahiagrass | Centipedegrass |

# Establishment rate

Here's a look at which grasses fill in the quickest after planting:

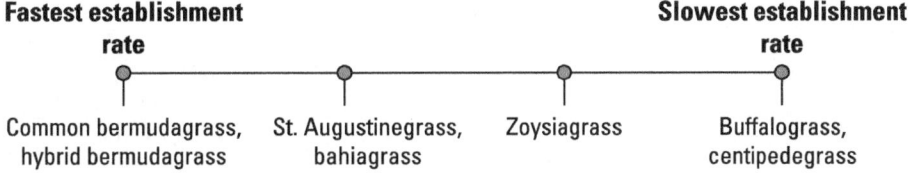

| Fastest establishment rate | | | Slowest establishment rate |
|---|---|---|---|
| Common bermudagrass, hybrid bermudagrass | St. Augustinegrass, bahiagrass | Zoysiagrass | Buffalograss, centipedegrass |

# Tendency to produce thatch

Thatch is a layer of organic matter that forms between the grass blades and the soil line and consists of tightly woven, living and dead grass stems, roots, and crowns. Thatch makes almost every step of lawn care more difficult, from watering to fertilizing to mowing. Here's a comparison of warm-season grasses' tendency to generate thatch:

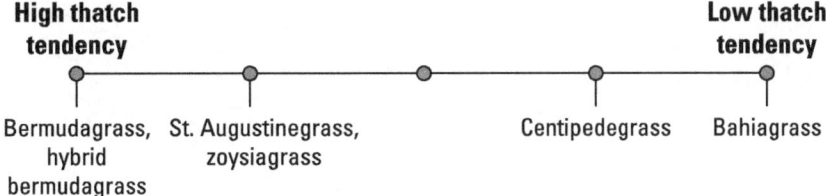

| High thatch tendency | | | | Low thatch tendency |
|---|---|---|---|---|
| Bermudagrass, hybrid bermudagrass | St. Augustinegrass, zoysiagrass | | Centipedegrass | Bahiagrass |

# Total maintenance, cost, and effort

Throw all the factors together for a comparison of how hard you have to work, how much time you have to spend, and how much it costs to maintain a lawn of each type of grass. Here's how grasses rate in total maintenance needs:

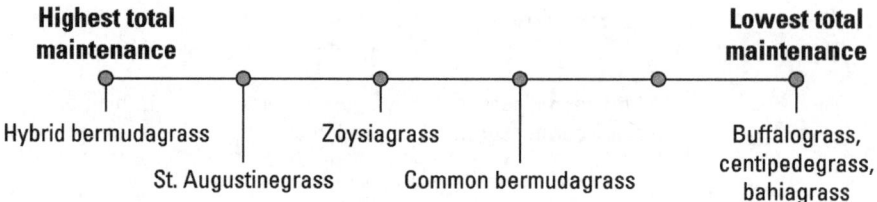

# Chapter 6

# Increasing Your Soil Sense

All plants, including lawn grasses, grow best in healthy soil. To have a good-looking lawn that's easy to manage, start thinking of your lawn as a garden of grass plants. Just like your flower or vegetable garden, your "grass garden" needs healthy soil to flourish. The way you treat your soil has a huge effect on how well it can support a lush, green lawn.

Healthy soil supports an astonishing array of subterranean organisms, including microscopic ones like bacteria and fungi, and visible ones like earthworms. Together they form a dynamic soil ecosystem that supports plant growth. Lifeless soil is just dirt.

In this chapter, you discover ways to determine the type of soil you have and find out how to take ordinary soil and turn it into great soil. Specifically, you discover why and how to take a soil test and how to adjust soil pH with lime or sulfur. You also dive into the benefits of organic matter and compost. The time you invest in learning about soil and how you can improve it is an all-important step toward a thriving lawn.

# What Kind of Soil Do You Have?

Before you can start improving your soil, it helps to know what kind of soil you have. Different soils have different strengths and weaknesses when it comes to supporting plant life.

>> **Sandy soils** drain water quickly — sometimes too quickly, leading to thirsty plants. Water drains right through these soils and, as it does, it takes nutrients with it. Sandy soils are well-aerated, quick to dry out, and need regular fertilizing to provide the nutrients that grass plants need.

>> **Clay soils** tend to be sticky when wet and rock-hard when dry. They drain poorly, leading to wet spots that can, in turn, lead to plant diseases. On the upside, they contain and hold onto plant nutrients, and they don't require frequent watering.

>> **Loam soils** are considered the ideal. They are well-drained while still being able to hold water and nutrients.

## Determining your soil's texture

Soil scientists group soil mineral particles into three groups based on size, and the proportion of these three mineral particles in a soil determines its *texture*.

**TECHNICAL STUFF**

>> **Clay** particles are the smallest, less than 0.002 mm across. You need a microscope to see an individual clay particle.

>> **Silt** particles are slightly larger, from 0.002 mm to 0.05 mm. Dry silt feels a lot like flour.

>> **Sand** particles are the largest, from 0.05 mm to 2.00 mm in diameter.

Here are three simple ways to get an idea of your soil's texture.

### Feel the grit test

Rub some moist soil between your fingertips. Does it feel gritty? If yes, it contains sand. Does it feel slick or sticky? It probably contains lots of clay.

### Ribbon test

Take a small clump of moist soil and try to form it into a ball. If it easily crumbles apart, it contains a lot of sand. If you can roll it between your hands into a cylinder or ribbon, then it contains a lot of clay. If you can form it into a ball, but the ball falls apart when you poke it, then it probably contains a mix of sand, silt, and clay.

## Soil shake test

To get a clear picture of your soil type, fill a clear jar two thirds full of water and then add enough soil to nearly fill the jar. Screw on the top, shake it, and then set it in a place to rest undisturbed so the particles can settle. The sand particles will quickly form a layer at the bottom, then the silt, and finally the clay will form the top layer. (See Figure 6-1.) Some of the clay may stay suspended in the water, making it cloudy. Organic matter will float.

Measure the overall height of the soil as well as the height of each layer. Divide the height of each component by total height of the soil sample and multiply times 100 to get the percentages. Consider the example shown in Figure 6-1, which has these characteristics:

The overall height of soil is 4"

The sand layer is 2"; 2 divided by 4 times 100 = 50%

The silt and clay layers are 1" each; 1 divided by 4 times 100 = 25%

This soil is about one half sand and one quarter each of silt and clay; it falls into the category of a loam soil.

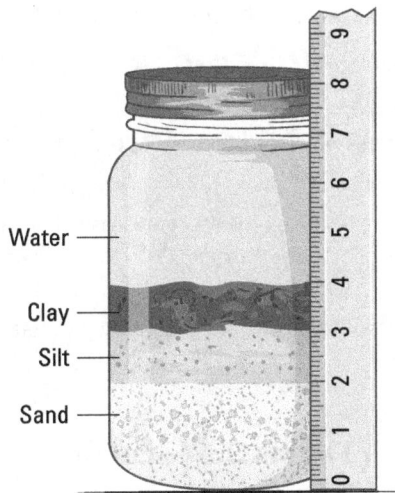

**FIGURE 6-1:**
Use the soil shake test to determine your soil texture.

Water

Clay

Silt

Sand

## Understanding soil structure

**TECHNICAL STUFF**

As important as soil texture is *soil structure*, which describes how the soil particles are arranged in clumps, called aggregates. A soil with good structure has lots of aggregates in a range of sizes. These create lots of spaces for water and air, both of which are critical for healthy root growth. Soil with good structure is moist, soft, and crumbly (think moist chocolate cake). One with poor structure looks like more like flour or sand — it will easily run through your fingers — or it might be baked into rock-hard nuggets.

**WARNING**

Don't add sand to clay soil (or vice versa) to try to improve it; it won't help, and it can actually make things worse. The best way to improve soil is by adding organic matter.

## Organic matter to the rescue

Soil organic matter describes any plant or animal tissue in various stages of decomposition. The most familiar type of organic matter commonly added to soil is compost. Organic matter improves soil in so many ways it almost sounds too good to be true.

Organic matter helps overcome some of the challenges if one of the mineral sizes is present in too high a quantity. It improves water and nutrient retention in sandy soils, and it improves drainage in clay soils. Organic matter also

>> Binds soil particles into aggregates so the soil can hold plenty of air and water.

>> Increases the soil's ability to hold onto nutrients, so they aren't lost through leaching.

>> Feeds beneficial microorganisms and other soil life that help keep plant-damaging organisms in check.

>> Acts as a reservoir of nutrients; as soil microorganisms break down the organic matter, they transform these nutrients into forms plants can use.

Find more information on organic matter, and how you can use it to improve your soil, later in this chapter.

## Checking pH and nutrient levels

Like many plants, lawn grasses are a bit fussy about the soil pH, which is a measure of acidity or alkalinity. The pH scale goes from 0 (extremely acid) to

14 (extremely alkaline) with 7 being neutral. Most soils fall into the 5.5 to 8.0 range, and most lawn grasses prefer slightly acidic to neutral soil with a pH between 6.5 and 7.0.

TECHNICAL
STUFF

Small variations in soil pH matter because the pH scale is logarithmic; that means that a soil with a pH of 6 is ten times more acidic than a pH of 7.

There are two ways to test your soil: do-it-yourself kits and soil testing labs.

## Do-it-yourself kits

These affordable kits, which are readily available at garden centers and home improvement stores, aren't the most precise, but they'll give you a general idea of whether your soil is acidic, neutral, or alkaline. Some kits also give you a snapshot of nutrient levels.

## Soil testing labs

Your local cooperative extension office or a private soil testing lab can conduct a more complete and reliable soil test. The benefits of using a professional lab are that results will be much more accurate than at-home kits, they can test for a larger range of nutrients, and they usually offer recommendations for soil improvements based on the types of plants you want to grow, such as turfgrass. Be sure to follow the instructions for collecting soil samples to ensure the most accurate results.

TECHNICAL
STUFF

A soil sample should be a representation of the soil throughout your lawn area, taken as several vertical cores of soil about 6″ deep taken at random throughout the lawn and mixed together.

# Interpreting soil test results

Soil pH is so important to plant health that it makes sense to test your soil. That said, it's possible to get a general idea based on where you live. Soils in areas of high rainfall, such as east of the Mississippi River, tend to be acidic (low pH). In arid regions west of the Mississippi, soils tend to be alkaline (high pH). Because pockets of unusually acidic or alkaline soils do occur, it's wise to test pH to be sure. Your cooperative extension office can also offer general information about the soils in your area. Find a link to your state extension office at `https://extension.org/ find-cooperative-extension-in-your-state`.

**TIP**

Some do-it-yourself kits include tests for nutrients, especially the big three — nitrogen, phosphorus, and potassium. The results can be useful indicators but generally aren't nearly as accurate as the results from a soil testing lab. A lab will not only offer more reliable results for these three nutrients, but they can also test for other nutrients plants need in smaller quantities, such as magnesium, calcium, and iron, as well as for levels of organic matter.

# Building Healthy Soil

Like the aboveground ecosystem of your landscape, the underground soil ecosystem is teeming with life, and it needs nurturing to ensure it can provide the best possible conditions for healthy root growth. Caring for your soil ensures that the myriad beneficial organisms, including bacteria, fungi, and earthworms, will thrive.

## Calculating the area of your lawn

It's always helpful to know the approximate square footage of your lawn, and it's a necessary step before you can calculate the quantity of soil amendments to add. Buy, rent, or borrow a 50- or 100-foot tape measure and then use these guidelines for making your calculations:

>> For a square or rectangular area, multiply the length by the width.

Example: 60-foot length × 40-foot width = 2,400 square feet

>> For a triangular lawn, multiply the height times the length of the base and divide by 2.

Example: 60-foot height × 30-foot base = 1,800 square feet. Divide by 2, and you have 900 square feet

>> For a circular lawn, take the radius (the distance halfway across a center line) and multiply that number by itself. Then multiply the result by pi (3.14).

Example: For a circle with a radius of 25 feet, 25 × 25 = 625, multiplied by 3.14 equals approximately 1,963 square feet

>> For an irregularly shaped lawn, break up the areas into circles, squares, and rectangles, calculate the areas for each section, and then add them up.

>> Remember that you don't have to be exact. Just a reasonably close estimate of the lawn size will suffice.

# Adjusting soil pH

TIP

It's important to adjust pH, if necessary, because pH affects how well grass plants can take up the nutrients in the soil. Some nutrients are only available to plants within a specific pH range. Outside that range, the nutrients can be locked up in forms that are unavailable to plants.

If your soil's pH is lower than 6.5, the soil is too acidic to grow healthy grass, and you need to add ground limestone (often shorted to lime). If the pH is higher than 7.5, the soil is too alkaline for grass, and you need to add soil sulfur.

All cooperative extension offices, any soil laboratory, and many lawn and garden centers have charts showing how much lime or sulfur to add to correct your pH. The scale is based on pounds of material to add per 1,000 square feet to raise the pH from its current level to 6.5, as shown in Tables 6-1 and 6-2. Now you know why getting your lawn's square footage is so important, as well as knowing what type of soil you have (sandy, loam, clay).

**TABLE 6-1**     **Pounds of Limestone Needed to Raise pH per 1,000 Square Feet**

| pH Change Needed | Sandy Soil | Loam Soil | Clay Soil |
| --- | --- | --- | --- |
| 4.0 to 6.5 | 60 | 161 | 230 |
| 4.5 to 6.5 | 51 | 133 | 193 |
| 5.0 to 6.5 | 41 | 106 | 152 |
| 5.5 to 6.5 | 28 | 78 | 106 |
| 6.0 to 6.5 | 14 | 41 | 55 |

**TABLE 6-2**     **Pounds of Sulfur Needed to Lower pH per 1,000 Square Feet**

| pH Change Needed | Sandy Soil | Loam Soil | Clay Soil |
| --- | --- | --- | --- |
| 8.5 to 6.5 | 46 | 57 | 69 |
| 8.0 to 6.5 | 28 | 34 | 46 |
| 7.5 to 6.5 | 11 | 18 | 23 |
| 7.0 to 6.5 | 2 | 4 | 7 |

The best way to apply these materials is with a drop spreader, like the type used to apply granular fertilizer. This simple tool doesn't cost very much, and it helps you spread materials more evenly than if you tried to spread things by hand. Follow the instructions on your equipment and make the necessary adjustments to spread the right amount evenly over the area. (For more information on spreaders, see Chapter 12.)

*Ground limestone* (also called pulverized limestone, or just lime) is the most common and inexpensive acid neutralizer. *Dolomitic limestone* contains magnesium as well as calcium and is used when a test indicates that your soil is low in magnesium. *Pelletized limestone* is a little more expensive than ordinary powdered limestone, but it's easier to apply and isn't as dusty. It's slower to change pH than more fine-textured types of limestone.

**TIP**

If you're starting a lawn from scratch, the best time to spread the limestone over the soil and till it in to a depth of 3 to 6 inches is before you plant. Tilling in the limestone allows it to break down and do its work more quickly and efficiently throughout the turfgrass root zone than if you apply it to the soil surface.

You can add either soil sulfur or limestone to existing lawns. In fact, you may have to add them regularly to keep the pH in balance. If you add sulfur after your lawn is planted, the sulfur can burn the grass if you apply it a high rate all at once. Break up the application into three or four parts and time them evenly over the next growing season or two.

**WARNING**

Be sure to wear a dust mask when applying limestone or sulfur because the materials can be very dusty and irritating if inhaled.

**TIP**

A complete soil test, done through a soil testing lab, is a good investment that you should do every three or four years. Besides providing soil pH and nutrient levels, a soil test can identify local problems. For example, in some dry-summer areas, you may have salty soil; the remedy is to add *gypsum*, a readily available mineral soil amendment. Gypsum can help create better soil structure in a clay soil with high sodium levels, as would be indicated on a soil test.

## Should you add topsoil?

**WARNING**

Adding topsoil to your lawn is an iffy proposition. Where did that topsoil come from? Is it full of weed seeds? Is it a similar texture to the soil in your lawn area? Is it full of rocks and other debris? These are good questions to ask your topsoil dealer before you sign up for delivery. Unless you're tackling the aftermath of a construction project that left you with nothing but lifeless subsoil, you probably don't need it unless your lawn area is very uneven and the topsoil could help even up the surface.

In most cases, you can improve your existing soil without adding topsoil. You can do so by getting your soil tested and adding lime or sulfur as needed, spreading generous amounts of organic matter, and then rototilling it all into the soil.

# Adding organic matter

The very best organic matter is *compost*, that dark, crumbly, soil-like material that gardeners call "black gold." Compost is the end product that results when organic matter such as leaves, kitchen scraps, and animal manures have fully decomposed. Purchased compost is easy to use and readily available in bags or bulk. Find tips on making your own compost below.

## Adding compost to new lawns

If you're starting a new lawn from scratch or completely renovating an area, you can increase soil organic matter by adding compost prior to sowing grass seed. Apply a layer of 1" to 2" and then till it in to a depth of 3" to 6".

Start by figuring out the amount of compost you'll need. (Precision isn't required here — the important thing is that by adding compost you're doing the single best thing you can for your soil.) To get the amount of compost you need in cubic feet, multiply the square footage of the area by the depth of the compost in inches and divide by 12. For example,

1,000 square feet × 1 inch / 12 = 83 cubic feet

Here's how that translates to real-world compost-buying:

» **Bagged compost** is usually sold in bags that contain either one cubic foot or 20 quarts (one cubic foot equals about 25 quarts). So you'll need about 80 to 100 bags to equal 83 cubic feet.

» **Bulk compost** is sold by the yard, which is a unit of measurement that's 3 feet x 3 feet x 3 feet, or 27 cubic feet, so you'll need about 3 yards to equal 83 cubic feet. You can get bulk compost delivered to your door or, if you have a truck or trailer, you can pick it up yourself at a garden center or farm supply store.

Use a peat moss spreader (sometimes called a compost spreader or topsoil spreader, Figure 6-2) to spread the material over the soil. If you don't have access to such a spreader, a lawn leveling rake works great.

**FIGURE 6-2:**
Rent, borrow, or
buy a peat moss
spreader to
spread compost.

## Adding other types of organic matter

**WARNING**

There are many other types of organic matter, but most pose some problems. Mixing sawdust or shredded leaves into the soil, for example, robs the soil of nitrogen until they are fully decomposed, which takes time. Livestock manures can be full of weed seeds. If you use manure, make sure that it's fully composted — in other words, that it's been sitting around for a year or two and very little of the original raw material is visible.

## Adding compost to existing lawns

Use a peat moss spreader (Figure 6-2) to spread a thin scattering of compost over your lawn. The compost will quickly disappear as it gets washed down into the soil by rain or irrigation, where it can do its good work. Doing this a few times a year will go a long way to improving soil health. Only about ⅓" to ½" of compost will benefit the lawn significantly.

# Making Your Own Compost

Get free soil-boosting, nutrient-rich compost for your lawn by making your own. There are countless commercially available compost bins that make the process mess-free and hassle-free (see Figure 6-3). You can also build your own bin, or even just make a simple compost pile.

**FIGURE 6-3:** Commercially available composters include wire bins, enclosed bins, and tumblers. You can also make your own tidy compost pile using wooden pallets.

**WARNING**

Some municipalities and homeowners associations (HOA) regulate the type and location of compost bins, so check with yours before purchasing or installing one. If your HOA bans composting altogether, consider asking them to reconsider by enthusiastically describing all the benefits of compost!

One of the keys to effective composting is to use a mix of "green" (fresh and moist) and "brown" (dry) materials. Green materials include vegetable scraps, weeds from the garden, and fresh grass clippings. Brown materials include dry leaves, straw, and dry grass clippings. Keep the materials damp but not saturated and turn the compost to incorporate air (a garden fork makes this easy).

Most commercial composters are designed to offer good airflow and include a cover to prevent the materials from becoming saturated after a rain. If you use an open bin or simply pile your ingredients in an out-of-the-way corner of your yard, be sure to cover it, turn the materials regularly, and use a garden hose to keep the pile evenly moist but not soaking wet.

**WARNING**

A pile made up solely of fresh grass clippings will quickly turn into a sour, smelly, slimy mess due to the type of microbes that thrive in wet, oxygen-poor environments. By layering fresh materials like grass clippings with dry materials like tree leaves or straw and turning the pile regularly, you'll create an oxygen-rich environment and encourage the type of microbes that create rich, dark, earthy, crumbly (and nonsmelly) compost.

**WARNING**

If you use pesticides or herbicides on your lawn, keep grass clippings out of your compost.

# Nurturing Soil Health

Improving your soil isn't a one-time deal. It's something you need to do on an ongoing basis as part of maintaining a healthy lawn. Keep in mind that your lawn is made up of grass plants, and just like a vegetable or flower garden, the soil beneath it needs regular attention to ensure it can support the healthiest plants.

This gardener's adage sums it up: Feed your soil, and your soil will feed your plants. The beneficial microbes in a healthy soil ecosystem slowly break down organic matter into a steady supply of nutrients for plants. This creates a natural cycling of nutrients that means you'll need to fertilize less often. It's win-win for you and your lawn!

Core aeration and compost topdressing can help bring oxygen into the soil to stimulate a more extensive grass root system and to build the soil over time. This is especially important in compacted clay soils.

## HEALTHY SOIL = HAPPY MOOD

There's another benefit to nurturing your soil. Scientists have discovered that healthy soils rich in organic matter contain robust populations of bacteria called *Mycobacterium vaccae* that triggers a release of serotonin (the "happy hormone") in the brain. No wonder that gardeners get the itch every spring to get their hands in the soil!

# 2

# Preparation and Planting

**IN THIS PART . . .**

Find everything you need to know about preparing your yard and soil for planting, including options for getting rid of old grass and weeds and evaluating and improving your yard's drainage.

Get help knowing when to plant your new lawn from seed, sod, plugs, or sprigs and choose the method that's best for your landscape, climate, and budget.

Find out how to care for your newly planted lawn.

# Chapter **7**

# Preparing Your Lawn Area for Planting

P reparing your yard properly is one of the most important steps in planting a lawn. Cut corners, and you'll have serious problems down the road. Planting a lawn is a lot like painting your house. You don't treasure the idea of scraping off the old paint because it's a tedious and dirty job. However, if you don't get rid of the old paint, patch holes, and fill in cracks, the new paint you put on quickly peels off, and you have to do it all over again. Lawns are the same. If you don't get rid of the weeds and debris, the weeds will just come right back.

In this chapter you find out all you need to know about preparing for planting, whether you're starting from scratch after new construction or embarking on a full makeover of an existing lawn.

## Do You Need to Replace Your Lawn?

Doing a complete makeover by replacing your existing lawn is a big job. It might be necessary if your lawn is more bare soil than grass, or if it's so overrun with weeds that it's beyond reasonable repair. Maybe you need to fix the slope of your yard to direct water away from your house or otherwise improve drainage. Or per-haps you just don't like the grass you have and want to start over with a new type of turf.

**TIP**

A complete makeover will likely entail lots of digging, hauling in new materials, grading, and other heavy labor. Before you commit to a time-consuming and expensive makeover of your entire lawn, ponder these questions:

>> Can bare spots can be patched, especially those in out-of-the-way areas? (Find tips for renovating bare spots in Chapter 14.)

>> Are there unused or lesser-used parts of your lawn that you can replace with shrubs, gardens, mulched areas, wildflowers, or other nonlawn uses? (Find ideas for lawn alternatives in Chapter 19.)

>> Are the biggest problem areas beneath trees or in other shaded spots? Because there are no lawn grasses that will thrive in deep shade, you'll want to consider other options (see Chapter 19).

>> Do you live in a climate that is arid or semi-arid? Maybe it's time to rethink having a thirsty lawn and consider other options for some or all of it, such as xeriscaping (a style of landscaping that incorporates drought-tolerant plants to reduce the need for irrigation). Some municipalities even offer rebates for replacing thirsty lawns with less water-intensive landscaping. Read more about xeriscaping in Chapter 23.

>> Have you taken steps to improve your existing lawn by ensuring it's being properly watered, fertilized, and aerated and/or by improving the soil by adding organic matter? (Read more about these techniques in Chapters 6 and 11 through 14.)

>> Does your municipality or homeowners association have any rules or regulations around lawn and landscape renovations?

If a complete makeover is right for you, read on. This chapter deals with preparing your yard for seeding, laying sod, or planting sprigs or plugs. If renovation sounds like the right path forward, go to Chapter 14 for details.

## Planning Ahead

The importance of planning and preparation can't be overstated. The more time and effort you put into proper and thorough preparation prior to planting, the more successful you'll be in your efforts.

**REMEMBER**

Keep in mind that the best time to plant cool-season grasses like Kentucky bluegrass or tall fescue is in fall or spring. Warm-season grasses are best planted in early summer. At those times, for those grasses, the upcoming weather is ideal for vigorous growth and the grasses become established quickly with a minimum of problems. You'll want to count backward from the optimal planting time to create a schedule of tasks. (Check out Chapter 2 to determine your lawn climate and learn more about what grasses are best suited to your region.)

Carefully plan your project well ahead of time so you can be sure that all the preparation work is completed by the appropriate planting time. If you have a lot of soil to move, you may want to start working four to six weeks or more prior to the ideal planting time. If you're using an herbicide to kill existing vegetation, you may need to wait up to six weeks before you can plant grass seed (check the product label), or you may need to repeat the application a couple of weeks later for difficult-to-eradicate weeds. Use a calendar to plan, making sure to build in extra time for bad weather and unexpected delays.

TIP

If you plan to deal with existing sod and weeds by smothering them (more on that later in this chapter in the "Smothering the sod" section) rather than by using herbicides, the process can take three months or longer. If you can plan far enough ahead (six months to a year), you can leave the smothered sod in place and it will decompose, adding organic matter and nutrients to the soil.

WARNING

Start by finding out if your city, town, or homeowners association has any regulations or permitting requirements around lawn and landscape renovations or turf removal. Better to learn about these before you get started!

As you begin planning your lawn makeover, sketch a landscape map that includes items that you plan to incorporate immediately as well as those on your long-term wish list. Now's the time to dream big — where could you put that new patio? Is there a sunny spot for a wildflower meadow or some fruit trees? How about some raised vegetable gardens? A gazebo? A greenhouse? (Find out how draw a landscape map in Chapter 1.)

## NEW HOUSE, NEW LAWN

Congratulations to those of you who are moving into a newly built home!

Chances are, you have a whole yard outside in immediate need of trees, shrubs, flowers, and grass to make your home landscape complete. The first thing you need to do is clean up the construction mess the builders left behind.

Get a wheelbarrow and start scouting the yard for nails and screws, broken slabs of wall board, piles of mortar and cement, pieces of wood, and any other debris.

*(continued)*

*(continued)*

If you're lucky, the contractors stockpiled the topsoil when the project started and placed it back on the landscape at final grading. (*Topsoil* is the uppermost layer of soil that provides good conditions for root growth. *Subsoil* is found beneath the topsoil and is less hospitable to plant roots.) If they simply leveled the huge dirt pile they created when they dug the hole for your basement and foundation, you may have a yard covered in rocky or clay subsoil, with little or no topsoil. If that's the case, you'll want to bring in enough topsoil to cover your yard with a layer at least 4 inches deep. For a large yard, that amount of topsoil adds up quickly!

Use this opportunity to create a level grade around your yard, making sure that the land slopes away from your house so that water drains away from your foundation (see the section "Making the grade" later in this chapter). If you have seriously sloping ground, you may want to consider terracing or filling in areas. A landscape contractor can help you do it properly (see the section "Hiring help" later in this chapter).

It's also the perfect time to brainstorm all the features you'd like to incorporate in your new landscape and then sketch a landscape map, as described in Chapter 1.

# Getting Rid of Old Grass and Weeds

If you've decided to go for the total lawn makeover, then the first order of business is to tackle the old lawn, weeds, and other debris. Chances are, you'll be doing some digging (and maybe a lot of it, depending on the method you use), so keep in mind the following:

**WARNING**

» Prior to doing any digging, call Dig Safe (by dialing 811), a free public utility locator that notifies member utilities of upcoming excavation projects so their teams can come out and mark underground utility lines. You don't want to accidentally cut off your (or your neighbor's) Internet! In some states, you must notify Dig Safe at least 72 hours before digging on public or private land.

» If you have an underground sprinkler system, be sure to flag the sprinkler heads so you can avoid damaging them with the tiller.

» Many trees and shrubs have shallow root systems that grow right at or just a few inches below the soil surface, and those roots usually extend beyond the drip line (as far out as the leaves on the ends of the branches). Try to avoid trenching or removing soil or adding more than 2 to 3 inches of soil to the area within the tree's dripline. You can damage trees and shrubs by digging too deeply or too closely to them, so use caution and dig down only an inch or so. You'd rather be safe than sorry.

# Nonchemical ways to remove old sod

If you prefer not to use herbicides, there are several tried-and-true methods of tackling sod and weeds. (The different types of herbicides and their use are described in the section "The herbicide approach," later in this chapter.)

## Tilling

For most small to modest-sized yards, a rotary tiller is a good, manageable tool for the job. You can rent a tiller by the day at many rental centers, home improvement stores, and garden centers. Be sure to get a tiller that has the rotating tines in the rear behind the tires. A rear-tined tiller is easier to handle and much more effective for the job of breaking up sod than a tiller with the tines in front. Till the soil to a depth of 4 to 8 inches, rake out the grass and weeds, and till again, repeating until all the green matter is gone. If perennial weeds are present, some parts will remain that can sprout into new weed plants, so a second tilling or selective hand removal may be needed a couple of weeks after the first round of tilling. Dump all this material in a pile where it will decompose over a period of months and transform into compost. (Another option is to bring the material to a municipal recycling center that accepts yard waste.) Note that it can be challenging to till an area with very dense turf or compacted clay soil.

TIP

Don't try to till dry or very wet soil. A tiller will just bounce over dry soil, and it will sink in and create a muddy mess if the soil is too wet. Ideally, the soil should be lightly moist. Water the whole area, let it dry for a few days, and then till.

## Renting a sod cutter

You simply guide the sod cutter over your old weedy lawn, and it cuts the turf at just below the soil surface. You can rent a sod cutter at large rental centers. Instead of saving the sod for replanting, turn the sheets of grass upside down and pile them in an out-of-the-way place. A pile of old lawn sod decomposes over time, yielding nutrient-rich compost. You also can haul the sod to your local recycling center that accepts yard waste.

## Smothering the sod

If your lawn is small — say less than 1,000 square feet — you can kill the grass by smothering it with a layer of something that deprives the sod of sunlight and water. The smothering process can take anywhere from a month to three months or more, depending on how hot and dry your season is. The longer you can leave the sod to smother, the more likely it will be fully killed and will begin to decompose.

The easiest (but not necessarily the most environmentally friendly) material to use is black plastic sheeting. Go to the hardware store or home center and buy enough heavy-gauge black plastic to cover the entire area. Spread out the plastic and stake it in place or weigh down the edges with logs, rocks, or something else heavy. Naturally, this method has an aesthetic downside. Your lawn looks pretty ugly covered in black plastic, but the method works.

Another option is to use sheets of corrugated cardboard (flattened boxes work well but remove any plastic tape or staples first). Be sure to overlap the edges so no light gets through to the ground. In windy spots, you may need to weigh down each piece of cardboard with a rock or other weight. As with black plastic, the aesthetic is, well, lacking.

A somewhat more aesthetically pleasing option is to lay down several sheets of wet newspaper, overlapping them as you go, and then cover them with a layer of bark mulch. Making sure to cover the edges of the sheets so they don't catch the wind. The mulch holds the newspaper securely in place and disguises it.

## Bulldozing

The idea of a bulldozer roaring back and forth across your yard may sound a little strange, but if you have a large area, a small, backyard-sized bulldozer (called a skip loader, skid steer, or Bobcat) may be a good option. Adjust the blade so that you're just scraping off the thin layer of grass and weeds, removing as little valuable topsoil as possible. Dump the weeds and grass into a pile and let them decompose or haul the material to your local recycling center that accepts yard waste.

# The herbicide approach

Most professional landscapers will tell you that the best way to get rid of weeds (or a dreary lawn) is to spray the entire area with an herbicide. This section covers tips for using herbicides to prepare your yard for planting; you'll find more details on using herbicides in Chapter 15.

**WARNING**

All herbicides — even organic ones — must be used with care to avoid damaging nearby plants and for the safety of people and pets. Always read the label instructions carefully and follow them to the letter — it's not only smart, but it's also the law.

For a large lawn, say over 1,000 square feet, you will want to rent or buy a backpack sprayer to apply herbicides. Some herbicides are sold in ready-to-use (RTU) formulas; others are sold as concentrates that you mix with water according to the manufacturer's instructions.

## Herbicide safety

Make sure that you precisely follow the herbicide label instructions and wear all recommended safety gear. At a minimum, wear a long-sleeved shirt, long pants, rubber boots, plastic gloves, and safety goggles. For other safety tips on using herbicides, see Chapter 15. Here are some additional guidelines for using herbicides.

>> Timing of application is often critically important; some products are effective only within a certain temperature range, and some work only when applied during a specific time of year. If you're unsure of how to use a product, reach out to the manufacturer or contact your local cooperative extension office for help.

>> Spray on windless days to prevent the herbicide from drifting onto nearby trees, shrubs, and gardens. Use a coarser droplet spray at a lower pressure to avoid creating a fine mist that can drift onto desirable plants nearby with the slightest breeze.

>> Cordon off the area you'll be spraying with tape, streamers, or some type of barrier. Keep kids and pets off the lawn and away from the yard.

>> Follow herbicide label instructions for the reentry time — this is the period of time after application you need to wait before allowing people and pets to enter the treated area.

## Types of herbicides

Herbicides can be broken into two categories: pre-emergent and post-emergent.

**WARNING**

>> **Pre-emergent herbicides** prevent seeds from germinating; they do nothing to control existing weeds. Worse yet, they'll kill germinating grass seeds so don't use pre-emergent herbicides to tackle existing sod and weeds prior to planting.

>> **Post-emergent herbicides** kill weeds that are already growing. These are the ones you'll want to use for killing existing sod and weeds. Within this group are the following types of herbicides:

- *Broad-spectrum (nonselective) herbicides:* These kill any plant they touch.

- *Selective herbicides:* These target certain types of plants, such as broadleaf weeds or grasses.

- *Contact herbicides:* These kill only the part of the plant they come into contact with.

- *Systemic herbicides:* These travel through the plant, often down into the roots, so they kill more completely.

**TIP**

Purchase a spray indicator (blue dye) product to include in the spray mix. This will help you know that you are not missing any spots and will prevent the need to respray later. The dye will wash off and/or break down in a couple of days so it's longer visible.

## Organic herbicide options

One of the key benefits of organic herbicides is that they break down quickly in the environment so there's minimal risk of long-term soil contamination.

**WARNING**

Note that organic herbicides are still potent and can cause eye, skin, and respiratory irritation; always wear goggles or a face shield as well as waterproof gloves, long sleeves, and long pants when handling and spraying them.

Organic herbicides fall into the broad-spectrum, contact herbicide categories. Spray them on foliage, and within a day or so, the foliage will brown and wither. These products don't travel through the plants, so roots remain alive and will likely resprout. Repeated applications are needed: Apply the product, wait a few days or a week to allow weeds to resprout, apply again, and repeat until plants don't resprout, indicating that the food reserves in the roots are depleted. Once it looks like the herbicide has done its work, you can rake off any debris.

**TIP**

These herbicide products work best on warm to hot, sunny days and are much less effective in cool, overcast weather.

Here are a few of the active ingredients found in organic herbicides:

>> **Vinegar:** While supermarket-variety vinegar (5 percent acetic acid) will knock back young weed growth, horticultural-grade vinegar (20 percent acetic acid) is four times stronger and much more effective.

>> **Essential oil-based herbicide:** Products containing certain essential oils, notably citrus, clove, and cinnamon, kill plants by disrupting their cell membranes.

>> **Caprylic acid and capric acid:** These plant extracts are derived from coconut oil and palm seed kernel. Herbicide formulations containing these ingredients cause plants to dry out and wither.

## Nonorganic (synthetic) herbicide options

While garden center shelves are usually well stocked with a variety of synthetic herbicides, the availability of individual products can change for a variety of reasons. For example, as new and improved formulations are introduced, others fall out of favor. Sometimes, active ingredients are subject to new regulations or bans. Also, states may have laws that are stricter than federal regulations; an herbicide available to your cousin living in the next state over may not be for sale at your garden center. Your cooperative extension office will have the latest information and can help you decide which herbicide is best for your needs. You can find a link to your state cooperative extension office at https://extension.org/find-cooperative-extension-in-your-state.

**WARNING**

Some herbicides prevent weed seeds from germinating and growing into weed plants (pre-emergent herbicides), whereas others kill weeds that are up and growing (post-emergent herbicides). Make sure you choose a post-emergent herbicide if you're trying to get rid of existing weeds. (See the section "Types of herbicides," earlier in this chapter.) Post-emergent products work best when the weeds are actively growing. Weeds under drought, cold, or heat stress will not be effectively controlled with post-emergent products. So, it can help to water the weeds well and then use the products several days later when the weeds perk up and begin growing!

**WARNING**

It's critical to read the product labels to determine the active ingredients. For example, "Roundup" was once synonymous with "glyphosate," but this is no longer the case. There are other formulations of Roundup brand herbicide, some of which contain no glyphosate but rather a variety of other herbicides. There are also products containing glyphosate sold under different brand names.

Like organic herbicides, synthetic herbicides may require multiple applications to fully kill existing vegetation. Apply the product, wait a few days or a week to allow weeds to resprout, apply again, and repeat until plants don't resprout, indicating that the food reserves in the roots are depleted. Once it looks like the herbicide has done its work, you can rake off any debris.

**WARNING**

Check the product label to determine how long you need to wait after applying an herbicide before it's safe to plant grass seed. This waiting period can be as short as a week or up to six weeks. This allows time for the herbicide to degrade in the soil so it won't harm germinating seeds.

For more information on controlling weeds and using herbicides, see Chapter 15.

# Determining the Effectiveness of Your Drainage

**WARNING**

Simply put, water *must* drain away from your house. If water accumulates around the foundation walls, it can build up and seep through, filling your basement with excess moisture. In cold regions, this water can freeze, causing cracks in your foundation.

If moisture seeps into wooden floor joists, they can rot, threatening the structural integrity of your home.

Avoid a wet foundation at all costs, or it will cost you. If water pools near your foundation for more than a few hours after a rain, you'll likely need to regrade your yard (more on that in the "Making the Grade" section later in this chapter), and if you don't have gutters, consider getting them. You may also need to install an underground drainage system.

Gravel-filled trenches and flexible drainpipes are the two most common forms of underground drainage systems. Such systems capture runoff water and channel it away from your house. You can channel the water to a low spot (a good area for a rain garden) or to a dry well, which basically is a large hole filled with gravel where water can collect and slowly drain or be pumped away (see Figure 7-1).

Drainage is so important that it pays to hire an experienced contractor to offer advice and, if necessary, install the drainage system.

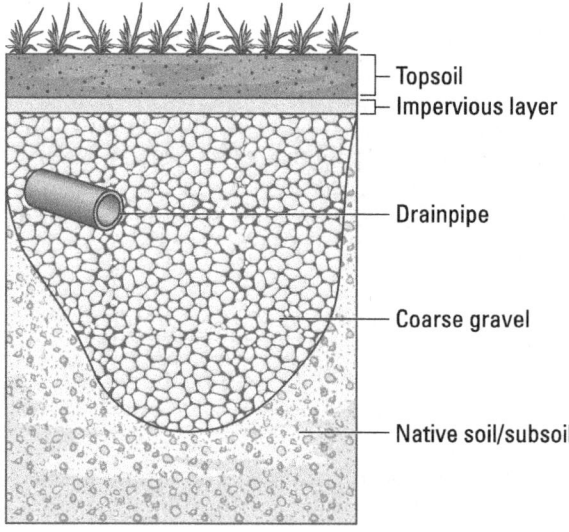

**FIGURE 7-1:** Some drainage systems include drainpipes that channel water away from the house to a dry well, where water can collect and slowly drain down into the soil.

- Topsoil
- Impervious layer
- Drainpipe
- Coarse gravel
- Native soil/subsoil

TIP

If an area of your yard away from your house collects water after a rainstorm, it might be a good spot for a rain garden (see Figure 7-2). Located in naturally occurring or human-made low spots that collect water draining from buildings and higher-ground areas, rain gardens are planted with water-tolerant shrubs and perennials that provide food and habitat for pollinators and other wildlife. Water slowly absorbs into the soil rather than running off into storm drains, reducing the strain on sewer systems.

**FIGURE 7-2:**
Rain gardens are
ideal for low
spots that collect
water. Plant the
lowest areas with
the most
water-tolerant
plants; the banks
are good spots
for plants that
tolerate
intermittently
wet soils.

# Making the Grade

The term *grading* describes how you reshape the surface of your yard to level it or to create the desired slopes. Depending on the existing slope of your yard (and how much you want to change it) as well as the soil type, leveling and grading the ground can be a fairly simple task or an expensive ordeal.

If your yard is small and relatively flat, you can probably rake the soil smooth by hand. If your yard is hilly or needs extensive reshaping, grading will likely require earth-moving equipment (and someone who knows how to use it).

**WARNING**

Proper grading is a critical part of the preparation process, so don't skimp on it! You may want to hire a landscape contractor to do the grading work. Contractors will have all the proper equipment and can recognize and fix drainage problems. If your landscape is complex, with lots of slopes and features, consult with a landscape designer or landscape architect ahead of time to help you create an overall landscape plan. See the section "Hiring help," later in this chapter.

## Why slope matters

As important as it is to grade the soil to achieve an attractive lawn, a more important reason is to preserve the foundation of your house. Your lawn needs to slope gradually away from your house so that rainfall and roof runoff can drain slowly away from the foundation.

Ideally, the ground around your house should slope away about ¼ inch for every foot or about 2 feet per 100 feet. In other words, at a distance of 100 feet from your house, the ground should be about 2 feet lower than it is at the perimeter of your house.

TIP

You can measure this slope with a string and stakes (see Figure 7-3). Start by driving a 3-foot-long wooden stake into the soil at the base of your house. Measure a distance 100 feet away from your house and drive another 3-foot-long stake into the ground.

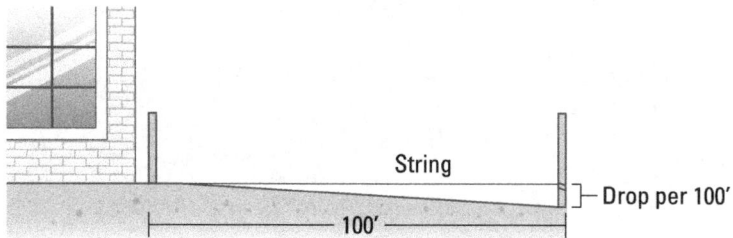

FIGURE 7-3:
Checking slope.

Attach a string at ground level on the stake near the house. Then run the string out to the other stake. Pulling the string as taut as possible, attach it to the stake so that the string is level. You can determine whether the string is level by holding a carpenter's level beside the string and raising or lowering the string so that the bubble appears within the grooves on the level. You can also use a line level, which you hang right on the string.

Now measure the distance from where the string attaches at the far stake to the ground. If the drop measures 1 to 2 feet, you may be able to do any light leveling yourself. If the ground is level or slopes upward, you should probably hire a professional to do the grading for you because it will likely involve moving quite a bit of soil. If you have really steep ground that slopes away from your house, consider building terraces (see Figure 7-4) or planting ground covers (see Chapter 19) because lawns on steep slopes are difficult to mow and to water efficiently.

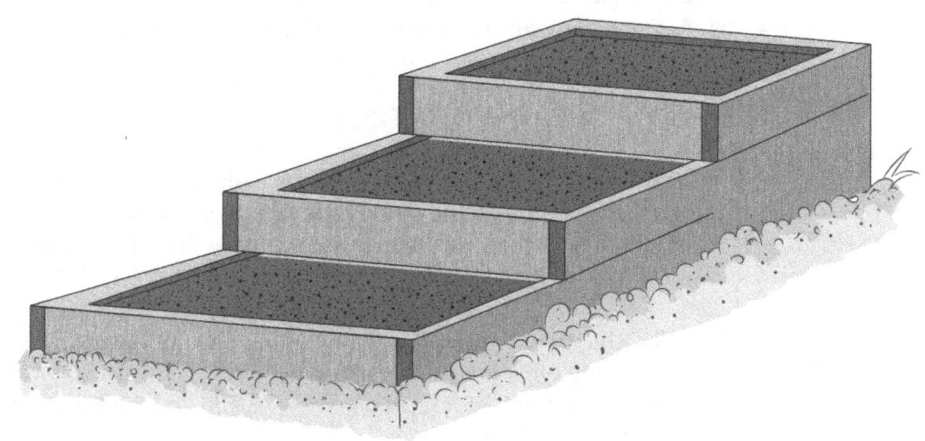

FIGURE 7-4:
Terraces are a good lawn alternative for steep ground.

**WARNING**

Before you or anybody else does any grading, call Dig Safe (by dialing 811) to ensure that you don't disturb any underground utilities. Dig Safe is a free service that notifies utility companies of planned excavation projects, so their teams can come out and mark the location of the buried lines. In some states, you must notify Dig Safe at least 72 hours before digging on public or private land.

If your house hooks up to its own well and/or you have a septic system, get out your surveyor's map. If you don't have one, you should be able to get one from your county or city planning or building department. Find the well and its water line, as well as the location of your septic tank and drain field (also called a leach field). If you can't get a survey map, call a company that installs and maintains septic systems and ask if they can help you locate the lines or recommend someone who can. Disturbing your well, water lines, septic tank, or drain field can result in costly repairs.

## Hiring help

If the job is reasonably straightforward, a *landscape contractor* should be able to perform the grading work. Landscape contractors often have state licenses to operate, and they should be bonded and insured to operate heavy equipment. Landscape contractors often provide design services and consultations.

For more complex jobs, you may want to start with a *landscape designer* or *landscape architect*. A landscape designer can help you create an overall plan for your yard, and they may be able to offer recommendations for landscape contractors. Landscape designers aren't required to have any professional degree or license. A *landscape architect* has a university degree and a license from the state you live in. In addition to drawing up a detailed landscape plan, a landscape architect can often hire the subcontractors to do the work under their supervision. Learn more about working with landscape professionals in Chapter 1.

**WARNING**

Whomever you hire, aim to get three estimates from three different architects or contractors and then get three references from each bidding company. This job is going to cost you a lot of money, and it directly impacts the value of your home. A bad grass-planting job is a relatively easy fix. A bad grading job, on the other hand, can mean years of nightmares and court action.

During a large grading job, your landscape contractor should start by taking off the topsoil and setting it to one side. Once they're done grading the subsoil and/or installing drainage, they'll replace and level the topsoil. Make sure your contractor plans to do this or has another plan to ensure you'll be planting your new lawn in topsoil, not subsoil.

**TIP**

If you have low spots that need filling or some other job that requires new topsoil, keep the following points in mind:

>> **Make sure that the topsoil you get isn't full of rocks, weed seeds, or toxic waste.** In other words, ask where it came from.

>> **Get compost added to your topsoil as a mix.** Many landscape contractors add compost to their topsoil, and your lawn benefits in the long run. Keep in mind that compost decomposes over time, resulting in some settling. Ideally, a topsoil/compost mix brought in for grading a lawn should contain no more than 20 percent compost to minimize the amount of settling.

>> **Try to work in any new topsoil with the subsoil or removed topsoil.** Mixing the two soils helps to eliminate *interfacing,* which is a line where different soils meet. Interfacing can impede water drainage and inhibit root growth.

Trees can pose a problem for any grading job. Don't pile up soil against the trunks of existing trees or lower the grade around their root zones. Either practice will likely kill the tree. To keep the grade around a tree intact, you may need to build retaining walls (see Figure 7-5). Reputable contractors and landscape architects know to grade without damaging tree roots; they also know not to cover tree roots with too much soil. How much is too much depends on several factors, including the age of the tree and soil type. It's highly advisable to contact a certified arborist to advise you (and any contractors you've hired) before doing any soil work. You can find certified arborists in your area at www.treesaregood.org/findanarborist.

Once your yard has been graded, it will still need some light grading and raking to smooth the soil around the foundation, near trees, along walkways, and anywhere else it needs a fine touch. You can pay your contractor to do this or do it yourself. Simply go around the yard with a wheelbarrow, knock off the tops of high spots, and use the soil to fill in low spots.

## Grading the ground yourself

If your yard is small and the ground is relatively level, gently sloped, and has no major impediments like huge boulders, you may be able to grade the area yourself. Of course, your first step is to remove all existing lawn and vegetation (see the section "Getting Rid of Old Grass and Weeds," earlier in this chapter).

The tools you need for soil grading by hand are simple. First, because you may need to haul soil from a higher spot to a lower spot, make sure that you have a sturdy wheelbarrow. Next, get a shovel with a squared-off blade. A pointed blade is good for digging, but a squared-off blade is better for skimming the soil to smooth out rough spots.

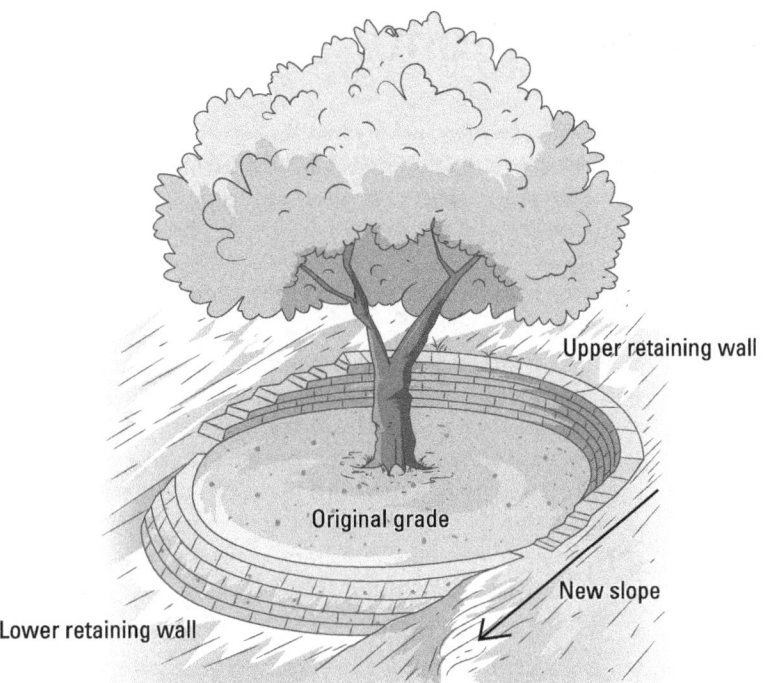

Upper retaining wall

Original grade

New slope

FIGURE 7-5:
Retaining
walls protect
tree roots.

Lower retaining wall

A long-handled metal rake is the next tool you'll need. The ideal type is a landscaper's rake, which has a wide head up to 3 feet across. You may be able to rent one from a rental center that carries landscaping equipment. You can level more ground with one movement than you can with a regular garden rake that is only 18 inches wide.

If you don't already have one, buy an 8-foot-long 2 × 4 piece of wood and a carpenter's level. As you rake soil, you can lay the 2 × 4 on the ground with the level on top to see whether your low spots are level and whether you're getting the gradual slope you need.

TIP

Make sure that your soil is slightly moist before you start grading. Dry soil just does not level as well as moist soil. If your soil appears powdery and dry or hard and dry, water it well (to a depth of at least 6 inches) several days before you start to level it. Likewise, wet soil is difficult to work with. Allow heavy, wet soil to dry before attempting to level.

If you haven't done so already, this is the time to decide how you'll water your new lawn. The online chapter that you can find at www.dummies.com/go/lawncarefd2e will help you decide if an in-ground irrigation system is right for you and, if so, how to install one. If you're ready to continue with site preparations, read on.

# Adding Amendments

It's best to do a soil test prior to adding any amendments to your soil (other than compost) to see if your soil is lacking in nutrients or needs the pH (acidity/alkalinity) adjusted. Chapter 6 offers information on soil testing as well as details on how to modify soil pH.

The following are amendments you may want to add to your soil:

» **Starter fertilizer:** A *starter fertilizer* — one that you work into the soil before planting — helps grass plants get established by providing the nutrients needed for healthy root growth. Starter fertilizers are usually higher in phosphorous than nitrogen because phosphorus stimulates root growth. (Having too much nitrogen at this point encourages too much leafy growth that young roots may not be able to support.) If your soil test shows that you have adequate phosphorus, you can skip the starter fertilizer. High-phosphorous fertilizers tend to be slow-release fertilizers — they release their nutrients at a slower pace, promoting even, sustained growth.

» **Lime or sulfur:** If your soil test indicates your soil is too acidic to support a healthy lawn, you'll want to add lime now. If it's too alkaline, you'll want to add sulfur. See Chapter 6 for details.

» **Compost:** Adding compost is one of the best things you can do to help get your lawn off to a good start. Learn more about the benefits of compost in Chapter 6. Applying a 1-inch layer over the entire lawn area should do the trick. If you applied topsoil/compost mix prior to grading, you can skip adding additional compost.

## How to add them

Use a fertilizer spreader to evenly spread the starter fertilizer as well as the lime or sulfur over the entire planting area. Then spread the compost, if using; a peat moss/compost spreader is the easiest way to do this.

## Mixing it in

The starter fertilizer (specifically the phosphorous in it) needs to be worked into the top few inches of soil because phosphorous doesn't readily move through soil like most other nutrients. In other words, you can't just spread it on the soil and expect the roots to be able to use it. Ditto for lime and sulfur — they need to be in contact with the soil to work their magic. Compost also benefits from being mixed into the topsoil.

You can mix the amendments into the top few inches of soil using a metal-tined rake or mini tiller. You can also use a larger tiller, but if you do, adjust the tilling depth to just 3 or 4 inches and go gently; you don't want to undo all the grading and leveling you've done to the site.

# Installing Edgings

Edgings not only help give your lawn a finished look, but they also help prevent grass from migrating into flower beds, gravel walkways, and mulched areas. Likewise, they keep ground covers like ivy from encroaching on your lawn. Edgings can be made from a variety of materials, including plastic, metal, wood, and brick.

» **Plastic and metal:** Durable and long-lasting, plastic and metal edgings are valued for their ability to bend into curves and relative ease of installation. To maximize their ability to keep grass out of garden beds (and ground covers out of the lawn), edgings should be tall enough so that, once installed, 4 to 6 inches of the edging are below grade, which helps keep roots contained. Installing edging so that a few inches remain above grade will allow it to also act as a barrier to prevent grass from encroaching, and it will also help keep grass clippings out of garden beds.

Some edgings are designed to be pounded into the soil using a wooden or rubber mallet. If your soil isn't soft enough to allow this, you can cut a narrow, vertical slice in the soil, guide the edging into the slice, and firm the soil around it.

» **Wood:** The best woods to use for edging are redwood and cedar because they're naturally rot-resistant. Pressure-treated lumber is another long-lasting option. Although it's possible to create curves using pliable bender boards made from wood or wood-like synthetic materials, it's easiest to use wood for edging that's limited to straight lines.

Dig a trench deep enough for the top edge of the wood to rest at ground level or at any height above ground level you choose and then place the wood in the trench. Use galvanized metal mending plates to attach lengths of wood to each other and corner braces for connecting boards at right-angles. Another option is to secure the boards using stakes pounded in at regular intervals. Refill the trench.

» **Bricks and pavers:** Bricks offer traditional good looks; however, rectangular concrete pavers are a good alternative because they're often more affordable and available in a variety of colors and styles. Bricks and pavers can be installed in several configurations depending on your aesthetic goals. For example, they can be installed at grade so that you can run the wheels of your mower along them (see Figure 7-6). Or they can extend above grade to create a raised edge that contains garden mulch or sidewalk gravel.

To install, dig a trench at least 6 inches deep that is slightly wider and as long as the bricks/pavers. Place a 3- to 4-inch layer of gravel in the trench, followed by a 1-inch layer of sand. The depth of the trench and gravel layer will depend on the thickness of the bricks/pavers and where you want the tops to sit relative to ground level. The gravel ensures good drainage, and the sand allows you to easily make small adjustments to the height of the bricks/pavers. Use a 4-foot carpenter's level to make sure that the bricks/pavers are properly aligned and level. Once they're in place, carefully fill in around them with gravel or soil and then use sand to fill in the cracks.

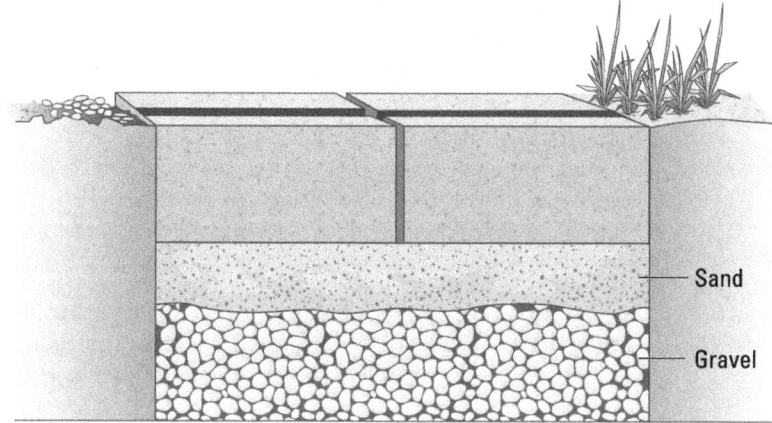

**FIGURE 7-6:**
Bricks and pavers make attractive edging. When set at ground height, they provide a place for your mower's wheels.

Sand

Gravel

# Final Leveling

Make sure the soil is at the right level for sowing seed or laying sod. If you plan on sowing seed, the soil should be level with surrounding walks, the tops of permanent sprinklers, and paved surfaces. If you plan to plant sod, you want the ground to be ½ to 1 inch lower to accommodate the thickness of the sod.

Take the time to smooth and even out the soil prior to planting. The ideal tool for this is a leveling rake, which you may be able to rent at a landscape supply store. Leveling rakes have a flat, wide head with tines or bars that pivot on the handle. As you pull the rake back and forth, it smooths out any bumps.

A landscaper's rake has a wide head that is toothed on one side and flat on the other. Use the toothed side to rake out an area, then flip over the rake and use the flat side for final leveling. If the soil is still uneven, go back to the toothed side of the rake and move the soil around to smooth it further, and then check it again. A water-filled lawn roller (Figure 7-7) is handy for further smoothing the soil surface prior to planting.

**FIGURE 7-7:**
Use a lawn roller to ensure a smooth, flat surface.

# Pre-Sprouting Weeds

Now that the ground is just right for planting, consider pre-sprouting weed seeds that are lying in wait. Gently water the prepared soil and give the weeds a week or so to come up. Then lightly rake to uproot them so that they dry out and die. Repeat every few days as needed. The whole process may take a few weeks, but it reduces the number of weeds in the future.

IN THIS CHAPTER

» **Understanding how grass seed grows and figuring out when to sow seed**

» **Knowing which grasses you can grow from seed**

» **Tallying everything you need to start a lawn from seed**

» **Sowing the seed**

» **Caring for your new lawn**

# Chapter **8**

# Planting a Lawn from Seed

S tarting a lawn from seed sounds simple and straightforward. You start with the most elemental form of plant life: seeds. You nurture them until they germinate, revel in the emergence of the young seedlings, and rejoice as they mature into flourishing turf. It's simple, yes, but that's not to say that you won't face some challenges. In this chapter, you find out what seeds need to sprout and what you can do to provide optimal conditions for the growth of your new grass plants.

## Knowing What Seeds Need to Grow

Every grass seed is a little miracle waiting to happen. The tiny grains are ready to transform into a lush, green plants — they're just waiting for their cue. To germinate and grow, seeds need water, oxygen, and the right environmental conditions.

Seeds appear lifeless, but they're simply in a resting state. Every seed contains a tiny embryo with rudimentary roots, stem, and leaves. In order to sprout, a seed needs the following:

>> **Water:** Water softens the protective seed coat, which allows the moisture to be absorbed by internal tissues. There, it causes chemical changes within the seed, and soon the tiny embryo, which had been lying dormant, begins to grow.

>> **Oxygen:** Just like animals, plants respire — that is, they consume oxygen as they metabolize food to create energy for growth. Because germinating seeds are so small and growing so quickly, they require an abundant, consistent supply of oxygen.

>> **The right temperature:** The seeds of different plants vary in their temperature requirements for germination, but all have a preferred range.

Getting seeds to germinate is just the first step, but it's a critical one on the road to establishing your new lawn.

# Determining When to Sow Grass Seed

Most garden plants have an optimal season of growth. You wouldn't want to plant heat-loving basil when the cool weather of fall is imminent. On the other hand, if you plant cool-loving spinach in the heat of summer it will bolt and turn bitter. Turfgrasses also have their preferences, and they differ depending on the type of grass. When you're starting a lawn from seed, it's especially important to get the timing right. You need to give those seeds the best possible conditions to germinate and grow healthy and strong.

## Soil temperature matters

The speed at which seeds germinate depends heavily on soil temperature. For example, say the optimum soil temperature for germination is 65°F, and at that temperature, seeds sprout in about ten days. If the soil temperature is cooler, then germination might take three weeks or more. If the soil temperature is too low, then seeds might not germinate at all.

The optimal soil temperature for sowing cool-season grasses is 50-60°F. For warm-season grasses, it's 70-95°F. (A soil thermometer is a useful tool for measuring soil temperatures.) Just as important as soil temperature is upcoming weather. You want to sow seeds just prior to the grass's season of most vigorous growth.

# Sow before the season of best growth

For cool-season grasses (which grow best in fall, spring, and, in some areas, winter), the best time to plant is late summer to early fall. At that time of year, the ground is still warm enough for quick germination, and the young grass plants have the entire upcoming cool season to become established. Early spring is the second-best time to start a cool-season lawn from seed. Although the young grass has less time to become established before the onset of hot weather, the results are usually satisfactory.

Warm-season grasses are best planted in late spring. At that time, the weather is still mild enough to let you get the grass established, but the hot weather of summer and the most vigorous growth are just around the corner.

# Other factors affecting germination and early growth

In addition to properly timing your seed sowing, other factors to consider include the freshness of the seed, the planting depth, and the soil conditions.

## Freshness of seed

Ideally, any grass seed you see on store shelves or order from a reputable source will be fresh enough to ensure good germination. Grass seed that has been stored properly under cool, dry conditions remains viable for two to three years. (After that, the germination rate will start to drop but the seed is probably okay to plant for a year or two longer; you'll just want to sow extra seed to compensate.)

**TIP**

The label on the box or bag of seed lists the month and year in which the germination rate of the seed was tested, which gives you a general idea of the freshness. Some states regulate the length of time grass seed can be sold after its last test date before it needs to be retested and relabeled. (Learn more on germination rates and seed labels in the "Understanding Seed Labels" section later in this chapter.)

## Planting depth

Seeds use stored energy to fuel their initial growth. When you consider the small size of a grass seed, it's clear that there isn't a lot of food available! Once a seed germinates, it must grow a tiny root and send up its first shoot into the daylight where it can start photosynthesizing — all before that stored food runs out. That's why planting depth is so important. If you plant a seed too deeply, the tiny plant will use up all its energy reserves before the shoot is tall enough to burst from the soil and reach the sunlight. Grass seeds should be covered by no more than ¼ inch of soil or mulch material (find ways to accomplish that in the section "Ready, Set, Grow," later in this chapter).

### Soil conditions

It's critical that the tiny roots that emerge from germinating seeds can easily make their way down into the soil because that's where the plants will be accessing the water and nutrients they need to grow. Moist, healthy soils allow emerging roots to quickly dive deep. In contrast, compacted soils inhibit root growth, leading to roots that are susceptible to drying out. (Learn more about building healthy soil in Chapter 6.)

# Planning for Watering

Seeds not only need water to germinate, but they also depend on a steady supply of moisture to support the tiny, vulnerable seedlings. If they dry out now, they're goners, and there's no going back; you can't turn on germination and then turn it off.

Now's the time to plan how you'll water your new patch of lawn — *before* you plant. (Learn more about watering options in Chapters 8 and 12.) At the very least, you need a hose and a hose-end sprinkler. (It's very time-consuming to water a lawn by hand and therefore it's easy to neglect this important task. It's much easier to turn on a sprinkler.)

TIP

Keep in mind that you want to avoid walking on the newly seeded area as much as possible until the grass plants are up and growing strong. If your sprinkler doesn't cover the entire lawn, you'll need to drag the sprinkler across the surface by pulling on the hose as you stand at the edge of the seedbed. You may end up disturbing the seedbed a bit so, if possible, set up a system that lets you water the whole area without needing to move the sprinkler.

# What Types of Lawns Can You Start from Seed?

You can start all cool-season grasses from seed. On the other hand, many warm-season grasses (including hybrid bermudagrass, St. Augustinegrass, and almost all types of zoysiagrass) are best started, or can only be started, from sod, sprigs, or plugs. If you're unsure of what types of grass grow well in your climate, Chapters 3, 4, and 5 offer more information on lawn climates and grass types.

Table 8-1 shows you which lawn grasses you can start from seed and how quickly the seed usually germinates. The table also shows you how many pounds of seed to sow over an area that measures 1,000 square feet.

**TABLE 8-1**      **Seeding Chart**

| Grass Type | Pounds per 1,000 Square Feet | Days to Germination |
|---|---|---|
| Bentgrass (cs) | ½ to 1 | 6 to 14 days |
| Bahiagrass (ws) | 6 to 10 | 10 to 28 days |
| Bluegrass, Kentucky (cs) | 1 to 2 | 14 to 21 days |
| Bermudagrass, common (ws) | 1 to 2 | 10 to 14 days |
| Buffalograss | 1 to 3 | 7 to 14 days |
| Centipedegrass (ws) | ¼ to ½ | 14 to 21days |
| Fescue, fine (cs) | 3 to 5 | 7 to 14 days |
| Fescue, tall (cs) | 6 to 10 | 7 to 12 days |
| Ryegrass, annual (cs) | 4 to 5 | 5 to 10 days |
| Ryegrass, perennial (cs) | 4 to 5 | 5 to 10 days |

**Note:** *(cs) = cool season; (ws) = warm season*

**TIP**      To facilitate spreading of tiny centipedegrass seeds, mix them with sand.

# Understanding Seed Labels

The people who package grass seed don't always put just one type of seed in each package. Sometimes they combine different types of seeds in different ways. (Because sod comes from seed, most sods sold are described similarly.)

Here are ways seeds may be packaged:

>> **Straights** are made up of just one type of grass or just one variety or cultivar (cultivated variety). Warm-season grasses, such as bermudagrass and centipedegrass, are sold this way.

>> **Blends** are combinations of several (usually two to four) different varieties of one type of grass. Cool-season grasses, especially tall fescues, are often sold this way.

>> **Mixtures** are combinations of different types of grasses. For example, Kentucky bluegrass commonly gets mixed with some fine fescue and perennial ryegrass. Sometimes mixtures include nongrass plants, such as clover.

TIP

Why are straights, blends, and mixtures important? Usually, a mixture or blend of grasses results in a stronger, more versatile lawn. That's because the conditions across your yard probably vary. Some areas might be sunny, some in light shade. The soil might dry out faster in some spots than others. By planting a blend or mix of grasses you ensure that the lawn grows well under all the different conditions and looks good over your entire yard.

For example, in a cool-season mixture, the red fescue grows better in shade, the Kentucky bluegrass in sun, and the perennial ryegrass in areas where people walk a lot. When you look at the lawn, you can't tell what's growing where. Instead, you see uniform turf throughout your yard regardless of varying conditions.

Improved disease resistance is another good reason to plant mixtures or blends. If a disease wipes out one variety in a blend of tall fescues, another resistant variety picks up the slack and takes over — and you probably won't even notice. If the lawn had been made up of just the one variety, you might have lost the whole lawn.

## What's on the label

A package of grass seed contains a wealth of information. In fact, because of the Federal Seed Act of 1939, all grass seed sold in the United States (other countries have similar programs) must be labeled pretty much the same way. Figure 8-1 shows a sample of the most important part of a grass seed label.

| Pure Seed | Water Miser<br>Turf Type Tall Fescue | Germ. | Origin |
|---|---|---|---|
| 29.40% | Tough Tall Fescue | 90% | OR |
| 24.55% | Real Tough Tall Fescue | 90% | OR |
| 24.55% | Mean Tall Fescue | 90% | OR |
| 19.65% | Exeter Tall Fescue | 90% | OR |
| 0.50% | Other Crop | | CMS 480 |
| 1.25% | Inert Matter | | Lot No. 67834 |
| 0.10% | Weed Seed | | TESTED 10/2025 |
| Noxious Weeds: | None | | IN CA SELL BY 10/2027 |

**FIGURE 8-1:**
Grass seed label.

A typical label shows the percentages of each type or variety of grass included in the package, where it originated from, and what percent of seeds you can expect to germinate under ideal conditions. The origin of the grass isn't important. (Most

grass seed is produced in Oregon, but where it's grown doesn't influence how well it growsw in your area.) The mixture or blend of varieties or grass types determines if the lawn can be expected to grow well in the area where you live, as well as the more specific conditions in your own yard.

Other information that must appear on a seed label includes the percentages of crop seeds (seeds not specified on the label but not considered weeds), inert matter (dirt and debris), and weed seeds. These numbers should be low; there should be no more than 1 — or at most 2 — percent of any of them.

In the final analysis, the best advice is to buy the highest-quality seed available. This isn't a place to skimp or shop for bargains.

### Beyond the label: Deciding what seed to buy

TIP

A label can only tell you so much. Ideally, local garden center staff and online seed companies can guide your purchase, but in the end it's up to you to determine what will grow best in your yard. Avoid impulse purchases; these can be costly if you end up needing to replace your entire lawn because the seed you chose wasn't a good fit. Instead, consider the following before you select your grass seed:

>> **Get localized help.** Ask knowledgeable staff at your neighborhood garden center or contact your local cooperative extension service for information on the best grasses for your area.

>> **Look for named varieties.** Quality grass seed usually includes at least some named varieties. If the label just says Kentucky bluegrass, this package may contain some outdated, less-than-desirable varieties, and you may want to shop around some more. The extensive (and ongoing) research that produces modern grass seed varieties pays off in healthy, disease-resistant lawns.

>> **Buy from reputable sources.** Discount seed suppliers abound. Although it pays to shop around and compare prices, remember that the quality of seed you purchase directly affects the quality of lawn you end up with. Always purchase your grass seed from a trustworthy source.

# Tools of the Seed-Planting Trade

The key to success in establishing any lawn is to properly prepare your soil before you plant. If you don't know how to get your soil ready, take a look at Chapters 6 and 7.

After you've prepared the soil properly, the site is nice and level, and the timing is correct, you're ready to sow the seed. Start by gathering the following supplies.

>> **Grass seed:** Buy quality seed and get enough to cover the square footage of your planting area at the rates recommended in Table 8-1 or on the label of the seed box. (Learn how to calculate the area of your lawn in Chapter 6.) More seed isn't better because using too much seed results in crowded seedlings and a weakened lawn.

>> **Organic matter for topdressing:** *Topdressing* refers to adding a thin layer of material over the soil surface. After sowing seeds, topdressing ensures that seeds are planted at the proper depth, helps prevent seeds from drying out, and keeps hungry birds at bay. Landscapers usually prefer peat moss for topdressing because it spreads easily with a peat spreader. However, if it's allowed to dry out, peat moss becomes hydrophobic — it repels water and can be difficult to rewet. If they're available, sifted compost or screened topsoil (no big clumps in either) are also good choices. You don't need much because you put down only a thin layer about ¼ inch deep. One cubic foot of topdressing material covers about 50 square feet. Another topdressing option is weed-free straw; one large bale will cover about 1,000 square feet.

>> **Peat spreader (also called a compost spreader):** This piece of equipment, shown in Figure 8-2, is a cylindrical wire cage that throws down a thin topdressing of peat moss or compost to protect your seed from hungry birds, drying out, or blowing away. You can buy one or rent one from a rental yard. A peat spreader is handy for top-dressing your lawn with compost (see Chapter 15), so it may be worth investing in one.

>> **Seed spreader:** You usually use a drop spreader for applying fertilizers, but you can calibrate it for grass seed. Handheld spreaders are relatively inexpensive devices that you can also use for fertilizer. For larger areas, use a wheeled or handheld spinning centrifugal spreader (also known as a broadcast or rotary spreader). You can buy one or rent one at a rental center. Figure 8-3 shows examples of spreaders.

>> **Starter fertilizer:** Once you determine the size of the area you'll be seeding, you can calculate the quantity of starter fertilizer that you need — that is, if you didn't work the starter fertilizer into the soil when preparing the site (see Chapter 7). You can skip the starter fertilizer if a soil test indicates your soil has adequate phosphorous. Follow the instructions on the fertilizer label.

>> **Water-filled roller:** Use this piece of gear to press the seed into the soil, ensuring good contact. (The roller also levels the planting surface after soil preparation; see Chapter 7.) The roller is a big, empty cylinder that you fill with water for added weight. You can buy one or rent one at a rental center.

>> **Water:** By now you (hopefully) know how you plan to keep your lawn watered. If not, there's loads more information in Chapters 8 and 12.

**FIGURE 8-2:**
A peat spreader
puts down an
even layer of
mulch over
grass seed.

**FIGURE 8-3:**
Handheld
spreaders and
drop spreaders
are ideal for
sowing
grass seed.

# Ready, Set, Grow

You have your supplies, the timing is right, the soil is ready, the site is level, and the watering system is in place. Now you can plant your grass seed.

TIP

Watering the soil a few days before planting will help ensure good seed germination.

1. **Spread the seed.**

   Make sure that you properly set your spreader rate for sowing seed. (You can check the manufacturer's instructions, but many times, the spreader has the necessary information printed on it.) Put half the grass seed in the spreader. Spread the first half of the seed by walking in one direction and then spread the second half crisscross to the first direction. This pattern ensures even coverage.

2. **Topdress the seedbed to hold moisture.**

   If you're using sifted compost, screened topsoil, or peat moss, open the door of the peat/compost spreader and fill it. Briskly push the spreader back and forth until you cover the entire area. Apply a very thin layer, no more than $1/_4$ inch deep. Adjust your speed until the spreader applies about the right amount. If you're using clean straw, you'll need to roll the area first (see step #3 below) and then scatter the straw in a thin layer; you should be able to look through the straw and see the soil.

3. **Roll the surface.**

   To ensure good contact between seed and soil, roll the entire area with a roller that you've filled halfway with water. Roll the perimeter first and then finish the entire area, as shown in Figure 8-4.

   If you don't have a roller, you can use a stiff metal rake and just lightly push and pull the tines back and forth to make shallow grooves and cover the seed. Don't push too hard, or you'll move the seed around or cover it too deeply.

4. **Water.**

   This may be the most important step. With the first watering, apply enough water to wet the soil down to 6 to 8 inches; this will encourage the young plants to grow deep roots. (For more details on watering, see Chapter 12.)

TIP

Apply the water gently so that you don't wash the seed away or create puddles. You may have to water several times in short intervals until the bed is thoroughly wet. After that, water often enough to keep the top inch or so of the seedbed moist until the seed germinates. Remember, seeds get only one shot at germination. Let them dry out, and they're dead.

In hot, windy weather, you may need to lightly water the seedbed daily (or even more than once daily) to get even germination across the entire lawn. However, you don't want to overdo it. Too much water causes the seed to rot. The surest way to determine if an area needs watering is to stick your finger in the soil in several places. If it's dry at or near the soil surface, it's time for a light watering.

5. **Protect the seedbed.**

Here comes the neighbor's dog! Oh, no, what a muddy mess. To keep kids, pets, or whatever off your newly seeded lawn, encircle it with brightly colored string attached to small stakes. However, that may not be enough for the dog. If the lawn is small, you can surround the whole area with some roll-out metal fencing available at hardware stores — or at least ask the neighbors to keep their dogs in their own yards.

## HYDROSEEDING

Hydroseeding involves spraying a slurry of seed and paper mulch over the planting area. Often used by landscapers, it's a fast and economical way to cover large areas. The mulch helps reduce erosion, keeps the soil moist, and protects the seeds until germination. You can rent a hydroseeding machine or hire a contractor to do the work.

# Caring for Your New Lawn after Germination

As your new lawn becomes established, you can start easing up on the water, depending on the weather. If you continue your everyday watering routine, you're likely to overdo it and rot the young seedlings.

**WARNING**

Showering your new lawn with frequent, shallow sprinkles encourages plants to grow roots at the soil surface rather than forming the deep, drought-resistant roots you want.

When you have a pretty even ground cover of new seedlings, try skipping a day of watering and see what happens. Watch the grass carefully. If the color starts to go from bright green to dull gray-green, the grass needs water. You may have to water some quick-to-dry areas with a handheld hose. If the grass doesn't dry out, keep stretching the intervals between watering until you're on a schedule of once or twice a week, or as needed. When you do water, apply the water deeply, getting the moisture down 6 to 8 inches. (You can check how deep the water penetrates by probing the ground with a long screwdriver; it will move easily through wet soil and then stop, or become difficult to push, when it reaches dry soil. More on this in Chapter 12.)

Once the grass is 3 to 4 inches high, depending on the type of grass, it's time to start mowing. Mow when the soil is on the dry side; otherwise, you may tear up the new turf. (For more information on mowing, see Chapter 14.)

About six weeks after the lawn seed has germinated, it's time to make your first application of fertilizer. (See Chapter 13 for more on fertilizing.)

IN THIS CHAPTER

» Taking advantage of sod

» Timing the planting stage

» Purchasing sod

» Planting sod step-by-step

» Caring for sod after planting

# Chapter **9**

# Starting a Lawn from Sod

People often describe planting a lawn from sod as creating an instant lawn, and in a way they're right. Planting sod is kind of like laying new carpet in your living room. However, instead of someone delivering a big roll of carpet, you get rolls or rectangular sections of grass growing in a thin layer of soil. You just roll out or place the sections of grass out where you want your new lawn, and bingo, it's time to bring out the lawn chairs and volleyball net, right? Not quite.

Establishing an attractive sod lawn is a little trickier than just laying down the stuff and starting the party. Although you get the look of an instant lawn, you still must prepare the soil prior to planting. After the sod is down, you have to water and care for it diligently until the grass becomes established. Then and only then can you start the party. You should also know that starting a lawn from sod involves some pretty heavy lifting, and it's more expensive than planting one from seed.

Nevertheless, you can't deny the appeal of instant gratification. You can wake up on a Saturday morning with a bare patch of soil in your yard and then go to bed that night with a lawn. With a little planning and sweat, your new instant lawn will have your neighbors stopping by to ask how you did it.

Starting a lawn from sod also has other advantages. Because it's already growing, the sod is not quite as susceptible to drying out as are the germinating seeds and young grass seedlings. Sod also does a good job of smothering weed seeds. Sod is often a better choice for slopes than seed, because the seeds can wash away when watered. And, as long as the soil is not frozen solid and a light rototilling is possible, you can plant sod almost any time of year. Tilling is helpful for loosening and smoothing out the soil surface. However, in a landscape with established trees, only very shallow tilling (3 to 4 inches deep) is recommended to avoid damaging tree roots. In contrast, you usually need to plant seed in spring or fall, depending on where you live and the type of grass you grow.

# How Sod Is Grown

TECHNICAL STUFF

Lawns grown from sod aren't exactly instant because the grass has been growing for some months at a sod farm, and sod farmers really know how to grow grass. They prepare the fields perfectly and work in just the right amendments and fertilizer. They level the soil and do everything possible to ensure weed-free growth. Then, at just the right time of year, they plant the grass.

After planting, sod farmers care for the grass just as other farmers care for their crops. They apply water and fertilizer to promote fast, dense growth. They mow it frequently and tackle any pest and weed problems to help it develop into a thick, sturdy turf.

When it's time to harvest the sod, the farmers hop onto their sod-cutting machine and cut the turf into neat little pieces about 6 to 8 feet long, 2 feet wide, and 1 to 3 inches thick, depending on the type of grass. Warm season southern turfgrasses are generally cut into rectangular sections to be laid out like pieces of flooring tile or a brick in a wall. The thickness is critical. Sod that's cut too thin doesn't hold together and dries out quickly. Sod that's cut too thick is heavy to handle.

TIP

Sometimes, with cool-season grasses, sod farmers lay down very fine netting before planting, just to make sure that the sod holds together when it's dug. However, this netting can become a problem in home lawns. In areas where people walk a lot, as the sod wears down, the netting may come to the surface. So, you may want to avoid netted sod.

The sod machine rolls or stacks the sod and places it on a pallet. After the sod is on the pallet, the sod gets rushed to the nursery or garden center for you to buy and haul home, or it gets delivered right to your house.

# Determining When to Plant Sod

Most grass types are available as sod; some warm-season grasses are also planted as sprigs or plugs (more on those in Chapter 10). You can find sod composed of a mix of different cool-season varieties or species of a single type of grass. This is similar to how seed mixes are sold, but you have fewer choices for sod.

Although you can plant sod pretty much anytime, the ideal time is just prior to the period of optimum growth for that type of grass. The best time to plant cool-season grasses is early fall or early spring. Warm-season grasses perform best when planted in mid- to late spring, although they can be planted throughout the warm season, and even through the winter in the southernmost parts of the country. Take a look at Chapters 3, 4, and 5 for information about lawn climates and details on cool- and warm-season grasses.

Good weather makes a big difference in how easily you can successfully plant a lawn from sod. Try to time your planting right before you expect some rain; that way, Mother Nature can help you out with some of the watering chores. If the weather's too hot and dry, you'll need to water the sod frequently to keep it from drying out and dying.

# Buying Sod

If possible, buy sod directly from a sod farm that will ship it right to your house. If that isn't possible, ask your local nursery how to arrange buying sod so that it gets to you as fresh as possible.

## How much do you need?

To order the right amount of sod, you need to know many square feet of planting area you want to cover and then add about 10 percent extra. You don't want to be short of sod on planting day. (Learn how to calculate the area of your lawn in Chapter 6.) So, if your planting area is 600 square feet, order 660 square feet of sod. If the planting area includes many irregular shapes, getting an accurate measure is more difficult, so it's a good idea to order even more — 10 percent more than your measurements.

## What healthy sod looks like

Sod is very vulnerable stuff after it gets harvested. With only a thin layer of soil and roots, the grass dries out quickly. If you leave the pieces rolled up, or rectangular sections stacked up, for too long, two things happen: The grass suffers from a lack of light, and it also begins to heat. Although the sod can't burst into flames, the temperature can get hot enough to kill the grass. (Sod begins to decompose slowly after it's cut, and that decomposition process produces heat.) In hot summer weather, sod should be planted the same day it arrives from the farm; otherwise, significant damage can occur. So, if sod handlers aren't careful from the minute they cut the sod until the time you plant it, you don't get the quality, instant lawn you're after.

How can you tell if sod is fresh and healthy? Look for these qualities:

>> **The sod, especially the roots and soil, should be moist, but not dripping wet.** The edges shouldn't be dry, cracked, or starting to curl; these are signs that the sod is too dry. If the sod is too wet, it will be heavy and messy to handle.

>> **The grass should be evenly bright green and a consistent length.** If the grass is starting to turn yellow or brown, don't buy it. Yellowing is a sign that the sod has been rolled up or stacked too long and will be slow to make a nice lawn when you get it home. If the blades are uneven in length, that's another sign the sod may have been stored too long.

>> **The sod should be thick enough so that it doesn't tear easily when handled.** You'll be moving this stuff around quite a bit when you get it home, so it needs to hold together. The total thickness of a piece of sod — grass blades, roots, and soil — can vary from 1 to 3 inches depending on the type of grass. That said, the roots must be at least ½ inch long to hold everything together.

**WARNING**

>> **The sod should feel cool to the touch, not hot.** If sod sits around too long, it begins to decompose, a process that generates heat. This heat can kill the grass.

>> **Be wary of sod that's been rolled out on the ground.** Sod can last a long time rolled out on plastic or even on asphalt or concrete, but it must be watered a lot, often several times a day. If rolled-out sod looks the least bit parched, pass it by.

# Being Prepared *Before* You Buy Sod

If one thing really ticks off sod farmers, it's when people don't handle sod properly after they've cut and shipped it. If they had their way, the sod would be cut just before dark and shipped to your house overnight so that it would arrive early in the morning. You'd have soil, tools, and irrigation ready to go so you could plant it immediately. The grass would barely know it had been moved.

**TIP**

All too often, freshly cut sod sits for too long before it's planted. The sod waits in the sun, getting too hot or dried out. Then, when the sod finally gets planted, it grows poorly, and everyone blames the sod farmer. Fresh sod should never sit around for more than a day in hot weather and three days in cool weather.

Getting fresh sod is only one part of the sod-success equation. Planting it as soon as possible is the other. If the sod arrives in perfect shape, but you're not ready to plant it, you've got a problem. Be ready to plant when the sod arrives. See Chapter 7 for details about preparing your yard for laying sod.

## If planting is delayed

TIP

If you can't plant the day the sod arrives, store the sod in the shade and keep it moist with a light spray from a hose until planting. If you really get stuck and can't plant for more than 24 hours in hot weather or three days in cool weather, unroll the sod, lay it out on a flat surface in the shade, and keep it moist. Don't cover the sod with anything, especially plastic. It's better to let it breathe.

## Preparing the planting area

Make sure the site has been properly prepared. It should be graded and leveled, and the soil should be rolled smooth (see Chapter 7). If your soil needs lime or sulfur, it's best to add them and lightly rototill them into the surface few inches prior to laying the sod. If a soil test indicates your soil has adequate phosphorous, you can skip the starter fertilizer. Otherwise, you'll also want to spread and mix in the starter fertilizer prior to planting.

## Gathering the equipment you'll need

Make sure you have the following tools and supplies ready:

>> **Knife:** To cut the sod to fit curves, corners, and small places (see Figure 9-1). An old kitchen knife works fine.

>> **Board or piece of plywood:** To kneel on so that you don't squash the sod with your knees.

>> **Wheelbarrow:** To move the pieces of sod around (sod is heavy).

>> **Water-filled roller:** To smooth the sod after it's on the ground (see Figure 9-2).

>> **Hose and sprinklers:** To keep sod moist and to water the new lawn.

>> **Steel rake:** To level soil as you go (see Figure 9-3).

Moving sod and laying it is hard work. If possible, get some strong friends to help. The more help you have, the faster you can lay the sod, and the less likely it is to dry out. (Think about having a sod-laying party. Provide snacks and plenty of fluids, and get creative with sod-themed party decorations.)

**FIGURE 9-1:**
Sharp knife for cutting sod.

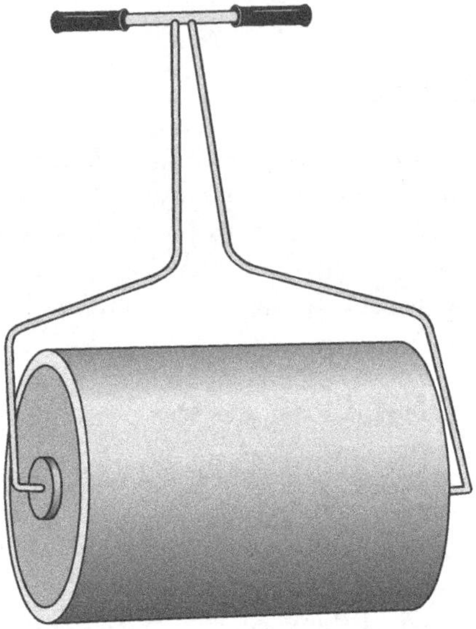

**FIGURE 9-2:**
Level the lawn with a water-filled roller after you lay the sod.

**FIGURE 9-3:**
Put a final level on the soil with a steel rake.

## Final preparations for sod-laying day

Because enough — but not too much — water is so important for sod to grow successfully, here are a few additional tips:

>> The soil in the planting area should be moist, not soggy or dry. Water thoroughly two days before the sod is delivered so that the top several inches of soil are moistened. Allow time for the water to be absorbed and excess water to drain so the area isn't muddy.

>> The sod should be moist to the touch but not dripping wet. Sprinkle it with water as needed to keep cool and moist, but don't soak it.

>> Have a hose with a hose-end sprayer ready to go so you can keep both the sod that's waiting to be rolled out and the sod you've laid watered throughout the day.

# Laying Sod, Step by Step

It's morning, the weather's right, your friends are here, and the sod is in perfect shape. Time to get down to business — laying the sod. Follow these steps:

**1.** **Start laying the sod along a straight edge, such as next to a walk or driveway, so that everything starts off straight.**

If your lawn has an irregular shape, run a string across the center of the lawn area, with each end of the string attached to a stake. Lay sod on either side of the string. To avoid roughing up the planting surface or the new sod, kneel on a board or piece of plywood as you work (see Figure 9-4).

**2.** **Lay the first piece of sod.**

Handle it with care so that it doesn't tear or fall apart as you move it. Place the edges of the sod tightly against any hard surfaces, such as cement edgings, walks, or driveways. Otherwise, you have empty gaps where the edges of the sod can dry out and from which weeds are more likely to sprout.

**3.** **Set the second piece tightly against the end of the first piece.**

**WARNING**

Make sure the edges are as close as possible without overlapping. Move the entire piece of sod to do this, rather than trying to stretch it to fit. The edges of the sod are the first parts to dry out, so you want to minimize the edges' exposure to the air.

FIGURE 9-4:
Avoid roughing up new sod by leaning or standing on a board.

TIP

4. **Stagger the pieces of sod as you lay them.**

   To avoid four corners from coming together in one spot — where they'll dry out even faster — stagger the ends as if you're laying brick (see Figure 9-5).

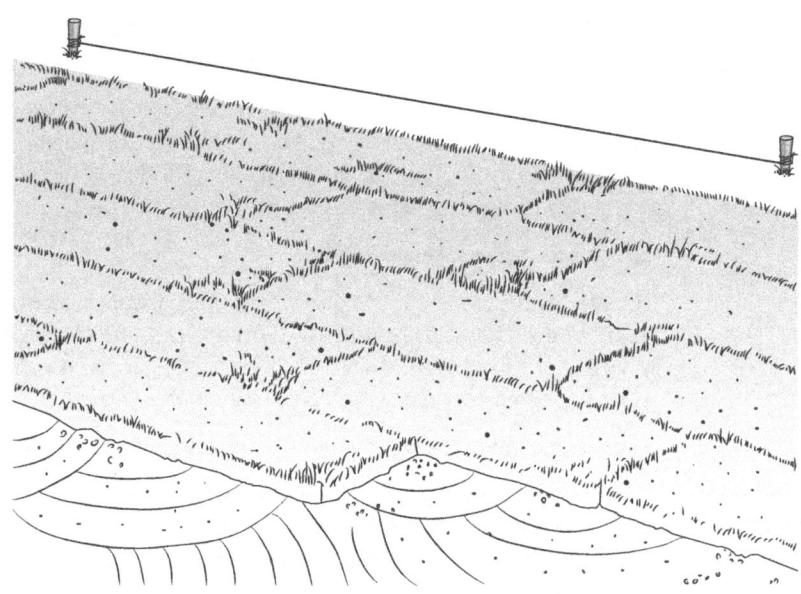

FIGURE 9-5:
Stagger the ends of the sod as if you're laying brick.

**5.** **If needed, level the planting surface with a rake as you go.**

If part of the planting surface gets roughed up, level it with a steel rake. Otherwise, you'll have a bumpy lawn. Occasionally, you may need to lift a piece of sod, rake the soil so it's level, and then replace the sod.

**6.** **When you come to the end of a row, roll the sod out over the edge and cut it to fit with a sharp knife.**

If you have in-ground sprinklers, cut small holes in the sod to fit it around them.

**WARNING**

A sharp knife gives you the clean edges you need to keep the pieces of sod tightly together so that they don't dry out, as shown in Figure 9-6. Be as careful with the knife as you would with any sharp object. Keep the knife out of the way where it won't get stepped on. You can even put brightly colored tape on the handle so that it's even more visible — and easier to find if it's lost.

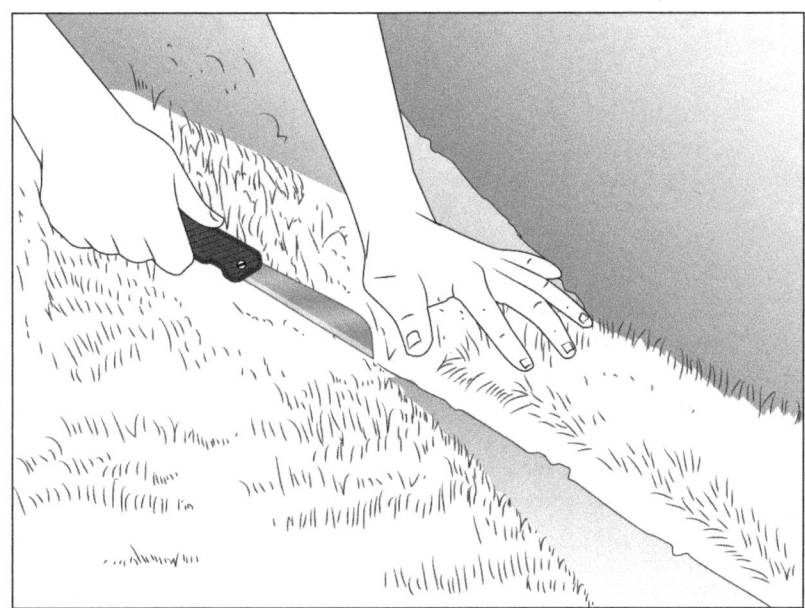

**FIGURE 9-6:**
Use a sharp knife to cut sod to fit irregularly shaped areas.

**7.** **After you lay out all the sod, place soil in any open seams between pieces of sod.**

You're bound to have a few narrow gaps where the sod may shrink and expand as it gets wetter or drier. Fill any gaps in the seams with topsoil from your yard. Don't try to fill the spaces with small pieces of sod, which dry out too fast and are likely to die.

If you're planting a big lawn or if it's hot and/or windy, you will likely need to use a hose to hand-water any dry areas of sod during the planting process.

8. **Roll the sod with a water-filled roller.**

   To help level the sod and ensure good contact between roots and soil, you need to roll the sod. Use a lawn roller that's half full of water. Roll perpendicular to the length of the sod.

9. **Water the lawn thoroughly, applying enough water to wet the soil 6 to 8 inches deep below the sod.**

   Probe the soil through the sod with a long screwdriver to see how far the water penetrates. For more information on how to check water penetration, see Chapter 11.

# Caring for Your New Lawn

You need to watch your newly sodded lawn carefully for the first few weeks until the roots grow into their new soil. The goal is to prevent the newly laid sod from drying out while not keeping the soil below continually saturated. If the soil is too wet beneath, the roots will be slow to penetrate the new soil. Water lightly every day for a week or so. In hot weather, your new lawn may benefit from a very light, twice-daily watering for the first week, followed by watering once a day for another week. Apply enough water so that the sod, plus the top of the soil, is moist. If you watered thoroughly after laying the sod, as described in Step 9 in the preceding section, the soil should still be moist several inches down. If it's not, water it until it is.

Pay special attention to the edges of the sod, which are the first areas to dry out. If the edges start to curl or look dry, you need to water. (Dry grass exhibits a dull, bluish-gray cast.) You may find that certain areas — such as sunnier spots, areas near a driveway (paving materials absorb heat, causing nearby soil to dry out), or a sloping part of the lawn — will probably dry out before the rest of the lawn. Water these areas in between your regular waterings with a handheld hose.

After a week or two, the roots will be knitting with the soil. (Gently lift a corner of the sod to see whether the roots are growing into the soil.) At this point, you can get by with less frequent watering, but you still need to scan for dry areas. Start by skipping a day or two to see how the lawn reacts. After two or three weeks, you should be able to get by on twice weekly waterings in most areas.

Let the newly planted lawn grow a little taller than normal before you mow it. You can find out about mowing heights for different grasses in Chapter 13. Mow only if the sod has knitted tightly with the soil. If you mow too early, you'll tear up the sod. Waiting is better than risking damage to your new lawn.

When you mow, cut off only about a third of the height of the grass. Mowing too low stresses the lawn and slows root growth. If you have to let the lawn grow quite tall before you can mow it, bring the height back down to size slowly by cutting just a little more off each time. A vigorously growing new lawn uses up a lot of nutrients, so fertilize six to eight weeks after planting. For more information on watering, fertilizing, and mowing, see Chapters 11, 12, and 13, respectively.

If all goes well, you should be able to use your new lawn in about four to six weeks. Check the progress by trying to lift the corners of the sod. If they don't easily lift, the roots are growing into the soil. It's time to put out the picnic table and enjoy your new lawn.

IN THIS CHAPTER

» **Identifying sprigs and plugs**

» **Comparing the different planting techniques**

» **Planting a lawn from sprigs**

» **Planting a lawn from plugs**

» **Caring for a new lawn**

Chapter **10**

# Planting Sprigs and Plugs

S*prigs* are tiny pieces of stolons and rhizomes from warm-season turfgrasses that are scattered evenly over the planting area and partially covered with soil. Sprigs are challenging to plant successfully and require frequent watering (up to five times a day!). *Plugs* are small pieces of turf with roots, leaves, stolons, and rhizomes. When properly cared for, sprigs and plugs gradually grow together to create a lawn.

Some warm-season lawn grasses, including hybrid bermudagrass, zoysiagrass, and St. Augustinegrass, are usually planted by sod or, in smaller areas, sometimes plugs. Seed isn't available for St. Augustinegrass, and all three of these types of turf establish much faster and more dependably when sod is used.

Bermudagrass can be planted with sprigs as well as sod (see Chapter 9); however, planting with sprigs is usually reserved for very large areas and irrigation must be frequent and precise, so this method is rarely used for home lawns. Bermudagrass is available by seed, as are a few types of zoysiagrass, but while seeding is more economical, it's also more difficult to obtain an even stand, and weed seedlings can quickly overrun new turf seeds.

Lawns of cool-season grasses are usually started from seed or sod; Chapters 8 and 9 explain how. Some types of cool-season grasses are also available as plugs; these are most often used to fix damaged areas of turf.

Read on for details, as well as for step-by-step instructions for planting sprigs and plugs and caring for your new lawn-to-be.

# Defining Sprigs and Plugs

**TECHNICAL STUFF**

Most warm-season grasses produce horizontal stems that grow either just under the soil surface or right on the soil surface. The underground stems are called *rhizomes*, and the aboveground stems are called *stolons*. At varying intervals along these horizontal stems, the plants send out new shoots and roots. Even a small piece of one of these rhizomes or stolons has the capacity to root and spread into a much larger plant.

The pieces of stem are typically 3 to 5 inches long and containing multiple nodes (growing points) where shoots and roots will form. Sprigs are sold without any soil.

The term *plug* refers to small pieces of sod, usually 1½ to 4 inches across, that are set at intervals throughout the planting area and eventually spread into a uniform lawn. They're grown and sold in soil-filled trays. Plugs can be used to repair damaged areas in existing lawns as well as to establish new lawns.

# Pros and Cons

**TIP**

On the upside, planting sprigs or plugs saves money compared to laying sod. That said, the downsides are substantial. Sprigs are particularly challenging. Because they are taken from warm-season grasses, and the planting season for these grasses can include hot and/or windy weather, it's very difficult to prevent the sprigs from drying out and dying in a home lawn setting. Lawns started from sprigs and plugs can take a long time to fill in, sometimes more than a year (although planting very densely can save you some time). You'll have to be patient. It will be quite a while before you can haul out the croquet set or soccer nets and enjoy your full, lush lawn. Also, you'll have to keep the weeds out between the spaces until the lawn fills in, which can be a lot of work.

# When to Plant

Late spring to early summer is the best time to plant sprigs and plugs of warm-season grasses. At that time, the weather is mild enough to let you set out the sprigs and plugs while allowing a few weeks of frequent irrigation to help them get established before the hottest weather arrives. Summer — the season of these grasses' most vigorous growth — is just around the corner.

**WARNING**

The earlier you plant, the sooner the grass fills in. Don't plant any later than two months prior to the average first frost date in fall. Otherwise, the grass may not be established before the onset of cool weather.

# Planting Sprigs

Bermudagrass is sometimes planted by sprigs in areas such as sports turf, and this method is generally confined to large municipal areas or commercial developments. Noting the challenges with planting and establishing sprigs, carefully consider if you want to go this route. If you decide to do so, you have two ways to get your sprigs:

>> **Order them by the bushel.** If you order by the bushel, the sprigs probably will be sent to you overnight, so you have to plan ahead and be ready to plant. How much you need depends on the type of grass and how close you'll be spacing the sprigs. The supplier can help you determine how much you need to order. (You'll need to know the square footage of the planting area; find out how to calculate this in Chapter 6.)

>> **Tear apart some sod into little pieces.** You can purchase sod and then cut it up using a knife, shovel, or edger, or you can tear it apart with your hands. Each sprig should have 2 to 4 swollen nodes where the roots will grow. Five square feet of sod will make 1 bushel of sprigs. This method will save you money, but it's a lot of work.

**TIP**

Whichever way you get your sprigs, keep them in a cool place and out of direct sun. Keep the sprigs lightly moist so they don't dry out and die.

Make sure the site has been properly prepared. It should be graded and leveled, and the soil should be smooth (see Chapter 7). If your soil needs lime or sulfur, it's best to spread and mix them into the soil prior to planting. If a soil test indicates your soil has adequate phosphorous, you can skip the starter fertilizer. Otherwise, you'll want to spread starter fertilizer and mix it into the soil prior to planting.

You can plant sprigs several ways. The soil should be lightly moist, but not so wet that it makes a mess when you walk on it. Spacing is really up to you. Closer spacing gives you faster fill-in, but you need more material to cover the area. Following are three ways to plant sprigs:

>> **Row planting:** With this technique, you use a hoe to create 1- to 2-inch-deep furrows, spaced 10 to 18 inches apart. Lay the sprigs in the furrow, with any tuft of foliage pointing up, spaced about 4 to 6 inches apart (see Figure 10-1). Then go back and fill the furrow with soil. About a third of the sprig should be above ground. Work in sections so that the sprigs don't dry out. Next, carefully smooth the whole planting area with a rake and then roll with a lawn roller filled halfway with water.

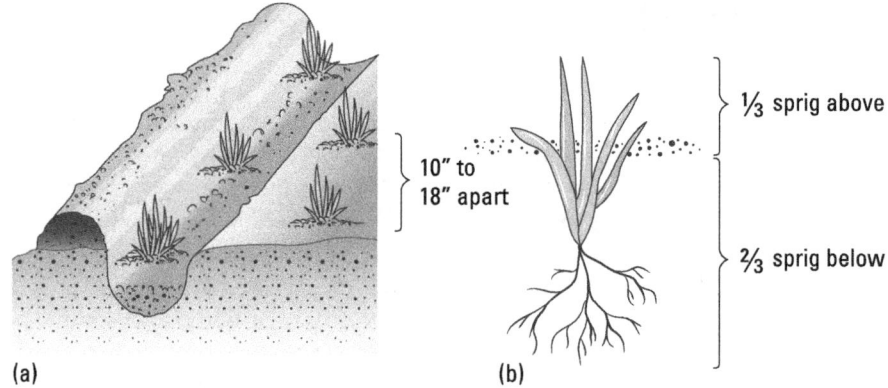

**FIGURE 10-1:** Row planting sprigs.

>> **Stick planting:** Here, you simply space the sprigs evenly over the planting area and gently push them into the ground with a small stick. Again, complete small sections at a time so that the sprigs don't dry out. Then roll the whole area with a lawn roller filled halfway with water.

>> **Broadcast sprigging (also called stolonizing):** With this planting technique, you spread the sprigs evenly over the planting area. You then use a peat spreader (also called a compost spreader) to spread about ¼ to ½ inch of mulch (peat moss, compost, ground bark, or the like) on top. You also can use a tool called a *stolon disc*, which you may be able to rent from your local nursery or rental center. The stolon disc lightly pushes the stolons into the ground as it rolls over them. You then add mulch on top. After the mulch is in place, roll the entire planting with a lawn roller that is half-filled with water.

It's absolutely critical that irrigation is applied to sprigged areas within 30 minutes of planting and continued about five times a day for the first few weeks, because sprigs will desiccate and die very quickly in warm weather, which is the norm when planting warm-season turf species.

# Plugging

**TIP**

Planting plugs — small pieces of sod — is usually a more reliable method than sprigging. A plug has more roots and is easier to get established. Plugged lawns, however, can take longer to fill in because you usually use less material. However, if you want a quicker fill-in, plant the plugs close together. The closest you should plant them is 3 inches apart; any closer, and you might as well plant sod.

You can cut your own plugs from sod or buy them growing in small plastic trays. Sizes usually range from 1½ to 4 inches across.

Plugs are commonly planted in staggered rows, with 6 to 12 inches between plants and between rows (see Figure 10-2). Zoysiagrass plugs are usually planted about 6 inches apart because this type of grass is generally slower to establish. Stretch out a long string or rope to keep your rows straight — the whole thing looks better as the plugs fill in.

**TIP**

Use some type of bulb planter to simplify digging all the holes (see Figure 10-3). Then set the plug in the hole and firm the soil around the sides. Gently level the ground with a rake. When planting is complete, roll with a water-filled roller.

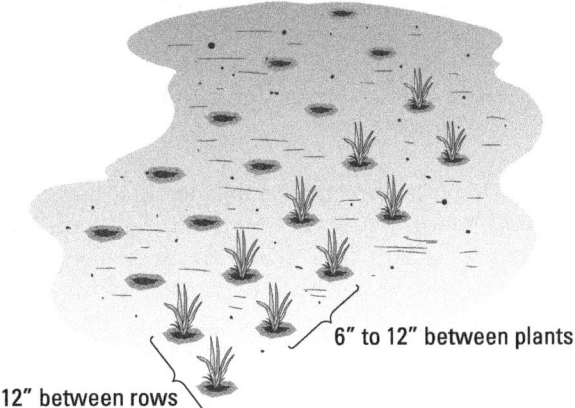

6" to 12" between plants

6" to 12" between rows

**FIGURE 10-2:**
Planting plugs.

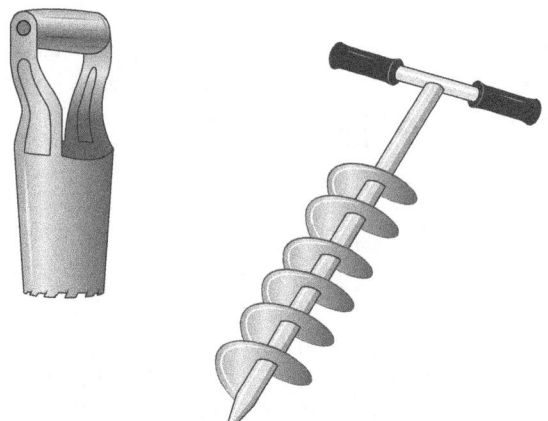

**FIGURE 10-3:**
Use a bulb
planter to
plant plugs.

# Post-Planting Care

After planting, keep the soil moist until the sprigs or plugs become established. Let them dry out just a little, and you might as well start over from scratch. Lightly sprinkle sprigs around five times per day and plugs at least twice a day for the first week or two. In hot weather, you may have to water more often. For more detailed information on watering, see Chapter 11.

**WARNING**

Watering or heavy rain may slowly erode some of the open soil between the pieces of grass. If this happens, add some sifted garden soil and level it with a rake; otherwise, you end up with one bumpy lawn.

You also need to eliminate weeds growing in the open areas — this can be a tough job. The best way to keep weeds under control is to use a hoe when the weeds are small, especially right after planting. For more information on weed control, see Chapter 15.

Four to six weeks after planting, fertilize the area. For more on fertilizing, see Chapter 12.

**WARNING**

When the grass pieces become established and are growing (four to six weeks after planting), mowing helps them spread and fill in. Set the mower higher than normal so that you don't scalp the grass. Remember, the mower wheels may be traveling on bare ground and be lower than normal, which can lead to scalping. If the mower pulls any of the plugs or sprigs out of the ground, stop and wait another week or two before trying to mow again. For more on mowing, see Chapter 13.

# 3

# Maintaining Your Lawn

**IN THIS PART . . .**

Find detailed information on how to water your lawn to keep it healthy while conserving this precious resource.

Keep your lawn healthy by knowing how to fertilize, which can sometimes be a confusing process. Discover the many different types of fertilizers, know how to choose the best one for your lawn, and find tips for applying the right type and amount of fertilizer to ensure healthy growth while minimizing the risk of runoff into nearby waterways.

Mow like a pro with the optimal mowing height for different types of lawn grasses. Discover tips for dealing with clippings and handling this essential chore that can make or break your lawn.

Discover what causes thatch — and what doesn't — as well as how to deal with thatch buildup, when to aerate your lawn, and when it's time for a complete renovation.

IN THIS CHAPTER

» **Understanding why watering your lawn is important**

» **Discovering how soil, weather, and shade affect watering**

» **Deciding how much, how often, and when to water**

» **Choosing, using, and maintaining sprinklers**

» **Conserving water**

Chapter **11**

# Watering Lawns

Ensuring your lawn has enough water — but not too much — is the most important aspect of caring for your lawn. You can get away with missing a mowing and skipping a fertilization, but if the weather is hot and you let your lawn go dry, the consequences can be serious. At first, the lawn might just look sickly, but then the weeds will start taking over. If your lawn goes thirsty for too long, it might die.

**WARNING**

However, watering your lawn is more than just making sure that the grass gets enough moisture. Water is a precious resource; you shouldn't waste it. Lawns and landscaping account for up to half of the average household's water use, especially in dry summer areas, such as the Southwest.

Therefore, applying water efficiently is just as important as applying enough water. Don't water so much that you end up with that precious resource flowing down street gutters, or ten feet below the deepest grass roots, or turning your lawn into a swamp.

And that's what this chapter is all about — everything you need to know about watering your lawn properly, from how soil type and health affect watering, to how often your lawn needs water, to the type of sprinkler you use.

# Creating a Water-Thrifty Lawn

Water is such a precious and limited resource, you need to use it wisely. This involves more than just how you irrigate your lawn. Water-conserving strategies start with how you maintain it.

**WARNING**

Water restrictions and rationing are becoming the norm in many parts of the country. Find tips for keeping your lawn healthy during dry spells in the "Caring for Your Lawn During Drought" section at the end of this chapter.

The way you fertilize, mow, and otherwise care for your lawn directly impacts the water it requires.

>> **Be judicious with fertilizer:** More isn't better. The more you fertilize, especially with nitrogen, the faster the grass will grow and the more water you'll need to apply to support that growth (and the more often you'll need to mow). Also, overfertilized turfgrass tends to have a more limited root system, which makes the grass more susceptible to drying out. Learn how to apply the right fertilizer, in the right amounts, at the right times, in Chapter 12.

>> **Mow high:** Set your mower at the high end of the cutting ranges listed in Chapter 13. Grass that grows on the tall side develops deeper roots and helps shade the soil, keeping it cooler and reducing the loss of water from the soil surface due to evaporation. This simple mowing adjustment also helps keep weeds at bay.

>> **Aerate and dethatch or verticut:** Aerating is the process of punching small holes all over your lawn with a core aerator that pulls out small cores of grass and soil. Dethatching involves raking through the thatch, which is a layer of tightly woven grass stems, roots, and crowns, and bringing it to the surface for removal. Verticutting slices through the thatch to the soil surface and is the preferred technique for warm-season turf species. Aerating, dethatching, and verticutting improve water penetration in compacted soils and those with a buildup of thatch. Find more details in Chapter 14.

**REMEMBER**

Smaller lawns require less water. They also require less fertilizing, mowing, and other maintenance chores. If your lawn is larger than you need or want consider planting some of it with ground covers, wildflowers, and other less thirsty plants. Chapter 19 has information on lawn alternatives.

# Getting to the Root of Watering

Your lawn's water cycle begins with the roots (see the sidebar "How plants use water"), and deep, healthy roots are the key to a thriving lawn. Figure 11-1 shows what a strong root system looks like. Roots need moisture, air, and nutrients for healthy growth. The way you water your lawn greatly influences the first two requirements: moisture and air. (It has some influence on how well plants can take up nutrients; more on that in Chapter 12.)

Because grass roots need both water and air, they need soil that is both moist and well aerated. Healthy soil has lots of small spaces in between the soil particles and, ideally, some of those spaces are occupied by water and others by air, so that roots have access to both. (Learn more about healthy soil in Chapter 6.)

**WARNING**

Grass roots can tolerate both dry and saturated soil for short periods of time. However, if soil remains parched or waterlogged for too long, the roots will suffer damage, and if conditions don't improve, they'll eventually die.

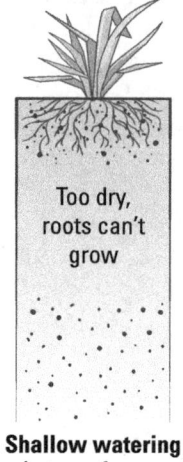

**Too dry, roots can't grow**

**Too wet, roots can't grow**

**FIGURE 11-1:**
Proper watering results in deep, healthy grass roots, while incorrect watering results in weak, shallow roots and a struggling lawn.

**Deep, infrequent watering** encourages a healthy, extensive root system.

**Shallow watering** leads to surface roots that are susceptible to drought.

**Overwatering** (watering too much/too often) leads to saturated soil that damages roots.

## When roots grow deep

Grasses differ in how deep their roots will grow, with some grass species growing roots that reach down 6 feet. That said, the roots of your lawn grass get most of their moisture from the top 6 to 8 inches of soil, so that's the target zone for watering.

**TIP**

In general, you want grass plants to grow the deepest roots possible so they can access the soil moisture that exists at various depths. To encourage deep roots, you need to moisten that entire zone when you water. Plants can't travel to seek out water, and their roots won't move from dry soil to wet soil in search of it.

## The peril of shallow roots

If you water only enough to moisten the top few inches of soil, then that's the primary place the roots will grow (see Figure 11-1). The resulting shallow roots translate to a lawn that dries out quickly, is more prone to damage during dry spells, and is more susceptible to grub damage. A shallow-rooted lawn is also less likely to spring back from drought or a missed watering. Deep roots are better for plants, and for you, too, because you'll need to water less frequently.

**TECHNICAL STUFF**

## HOW PLANTS USE WATER

Like most plants, grasses absorb water through their roots. It travels up through the stem and into the leaves (called *blades* on grasses), where's it's used for photosynthesis and other basic life processes.

The mechanism by which plants pull up water against the force of gravity is called *transpiration*. When tiny pores on the undersides of the leaves, called *stomata*, are open, moisture contained in the plant tissue evaporates and escapes into the air. This evaporation pulls water from the soil into the roots and moves it up to the leaves. When there's adequate water, the leaves stay hydrated and upright so that they're positioned to gather energy from the sun. During photosynthesis, the leaves use the sun's energy to manufacture food in the form of carbohydrates.

The hotter and drier the weather, the more water the plant needs to keep these processes going. If water isn't available, the grass blades go limp. (Although the plant can close its stomata to conserve water, doing that also shuts down photosynthesis, so it can't do that for long.) Your lawn needs a consistent supply of moisture to keep these life processes going.

# Getting to Know Factors Affecting Water Needs

Numerous factors affect how much water any plant uses or needs, including lawn grasses. Being familiar with these factors helps you adjust your watering practices.

## Soil conditions

Different kinds of soil — sand, clay, loam, and everything in between — have different water-holding capacities. The different soil types also absorb water and dry out at different rates. Here's a quick run-down of soil basics. See Chapter 6 for the full dirt on soil.

>> **Sandy soils** are composed of relatively large soil particles and are generally well aerated. Because water drains through them quickly, sandy soils hold the least amount of moisture, and they dry out the fastest. Consequently, lawns growing in sandy soils need more frequent watering. That said, it takes less water to penetrate the soil to the proper depth.

>> **Clay soils** are the opposite of sandy soils. Made of tiny particles that pack tightly together, clay soils are often poorly aerated, slow to absorb water, and once wet they stay saturated and are slow to dry out. Then, if they're allowed to dry out too much, clay soils can bake hard — think clay pottery. In general, lawns growing in clay soils need to be watered less frequently than those in sandy soils. When clay soil does need water, you need to apply more of it in order to get the moisture deep enough. You also need to apply water slowly so that the soil has time to absorb it without pooling or running off the lawn.

>> **Loam soils** fall between heavy clay and very sandy soils. Loam is composed of a good mixture of different-sized soil particles and is considered an ideal soil for gardens and lawns. Loam soils tend to have both good aeration and moisture-holding capacity.

**REMEMBER**

These are general categories of soil, but in reality every soil is unique. The good news is that adding organic matter to your soil can help overcome some of the challenges if one of the mineral sizes is present in too high a quantity. When you add organic matter to sandy soils it improves water and nutrient retention. When you add it to clay soils it improves aeration and water absorption.

Organic matter benefits all soils, even "ideal" loamy ones. It also nurtures the soil ecosystem which, in turn, encourages your lawn grasses to develop deep, healthy roots. Learn more about organic matter and how to add it to both new and existing lawns in Chapter 6.

**TIP**

Other factors can affect how your soil behaves. For example, years of romping children may have compacted the soil, slowing water absorption. Or your lawn may have a buildup of thatch, which can prevent water from reaching the soil. Find remedies for both in Chapter 14.

**TIP**

Take a look at Table 11-1 to get an idea of how much water and time you need for different soil types to reach an optimum watering depth of 6 to 8 inches. Keep in mind that these are just guidelines. As you sharpen your observation skills, you'll gain insights into how to adjust your watering according to how your soil reacts to water.

**TABLE 11-1**

## Amount of Water and Time Necessary to Soak Soil 6 to 8 Inches Deep

| Soil | Amount of Water | Absorption Time |
|------|-----------------|-----------------|
| Sandy | ½ inch | 30 minutes |
| Loam | 1 inch | 2 hours |
| Clay | 1 to 1⅓ inches | 5 hours |

# Weather and climate

Lawns react to weather a lot like humans do. Lawns need more water during hot, sunny weather than on mild, cloudy days. Likewise, lawns need more water in high summer than during cooler, shorter days of spring and fall. Lawns also dry out faster in windy weather than in calm weather.

Table 11-2 shows you how to use the weather as a watering guide. You can find out more about how weather and climate affect watering in your area in Chapter 2.

**TABLE 11-2**

## Watering According to the Weather

| Water Less | Water More |
|---|---|
| Cooler temperatures | Warmer temperatures |
| Cloudy or overcast | Bright sunlight |
| Low wind | High wind |
| High humidity | Low humidity |
| Rain | No rain |

# Shade

A lawn growing in the shade generally needs less water than one growing in full sun. However, if trees are creating the shade (as opposed to a building, for example), the trees' roots may use up a lot of the water you apply, so you'll still want to pay attention to soil moisture. The water requirements in a shady area depend on the type of grass and the type and age of the tree. Learn about lawn alternatives for shady areas in Chapter 19. Find tips for growing grass under trees in Chapter 20.

# Cultural practices

Lawns mown short need more frequent watering than those mown higher. That's because taller grass shades the soil, so less moisture evaporates from the soil surface. Taller grass also tends to have a deeper, more extensive root system. In general, for the healthiest, most water-thrifty lawn, mow at the upper end of the appropriate mowing height range for your species of turfgrass.

Also, lawns that receive more fertilizer grow faster and — you got it — need more water. See Chapters 12 and 13 for information on the best ways to fertilize and mow for both optimal lawn health and wise water usage.

# Type of grass

**REMEMBER**

In general, warm-season grasses such as bermudagrass and zoysiagrass are better adapted to hot weather and dry conditions compared to their cool-season cousins. Warm-season grasses can get by on less water than cool-season grasses, such as Kentucky bluegrass or tall fescue, in hot weather. Even within the cool-season and warm-season groups, some grasses look better with less water than others. Tall fescue, for example, withstands drought better than Kentucky bluegrass. You can even find varieties of grasses within grass types that need less water than others.

Table 11-3 shows you the relationships between grass types and water needs, from those requiring the least water to those requiring the most.

**TABLE 11-3**

## Grasses and Relative Water Needs

| | Type of Grass |
|---|---|
| *Least* | Buffalograss |
| | Bermudagrass |
| | Zoysiagrass |
| | Bahiagrass |
| | St. Augustinegrass |
| | Centipedegrass |
| | Hard fescue |
| | Chewings fescue |
| | Red fescue |
| | Perennial ryegrass |
| | Tall fescue |
| | Bentgrass |
| *Most* | Kentucky bluegrass |

**TIP**

The amount of water a lawn grass uses under ideal conditions and its ability to recover from drought (or still look okay with less than optimum amounts of water) are not necessarily the same thing. For example, most cool-season grasses start to decline quickly and look bad when their water supply is less than optimum. However, some grasses, like Kentucky bluegrass, may die altogether if they go completely dry. Others, like tall fescue, just go dormant and recover when watered again. In general, warm-season grasses can go very dry and still look pretty good — or at least still have a hint of green. Bermudagrass and zoysiagrass have underground rhizomes that can store water and help them recover better after a drought.

# Understanding the How Much, When, and How Often of Watering

**REMEMBER**

The frequency and amount of water you apply to grass vary, depending on soil, weather conditions, type of grass, and so on. (See the section "Getting to Know Factors Affecting Water Needs" earlier in this chapter for details.) Use the guidelines in this section for watering an established lawn. Then, as you observe your lawn, you'll gain insights into how to adjust your watering according to how the turfgrass and soil react. (Newly planted lawns have different water needs than established ones; see Chapters 8 through 10 for more information.)

## Use deep, infrequent irrigation

When you irrigate, apply ½ to 1 inch of water to turf. (See the section "Measuring How Much Water You've Applied" at the end of this chapter for an easy technique to measure this.) The moisture should penetrate to about 6 to 8 inches deep. Watering less deeply results in a shallow-rooted lawn that dries out quickly. On the other hand, applying water that penetrates much deeper than 6 to 8 inches is wasteful because the majority of lawn grass roots grow in that zone.

**TIP**

You easily can check how deep the water penetrates by probing the ground with a stiff metal rod or long screwdriver. The rod moves easily through wet soil and then stops, or becomes difficult to push, when it reaches dry soil. You can also buy a soil probe at a local nursery or irrigation supply store. The probe removes small cores of soil that you can feel to see how wet they are. Finally, there are several types of soil moisture meters available. Don't skip this step. You can't tell how deeply water has penetrated by looking at the lawn; you have to check.

## Apply water slowly

If you apply water faster than the lawn can absorb it, the water runs off onto sidewalks and into street gutters. Runoff is especially problematic on slopes and on compacted or clay soils. Avoid this waste by adjusting your irrigation to the "cycle and soak" method. Apply water in short intervals of about 10 to 15 minutes, turn off the water for 30 to 40 minutes to allow the water to soak in, and then turn the sprinkler back on for another 10 to 15 minutes. Repeat this procedure until you get the water down to about 6 to 8 inches deep.

Using sprinklers that water very slowly (see the section "Choosing Sprinklers" later in this chapter) along with a programmable irrigation timer make this procedure much easier. Better yet, consider getting an intelligent controller to really fine-tune your watering (see the section "Using Smart Technology in Irrigation," later in this chapter).

If water is getting absorbed slowly or is pooling on the surface, check to see if there's a buildup of *thatch,* a layer of stems, rhizomes, and dead organic matter that forms between grass blades and the soil line. Thatch can dramatically decrease water absorption; learn more about dealing with it in Chapter 14. Compacted soil will also cause water to pool on the surface; Chapter 14 explains how to aerate soil to improve water infiltration.

## Water in the morning

Early morning is the best time to water for a number of reasons. First, the weather is usually cool and calm, so less water is lost to evaporation. (Less wind also means that water doesn't blow into the street.) Second, morning watering gives the lawn a chance to dry off before evening, which is important for preventing lawn diseases. Wet foliage favors the growth of many fungal diseases, and their spores are spread via water droplets. Learn more about preventing lawn diseases in Chapter 17.

Your municipality's water restrictions may prohibit irrigation during certain times of the day to conserve water and minimize wasteful evaporation. Water restrictions will vary based on location, season, and weather and drought conditions; however, if watering is allowed, the restrictions will generally favor early morning watering.

## Water your lawn only when it needs it

You'll find lots of resources that tell you that your lawn needs 1 to 2 inches of water per week, but that's just a very general guideline. Rather than watering on a strict schedule, water when your lawn needs it. Smart irrigation tools can help you know when to water — or even take control of your irrigation system! See the section "Using Smart Technology in Irrigation," later in this chapter.

Until you get to know your lawn and, most importantly what it looks like when it needs water, start by assuming it needs an inch of water per week. If nature doesn't cooperate in the form of a good, steady rainfall in that amount, you'll need to irrigate. (Ignore short showers and heavy downpours because the water may not get absorbed deeply into the soil.)

You want your lawn to dry out a bit between waterings. Plant roots need both water and oxygen; too much water is as bad as too little. Your lawn will show you when it's getting dry and needs water: When you walk on the grass, you can look back and see your footprints. The grass doesn't spring right back as it does when it has enough water. You also can see that the grass changes color when it's dry, from bright green to a dull, almost smoky, grayish blue. (You can also use a soil moisture meter to measure the soil moisture.)

If your lawn tells you it needs water between its regular irrigation cycle, give it a good drink. If just one or a few areas get thirsty before the rest, see if you can find a way to spot water only those sections to carry them over until it's time to water the entire yard.

If your lawn is thriving, you can try reducing how often you water. Don't reduce the amount of water applied at each irrigation, just the frequency. You want the water to soak in deeply. If you apply water in light sprinkles, the grass will respond by growing shallow roots, rather than deep, healthy ones.

## Water only when grass is actively growing

Lawns planted with warm-season grasses do not generally require irrigation during winter months when they are dormant. Watering during this time can be wasteful and can lead to weeds and disease that can harm your lawn. Cool-season grasses slow their growth in hot weather and may even turn brown. Unless conditions are severe, the grasses will recover when temperatures cool. Tall fescues are notably able to withstand drought and recover quickly, while Kentucky bluegrass is less tolerant of dry conditions and should be watered during hot spells.

## Watch your lawn and make adjustments

If the lawn doesn't seem to dry out between waterings, stretch the intervals in between. If the water doesn't get deep enough, apply a little more at each watering, but water less often. If everything seems fine, try cutting back on the amount you apply anyway and see what happens. Maybe you can conserve some of that valuable resource. Don't forget to adjust irrigation with the season. If you get a lot of rain in summer, maybe you don't need to water at all.

**WARNING**

Keep an eye out for watering restrictions in your municipality. You may need to alter the days and times of your irrigation, or you may need to stop watering entirely if drought conditions are severe. Fines for violating the restrictions can be hefty. Keep in mind that most lawn grasses will endure drought by going dormant, and they'll resume growth when conditions improve. Contact your local cooperative extension office for more information about watering restrictions and how they affect lawn care in your area.

**WARNING**

If you're idea of watering is standing out on the lawn in the evening after work, garden hose in hand, consider that you may end up doing more harm than good. Not only is evening the worst time to water, it's also nearly impossible to get thorough, even coverage watering with a hand-held hose. For all but the smallest patches of lawn, you'd likely have to stand there for hours, swatting mosquitoes. When watering is a chore like this, you're less likely to do it, or you'll quit before you've done a thorough job — and it bears repeating: Shallow watering leads to weak, shallow roots. Find tips for choosing irrigation methods later in this chapter.

**REMEMBER**

Watering newly planted lawns is a whole different ball of wax from watering established turf. You need to water new lawns more often until the grass plants are growing strong. Learn more about caring for your new lawn in Chapters 8 through 10.

# Using Smart Technology in Irrigation

Smart irrigation systems are a win-win-win for you, your lawn, and the planet. They save you money, promote the health of grass plants, and reduce use of our precious water resources. Products that leverage technology and artificial intelligence (AI) to enable precision watering include these tools:

» **Intelligent controllers:** These devices gather data on current conditions from a variety of sources, such as on-site sensors and nearby weather stations, and they also factor in weather forecasts. Using information from your precise location, the controllers can reliably and effectively automate your irrigation system's watering schedule by calculating the amount of water plants will need. (See the "Evapotranspiration" sidebar, later in this chapter, for the science behind these calculations.)

» **Irrigation system mapping:** Are you considering installing an in-ground sprinkler system? Some irrigation supply companies now offer you the option of entering your street address. Almost immediately you'll receive a design for your sprinkler system, including sprinkler and line placement, supply lists, and even your expected cost savings over traditional, more wasteful watering systems.

» **Mobile apps:** Some smart irrigation systems let you manage your lawn watering remotely using a mobile app. Various apps offer different functions and options, such as monitoring conditions in real time and sending notifications to you. Also, some state cooperative extension services, particularly in hot-summer regions, offer mobile apps that help you determine how much water your lawn needs. For example, the "Water My Yard" app, a free program of the Texas A&M AgriLife Extension Service, monitors weather stations in some parts of Texas and sends you weekly watering advice.

» **Advanced soil sensors:** These wireless devices can be inserted into the soil to track information and send real-time updates on soil moisture levels. When they're integrated into an automated watering system, the sensors will shut down irrigation when the sensor's probe indicates that the soil has reached the desired moisture level.

- >> **Rain sensor or rain switch:** These devices are connected to an automatic irrigation system. When activated by a sufficient rainfall event, they shut off the irrigation system during rainfall and for a short time afterward.

- >> **Drones:** Originally implemented for the care of golf course turf, drones have made their way into everyday lawn care. By capturing bird's-eye footage, they enable users to gather data over a large area, which can then be used to assess water, fertilizer, and pest care needs.

- >> **Advanced sprinkler head designs:** Rather than spraying in the usual circle, semi-circle, or other standard pattern, digitally designed sprinkler heads have finely tuned spray patterns that are customized to the unique shape of your yard. This allows you to effectively water your yard with just one or a few sprinkler heads, in contrast to systems that utilize sprinkler heads placed at close intervals around your yard's perimeter. It also minimizes the spray overlap that is otherwise built into systems that use sprinkler heads with limited spray patterns.

Gone are the days (hopefully, anyway) when we walk by a torrent of water washing down the street, the result of sprinklers that someone forgot to turn off. Smart irrigation technology is a game-changer for water conservation, and it can even play a role in wildfire mitigation plans by automatically watering vulnerable areas prior to fire events. We are just scratching the surface of all the ways smart technology will make watering our lawns easier and more efficient.

**TECHNICAL STUFF**

# EVAPOTRANSPIRATION

Because water is so precious and so much of it goes toward lawns (up to 50 percent of the average homeowner's water use in some municipalities), scientists continue to look for ways to help us reduce the amount of water our lawns consume. One development involves *evapotranspiration,* or ET for short. Evapotranspiration, measured in inches, is the amount of water that evaporates from the soil, combined with the amount of water that transpires from the leaves of a specific plant over a given time.

ET translates to a very accurate way of telling you how much water plants have used in the past week or longer based on weather statistics and precise formulas. Developed for agricultural crops, you can now use ET for determining water needs for lawns.

For example, say you live in Omaha, Nebraska. Historical ET figures reveal that on the average summer day in Omaha, the ET for Kentucky bluegrass is about ⅕ inch of water. For a week, it totals 1⅖ inches. Bingo! If you know how much water the lawn uses, you

*(continued)*

*(continued)*

know how much you have to replace. Once the grass begins to display symptoms of drying out, you need to begin applying about ¾ inch of water twice a week — that is, if the rain hasn't supplied it for you.

ET figures are particularly important in dry summer areas, such as the southwestern United States, where water conservation is a prime concern. In California, Arizona, New Mexico, Utah, Colorado, Texas, and many other areas, you can get seasonal ET guidelines from either your local water supplier or from your cooperative extension service.

Lawn-watering requirements are usually 20 percent to 40 percent less than what is usually published as a base ET (the average figure for all plants). Keep in mind that ET figures are only guidelines. The numbers don't take into consideration specific conditions in your yard, such as shade, compacted soil, or sloping ground. You still have to be a good observer and make adjustments according to how your lawn reacts.

# Choosing Sprinklers: Portable or Permanent?

The goal of watering your lawn is simple: keep it healthy without wasting water. One of the more important decisions you make involves how you'll go about applying that water. You have two choices: portable sprinklers attached to hoses or an in-ground irrigation system with permanent/fixed sprinklers.

## Portable sprinklers

Portable sprinklers come in myriad styles with varying application rates (how fast they apply water) and application patterns (covering square, round, or rectangular areas). Portable sprinklers also vary by how large an area they can cover, but that area is further influenced by how high you turn on the hose and the amount of water pressure. Portable sprinklers vary in price from very inexpensive to quite costly.

The main disadvantage of portable sprinklers is that you need to move them around by hand. On large lawns, this task can be a real chore. You end up dragging the sprinkler around from place to place every half hour or so — especially if you live in a dry summer area where you need to water lawns frequently. You also need to move portable sprinklers when you mow or when someone wants to play on the lawn.

**WARNING**

Another problem with portable sprinklers is uneven distribution of water within the sprinkler pattern, with some areas getting more water than others. Also, application rates can be too heavy — water is applied too fast for the soil to absorb, causing runoff. For many sprinklers, adjusting the faucet to lower the water pressure makes the coverage area smaller.

**TIP**

Portable sprinklers are most useful in regions where watering is necessary only to supplement rainfall. You just need to drag out the hoses and sprinklers during dry spells. Portable sprinklers are also useful on small lawns (less than 1,000 square feet) where you don't need to move them around too much.

When considering a portable sprinkler, start by looking at the area it covers. Some models are adjustable to cover different sizes and shapes of lawn — a particular advantage if you have an oddly shaped lawn. Oscillating sprinklers sweep back and forth in a rhythmic pattern that just begs you to run through them on hot days. Traveling sprinklers look like small tractors and move along the length of a hose, which can reduce the number of times you need to move the hose and sprinkler to water your entire lawn.

Once you've bought your sprinkler, perform the trusty "can test," described in this chapter's section "Measuring How Much Water You've Applied," so that you know how long to run the sprinklers and how you need to overlap the patterns to provide complete coverage.

### Avoiding the "Whoops, I forgot to turn off the sprinkler" syndrome

This scenario sound familiar? You turn the sprinklers on and then forget about them. At least set an egg timer or stove clock so that you remember to turn off the sprinklers. Better yet, buy a timer and install it between your faucet and your hose. A simple model (see Figure 11-2) will allow you to set the amount of time you want the sprinkler to run and the timer shuts it off when the time is up. Battery-powered timers offer more options, such as settings that let you turn the sprinklers on and off at the days and times you choose.

**FIGURE 11-2:**
A timer shuts off the sprinkler after a set amount of time.

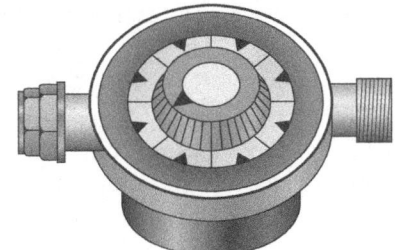

## Choosing hoses

**WARNING**

You can't talk about portable sprinklers without considering what they hook up to — a hose. The most important piece of advice about hoses is this: *Don't buy a cheap hose.* Spend a little money and buy one made of high-grade rubber, polyurethane, or other quality material. Buy a hose that rolls up easily, even in cool weather, and doesn't kink. If you'll be using the same hose to water your vegetable garden, look for a hose that's labeled as drinking water safe.

Other factors to consider when buying a hose:

>> **Length:** You need a hose long enough to reach your entire lawn. Or maybe you need more than one if you have a couple of faucets and a large garden.

>> **Diameter:** The hose's diameter determines how much water you can supply and at what pressure. In most situations, a ⅝-inch or ¾-inch diameter works best. At higher water pressures, the wider hose applies more water faster.

>> **Accessories:** Simple fittings, such as Y-connectors and end-of-hose shut-offs, can take some of the hassle out of watering with portable sprinklers. Buy high-quality fittings; cheap ones will invariably break or leak, wasting both money and water.

# Permanent sprinklers

Permanent, in-ground sprinkler systems have many advantages over portable sprinklers and are really the best choice where summers are dry or where lawns are large. Here's a roundup of some of the advantages; find details in the bonus chapter at www.dummies.com/go/lawncarefd2e:

>> They eliminate the need to drag hoses and move portable sprinklers.

>> You can connect them to controllers and fully automate them.

>> A well-designed system with precise sprinkler head placement ensures all parts of the lawn are watered evenly.

>> You can hook them to soil moisture sensors and rain sensors so that the lawn is watered only when needed.

The main disadvantage to permanent irrigation systems is their cost. However, that investment can quickly pay off with savings on your water bills due to more efficient water use. And don't forget the time and effort you'll save compared to the dragging-around-the-hose method.

**WARNING**

Even if you have an automated, in-ground irrigation system, you're not off the hook regarding maintenance. You still have to keep an eye on the system to make sure that it operates properly. Depending on your climate and the type of controller, you might still have to adjust the timer with the seasons and maybe even turn it off in winter — and in cold-winter climates, you'll need to drain the system.

## Tips for in-ground systems

Here are some other points to keep in mind. (Refer to the bonus chapter at `www. dummies.com/go/lawncarefd2e` for a rundown of the parts and pieces that make up an in-ground irrigation system.)

>> **Watch your sprinklers operate.** If the system runs early in the morning before you're even out of bed, how are you going to know if it's working properly? Turn on the system once in a while and see what's happening. Repair or replace broken sprinklers and unclog ones with disrupted spray. (Take apart to remove small particles or use a pin to dislodge them.)

>> **Observe your lawn and garden.** If part of your lawn suddenly starts to dry out and die, the sprinkler head might have a clog or is broken. If your sidewalk or driveway is soaking wet in the morning, one of the kids may have run into a sprinkler head with their bike and knocked it out of alignment. In any case, you need to turn the system on to find out the problem. If one section of the lawn is a soggy mess, you may have an underground leak that needs repair.

>> **Check the valve box.** If the valve box is full of water, that valve is probably leaking, and you need to replace a worn washer or gasket. Another sign of a valve box problem is if the lowest sprinkler leaks constantly.

## Common sprinkler heads used with in-ground systems

Here's a rundown of common styles of sprinkler heads.

>> **Pop-up sprinkler heads** automatically pop up when the water is turned on and then retract when the water is turned off. Although taller styles are available for garden beds, the most popular size for lawns is 4 inches high. There are different types of pop-up sprinkler heads.

>> **Spray-style heads** remain stationary and don't rotate when running. They are best suited for relatively small areas. Most can be adjusted to spray in a full circle, half circle, or quarter circle and have a spray radius of up to about 15 feet. (Some models spray in a rectangular pattern.) They have a relatively high precipitation rate — the rate at which water is delivered — and can deliver water at a rate of 1 to 2 inches or more per hour.

## MORE ABOUT ROTOR HEADS

Sprinkler heads with low precipitation rates are especially useful for lawns with clay soil, which absorbs water more slowly than sandy soil, and for slopes where faster application rates can lead to runoff.

The spray pattern of a rotor head depends on the model. Some are fully adjustable and can be set at any angle from 15° up to full circle. Others can be adjusted at specific increments. And some only spray in a full circle.

Rotor heads commonly used for lawns include *impact* and *gear-driven*. Impact heads change the direction of rotation when the water stream coming from the nozzle hits a spring-loaded arm. They are durable but can be noisy. Gear-driven heads use the flowing water to turn a series of gears that rotate the head; they are quieter than impact heads.

>> **Rotor-style heads** rotate as they distribute a spray of water. Because they throw water farther than pop-up heads, they're ideal for large lawn areas. Rotors have much lower precipitation rates, meaning they take longer to apply the same amount of water compared to a spray head. They generally deliver water at a rate of ¼ to ¾ inch per hour.

# Measuring How Much Water You've Applied

Sometimes simple is best, and this is true when it comes to measuring the amount of water your sprinklers are applying. The easiest method is with a "can test" (see Figure 11-3).

Randomly place five to seven straight-sided cans or cups (coffee mugs or empty soup cans work well) in the area that your sprinklers cover. Run the sprinklers for 10 or 15 minutes and then use a ruler to measure the water that accumulates in each can. That measurement is the amount of water your sprinklers apply over a given time. For example, say that each can accumulates about ¼ inch of water after 10 minutes. If you want to apply ¾ of an inch with each irrigation, you need to leave the sprinklers on for a total of about 30 minutes.

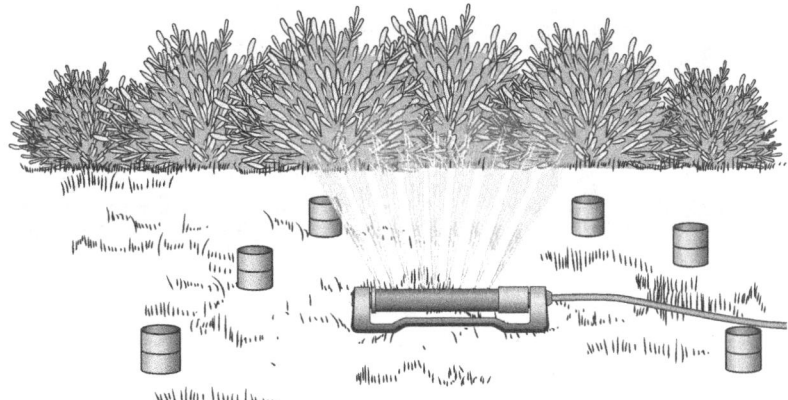

**FIGURE 11-3:**
The can test
reveals the
amount of water
sprinklers apply.

TIP

When you conduct a can test, you likely find that the amount of water accumulated in each can is slightly different. That's just the nature of most sprinklers — they don't apply water perfectly evenly. Ideally, the difference among the cans is not too drastic. If the greatest difference is more than 50 percent, you can clean the heads or, if needed, replace them. In any case, use the can that has accumulated the least amount of water to estimate how long you need to leave on your sprinklers. That way, you can be sure that the whole lawn gets enough water.

# Watering Tough Spots

Two areas of a lawn are particularly hard to water:

>> **Hillsides or steeply sloping ground:** The best advice is this: Don't plant grass on steep slopes. They're difficult to mow and water runs off before it can soak in. Plant a ground cover (see Chapter 19 for lawn grass alternatives). But if you must have grass on a hill, use sprinklers that apply water very slowly or water in short cycles.

>> **Narrow areas:** That little strip of grass between the sidewalk and the street and areas like it are just about impossible to water without waste and overspray. If possible, replace the lawn grass with drought-tolerant plants (check with your city planning department or homeowners association first to make sure that it's okay).

If needed, install drip irrigation or soaker hoses to water the plants. Drip irrigation applies water slowly and precisely through small emitters in plastic pipe. Soaker hoses are made from recycled tires and ooze water at a very slow rate along their entire length (see Figure 11-4).

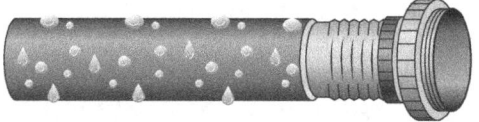

# Caring for Your Lawn during Drought

When the skies dry up and every drop of water becomes precious, your lawn may be the first place you want to — or have to — cut back on watering. Dry spells and drought conditions are common in the western United States but can happen almost anywhere. If the situation is severe enough, you may need to follow mandatory watering restrictions or even water rationing. In some dry summer areas like California, city water districts estimate that outdoor watering makes up about half of an average family's water consumption, and much of that goes on lawns. That makes lawns a major target for water conservation.

Following are some water-conserving strategies for your lawn. Although they can be followed any time, they are especially useful during dry spells.

» **Fertilize less:** Cutting back on the nitrogen you apply causes grass to grow slower and need less water. You may want to limit your fertilizer application prior to or during a period of drought. (Learn more about fertilizing in Chapter 12.)

» **Mow higher:** Set your mower at the high end of the cutting ranges listed in Chapter 13. This is a good idea any time, but it's especially important during times of drought. Letting grass grow on the tall side encourages it to develop deeper roots. Taller grass also helps shade the soil, keeping it cooler and reducing water loss due to evaporation.

» **Cut way back on watering:** Water less frequently. Start by cutting back on how often you water, keeping the amount you apply at each irrigation the same. For example, if you water every four days, cut back to once a week. If the lawn still looks good, cut back further. Even if the lawn starts to look a little rough, it will spring back when things get back to normal. Don't try to save water by applying light sprinkles; the grass will respond by growing shallow roots, rather than deep, healthy ones.

» **Let the lawn go brown:** Just stop watering altogether. Many grasses can go dormant for two or three weeks or longer and will come back when water becomes available.

>> **Reduce the size of the lawn:** Maybe all you really need is a small green spot in the backyard where the kids can play. So water only that area. When the rains return, you can water the whole lawn again or tear out part of it and replant with less thirsty plants. Chapter 19 has information on lawn alternatives.

>> **Aerate and dethatch:** These will improve water penetration in compacted soils and in those with a buildup of thatch (see Chapter 14).

## USING GRAY WATER

Gray water (other spellings include grey water, graywater, and greywater) is the water left over after you take a bath or wash clothes. On average, 60 to 65 percent of domestic wastewater is gray water. Where droughts are common, gray water can be an important alternative to using water fresh from the tap. Gray water use is subject to state and local regulations and building codes, so it's crucial to check with your local health jurisdiction and water authority before using gray water on plants, including lawns. Because gray water can contain debris like food particles and oils, some states ban its use.

Even where gray water is allowed for irrigation, there are practical considerations, such as how you'll actually get the gray water from your house to your plants. For example, regulations may stipulate that gray water be run through a colored pipe to identify it or applied at the soil line. You may not be able to use it in a sprinkler system. Also, if you plan to use gray water from your washing machine, you'll need to avoid certain laundry products, including those containing bleach. Contact your local cooperative extension office for guidelines on using gray water in your area.

IN THIS CHAPTER

» **Understanding which nutrients your lawn needs**

» **Deciphering fertilizer labels**

» **Figuring out how much fertilizer to apply**

» **Knowing when and how often to fertilize**

» **Applying fertilizers without polluting the environment**

Chapter **12**

# Fertilizing Lawns

A ll plants — including grass plants — need nutrients to grow and flourish. When you fertilize your lawn, you're supplying it with the necessary nutrients to create a lush carpet of green.

But there are more benefits to fertilizing than just keeping a lawn looking good. Proper fertilizing makes it more resistant to insects and disease and helps keep weeds at bay. It also makes your lawn better able to withstand extremes in cold, heat, and drought, and to recover from wear and tear.

So that's what this chapter is about — how to fertilize your lawn to keep it healthy and happy.

## Getting Started with Fertilizing

As you read through this chapter, consider the following.

> » **What are your goals?** Are you dreaming of a picture-perfect lawn? A pretty good lawn that keeps your neighbors content? A patch of green where the

kids can play? Knowing your goals will help you decide how often you want to fertilize and what products to use.

TIP

>> **Regularly test your soil** to ensure you provide enough — but not too much — fertilizer. There is no benefit to applying more fertilizer than your lawn needs. Overdoing it can stress the grass and lead to fast, weak growth that is susceptible to problems with pests and diseases. It also wastes money.

TIP

>> **Maintain soil health** by topdressing with compost, adjusting soil pH if needed, and leaving grass clippings on the lawn to decompose naturally. These efforts will go a long way to ensuring your lawn has plenty of nutrients. You may still need supplemental fertilizer, but you'll need less.

WARNING

>> **Know the regulations in your area.** Some cities are enacting regulations or passing bans on lawn fertilizers to protect local water sources. That's because the nutrients in fertilizers, although important for lawns, can cause algae blooms that kill aquatic life. See the sidebar "When fertilizers pollute waterways" later in this chapter. Contact your natural resources agency or local cooperative extension service for information about regulations and restrictions.

# Understanding Plant Nutrients

Grass, like other plants, requires 17 elements (or nutrients) for healthy growth. When enough of each of these are available, plants grow optimally. If even one of these is in short supply, plants can't grow as well.

Fortunately, some of these nutrients are readily available to plants. They get carbon and oxygen from the atmosphere and hydrogen from water in the soil. During the miraculous process of photosynthesis, green plants use energy from the sun to transform carbon, oxygen, and hydrogen into sugars — the "food" that fuels plant growth.

TECHNICAL
STUFF

Although it's common to say that we're "feeding" plants when we fertilize them, that's a misnomer. Plants create their own food — sugars and other carbohydrates — during photosynthesis. When gardeners talk about feeding their plants, they're really providing plants with mineral nutrients the plants need to manufacture their own food.

Most plants must get the other 14 nutrients they need from the soil or from applied fertilizer. (Carnivorous plants get nutrients from the insects they trap, but those are the exception.) Plants need some of these nutrients in relatively large quantities and others in minute amounts, but they need all of them to thrive.

The nutrients plants need in the largest quantities are called *macronutrients* and consist of nitrogen, phosphorus, potassium, calcium, magnesium, and sulfur. Of these, plants need the largest amounts of nitrogen, phosphorus, and potassium, so these are sometimes referred to as *primary nutrients*.

**TIP**

If you've been using conventional synthetic lawn fertilizers and are considering a more natural approach to lawn care, know that it's possible to have a lush lawn using organic fertilizers and techniques. Find out more in the section "Using Organic Fertilizers" later in this chapter.

## The big three: Nitrogen, phosphorus, and potassium

When you see N-P-K written on a fertilizer bag, those letters represent nitrogen, phosphorus, and potassium. The letters come from the periodic table of elements — remember chemistry class?

**TECHNICAL STUFF**

The abbreviation for nitrogen (N) is easy. Phosphorus (P) is kind of easy. Potassium (K) makes no sense until you learn that the abbreviation is from the Latin term, which was, in turn, taken from an Arabic word.

Nitrogen, phosphorus, and potassium each play a critical role in plant growth.

### Nitrogen (N)

Nitrogen is responsible for healthy green foliage and vigorous growth. It's vital for the development of chlorophyll and protein. Chlorophyll is the pigment that makes plants green and plays a critical role in photosynthesis.

Plants use a lot of nitrogen during the growing season, so they need a steady supply. If your lawn doesn't get enough nitrogen, it turns pale and yellow, grows slowly, and starts to thin out. Once that happens, weeds take notice and move in. That's why lawn fertilizers almost always include nitrogen.

Nitrogen is different from most plant nutrients because it moves easily through the soil, so it can easily *leach,* or wash, through the soil with rain or irrigation water. Once it leaches beyond the depths of plant roots, it's effectively gone. Nitrogen that leaches away doesn't just represent a waste of the money that you spent on the fertilizer; it can also pollute groundwater, streams, and lakes. See the sidebar "When fertilizers pollute waterways" later in this chapter.

**WARNING**

The type of nitrogen fertilizer you use and how you apply it are critical. Fast-acting nitrogen fertilizer can give you a fast green-up, but applying too much can burn the lawn like a blowtorch. (This is due to the high salt content, which dehydrates plant tissues.) Even if excessive nitrogen doesn't burn your lawn, it can cause a flush of lush growth that diseases and insects love to devour. You'll also need to mow more often. Discover more in the "Understanding the Nitrogen Component of Fertilizers" section later in this chapter.

## Phosphorus (P)

A ready supply of phosphorus is very important to the development of healthy roots and to the establishment of new lawns. It also plays a role in disease resistance and overall plant vigor. Phosphorus — which in fertilizers is usually in the form of *phosphate* (listed as $P_2O_5$ on a fertilizer bag) — doesn't move into the soil with water as nitrogen does. The best time to apply phosphorus is before you plant. You can work it into the soil where roots can get it.

**TIP**

Depending on where you live, your soil may already have plenty of phosphorus. However, sometimes the nutrient isn't readily available to plants. Whether the phosphorus is available to plants depends on several factors, including soil temperature and pH, as well as the soil levels of other nutrients, notably calcium, iron, and aluminum.

Although phosphorus doesn't tend to leach as quickly as nitrogen, under some conditions, such as in sandy soils, it can leach through the soil and end up polluting waterways. A bigger source of phosphorus pollution is caused by runoff, when fertilizer that's been spread over your lawn surface runs off with irrigation or rainfall. Because of this risk (and because many soils contain adequate phosphorus) phosphorus-free fertilizers are now readily available. See the sidebar "When fertilizers pollute waterways" later in this chapter.

## Potassium (K)

Potassium is critical for lawn grasses' hardiness, disease resistance, and wearability. It moves into the soil with water better than phosphorus but not as readily as nitrogen. Many soils have sufficient amounts of potassium, and it's generally needed by turfgrass in levels less than nitrogen but more than phosphorus. Very sandy soil often needs additional applications of potassium. Avoid adding too much potassium because it can make other nutrients — such as magnesium, calcium, iron, and zinc — less available to plants.

**WARNING**

# WHEN FERTILIZERS POLLUTE WATERWAYS

Excess nitrogen and phosphorus entering waterways, either through leaching or running off, can cause an overgrowth of algae, which in turn reduces the amount of dissolved oxygen in the water. This is called *eutrophication,* and the reduced level of oxygen ends up suffocating fish. The damage caused by phosphorus runoff is so great that some municipalities have banned phosphorus-containing fertilizers for lawns. Fortunately, in most areas, soils contain adequate phosphorus and can be managed to make that phosphorus available to plants.

Although pollution from excess nitrogen is also a problem, this nutrient is needed by plants in such quantities that it's problematic to ban it. Potassium runoff can also pollute waterways; however, it's usually applied in smaller quantities than nitrogen and is less prone to leaching, so there's less concern about it.

This chapter includes information on fertilizing best practices that will minimize the risk of leaching and runoff.

Fertilizer potassium is sometimes called potash, a term that derives from a time when potassium was extracted from big pots of wood ashes (pot-ash). Today, most of the potassium used in fertilizers is extracted from ancient marine deposits, though it's often still called potash. In fertilizer, the potassium component is expressed as $K_2O$ (potassium oxide), even though most fertilizers contain potassium in the form of potassium chloride (KCl).

## Secondary nutrients and micronutrients

Calcium, magnesium, and sulfur are nutrients that plants need in relatively large amounts, but not so large as the big three, N, P, and K. They're sometimes called *secondary nutrients.* Plants also need some nutrients in tiny amounts. These are called *micronutrients* and include boron, copper, iron, manganese, molybdenum, zinc, chlorine, and nickel.

**REMEMBER**

Most healthy soils contain sufficient quantities of the secondary nutrients and micronutrients your lawn needs. The only way you can be sure, however, is to have your soil tested. Plan to test your soil every three to five years. Repeatedly adding nutrients to your soil that are already present not only wastes money and resources, but it can also cause excesses that block uptake of other nutrients and risk polluting the environment. For information on how to test your soil, see Chapter 6.

Even if your soil contains all the needed nutrients, the soil's pH (a measure of its acidity/alkalinity) may restrict the availability of some. For example, iron is hard for plants to absorb in alkaline soils. If you live in an area where soils are commonly on the alkaline side, such as in parts of the desert Southwest, lawns are often pale yellow, even though the soil has plenty of iron and nitrogen. The solution is to adjust the soil pH, by adding sulfur to the soil. Find out more about soil pH and nutrient uptake in the "How soil pH affects nutrient uptake" sidebar later in this chapter. Learn how to adjust pH, if necessary, in Chapter 6.

**TECHNICAL STUFF**

## HOW SOIL pH AFFECTS NUTRIENT UPTAKE

Soil pH is a measure of soil acidity or alkalinity. The pH scale extends from 0 (very strongly acidic) to 14 (very strongly alkaline). Pure water is considered neutral with a pH of 7. Most soils have a pH in the range of 4 to 8.5. If a soil has a pH of 6, it's mildly acidic. If it has a pH of 8, it's moderately alkaline. Most plants grow best in soils that are neutral to slightly acidic, in part because soil pH affects nutrient availability.

Soil pH affects whether nutrients are available in forms that plants can use. In general, plants take in nutrients that are dissolved in the water they take up from the soil. In alkaline soils (with a high pH), many micronutrients get bound up in chemical compounds that render them insoluble in water and are therefore unable to be taken up by plants.

For example, plants growing in alkaline soils can suffer from a deficiency of iron, an important micronutrient, even when there's plenty of iron in the soil, because the iron is bound up in a form that isn't soluble in water. Plants that are deficient in iron become chlorotic (their foliage becomes pale green or yellow) because the plant can't produce enough chlorophyll, the green pigment critical for photosynthesis. Adding a fertilizer containing iron can help, but it's also important to address the underlying cause of the deficiency, which is soil that's too alkaline.

In acidic soils (low pH), the availability of macronutrients and secondary nutrients is reduced. In particular, the availability of phosphorus is affected; it reacts with other elements in the soil to form insoluble compounds, effectively tying it up in forms plants can't take up. Potassium, calcium, and magnesium availability is also reduced in acidic soils. In addition, the solubility of certain elements, such as aluminum, increases in acidic soils, which can affect the uptake of nitrogen, phosphorus, calcium, magnesium, and manganese; in extreme cases, excess soluble aluminum can be toxic to plants.

Finally, soil pH also affects the types and populations of soil microorganisms, which are responsible for breaking down organic matter. Materials like compost contain abundant nutrients, but these are held in complex organic forms that require the work of microorganisms to break them down into forms plants can take up.

Soil pH in the range of 6 to 7 optimizes the solubility and availability of most nutrients and creates a good environment for microorganisms.

# Deciphering Fertilizer Terminology

Here's a rundown of terms you'll see throughout this chapter, as well as on fertilizer descriptions and labels:

» **Quick release:** Sometimes called fast release, these types of fertilizer contain water-soluble ingredients that delivery nutrients in a form that plants can use right away. Quick-release fertilizers are like energy drinks; they deliver a quick jolt but don't offer much in the way of long-term benefits. Quick-release fertilizers don't contribute to soil health, and in many cases can harm soil life.

» **Slow release:** The nutrients in these fertilizers are in forms that are released slowly, over time, creating a sustained nutrient source that plants can draw on as they need them. Some fertilizers are made from materials that are naturally slow release, such as certain organic materials and slow-dissolving powdered minerals. Others are made from fast-release types of fertilizers that are compressed into granules or pellets that gradually release their nutrients into the soil. Many slow-release fertilizers rely on the activity of soil microbes to make the nutrients they contain available to plants, and the rate of this microbial activity depends on soil temperature and moisture conditions.

» **Controlled release:** These fertilizers are manufactured so that they release their nutrients at specific rates under specific conditions. For example, some coated fertilizers release nutrients in response to soil moisture. The nutrients inside the tiny beads "osmose" through the coating's membrane.

Another example is sulfur-coated urea. This fertilizer releases nutrients only after soil microorganisms work on the sulfur coating. Nutrients get released fastest during warm weather.

Some controlled-release fertilizers formulated for lawns can release nutrients for as long as eight months. Controlled-release fertilizers are convenient but expensive. And once they're applied, you lose some control over when and how much of the nutrients your lawn receives. For example, if you apply an eight-month timed-released fertilizer to a cool-season lawn in spring, it will still be releasing nitrogen in midsummer, when you really don't want it to.

**WARNING**

Some controlled-release fertilizers are manufactured by encapsulating the nutrients in a plastic coating. As the coating deteriorates, the nutrients are released. The process leaves behind a residue of tiny plastic particles that contribute to microplastic pollution.

» **Organic:** Most organic fertilizers are made from a variety of natural materials derived from plants and animals, as well as manures and pulverized rock. Examples include bone meal, fish emulsion, seaweed extract, compost, and aged cow manure. Many organic fertilizers require the presence of soil microbes to break them down into forms plants can use. This provides a slow, sustained release of nutrients and contributes to the overall health of the soil ecosystem. In essence, you feed the soil, and the soil feeds the plants. Organic fertilizers usually contain a wide range of nutrients, including micronutrients. Find out more about organic fertilizers in this chapter's section called "Using Organic Fertilizers."

>> **Synthetic:** Sometimes called conventional fertilizers, synthetic fertilizers are made through a manufacturing process and usually contain only a few nutrients. They tend to be in a concentrated form, in contrast to the bulkier organic fertilizers. Because they're created through controlled chemical processes, they contain well-defined amounts of nutrients in specific forms. They provide nutrients to plants but generally don't contribute to soil health.

>> **Complete:** Fertilizers that contain nitrogen, phosphorus, and potassium are called complete fertilizers. This doesn't mean that they contain all the nutrients plants need, just that they contain these important ones.

>> **Incomplete:** Incomplete fertilizers lack one or more of the big three: nitrogen, phosphorus, or potassium. A complete fertilizer isn't necessarily better than an incomplete one. If a soil test indicates you have plenty of phosphorus, then an incomplete fertilizer with nitrogen and potassium, but no phosphorus, is a better choice than a complete fertilizer.

**WARNING**

>> **"Weed-and-feed" and other combination fertilizers:** Some fertilizers include an herbicide, fungicide, or insecticide in their formulations. "Weed and feed" products, for example, contain fertilizer to supply nutrients and herbicide to control weeds. Although popular, combination fertilizers pose problems. For example, the optimal timing for fertilizer and herbicide applications often doesn't coincide. If you apply products at the wrong time, they won't be as effective. In addition, the herbicide in the product may not be effective on the weeds you're trying to control. Finally, applying these products to lawn areas under trees and near shrubs and garden beds can result in root damage from the herbicide.

Fertilizers containing insecticides and fungicides are often used as a preventative pill — to prevent problems you don't have and may never have. Repeated applications of unnecessary chemicals are a waste of money and resources and may end up causing pollution. It's much better to learn what problems you're most likely to encounter, identify them if they arise, and treat them only if needed. For more information about lawn problems, see Part 4.

# Understanding the Nitrogen Component in Fertilizers

Even though nitrogen is the most important nutrient your lawn needs, you have to apply it thoughtfully and at appropriate times.

Lawn fertilizers contain two forms of nitrogen: quick-release and slow-release. Quick-release forms of nitrogen provide quick green-up, but the grass uses them up quickly, and you need to apply them more often to sustain growth. Slow-release forms of nitrogen don't act as quickly but provide more consistent, sustained growth, and you don't need to use them as often. Many fertilizers formulated for lawns contain a mixture of quick-release and slow-release forms of nitrogen.

>> **Quick-release** forms of nitrogen, such as ammonium nitrate, ammonium sulfate, ammonium phosphate, and urea, are immediately available to the plant. In other words, you apply them, and the grass roots suck up the nitrogen right away. The following are characteristics of quick-release nitrogen:

- Lawn responds quickly

- More likely to burn the lawn

- More likely to leach through the soil

- Effects short-lived

>> **Slow-release** forms of nitrogen include ureaform, IBDU (*isobutylidine diurea*), methylene urea, nitroform, sulfur-coated urea, and organic materials like alfalfa meal, fish meal, biosolids, and animal manures. (The grass clippings you leave on the lawn to decompose are a source of slow-release nitrogen.) Plants can't absorb this type of nitrogen right away. Slow-release forms are so-called for two reasons: (1) The nitrogen needs to go through a conversion process (performed by microorganisms in the soil) before grass roots can absorb nutrients; and (2) the nitrogen has a coating of material that physically slows their release. The following are characteristics of slow-release nitrogen:

- Lawn responds slowly

- Less likely to burn the lawn

- Less likely to leach through soil

- Effects last longer

TIP

Grass clippings left on the lawn can provide up to 30 percent of a lawn's seasonal nitrogen needs (learn more about grass clippings in Chapter 13). Adding clover to your lawn also reduces the need for synthetic nitrogen fertilizers. Like all legumes, clovers form a mutually beneficial relationship with soil bacteria, allowing them to "fix" nitrogen — that is, to convert nitrogen in the air into a form that plants can use. That nitrogen helps feed nearby grass plants. Learn more about incorporating clover into your lawn in Chapter 19.

**REMEMBER** Acid soils are common in areas with very high rainfall, such as the eastern and northwestern United States. As soil pH drops below 6.0, phosphorus, potassium, calcium, magnesium, and even nitrogen become less available to plants. That's why maintaining proper soil pH is so important to keeping your lawn healthy. Find out how to test your soil and how to adjust soil pH in Chapter 6.

# Making Sense of Fertilizer Labels

If you visit a nursery or garden center, you may find the myriad fertilizers confusing. But, if you realize that all fertilizer labels contain the same information, making sense of them isn't as hard as you may think.

When you buy a commercial fertilizer, the label lists its guaranteed nutrient analysis, as shown in Figure 12-1. The first number indicates the percentage of nitrogen (N), the second the percentage of phosphate (P), and the third the percentage of potassium (K). A 100-pound bag of 20-4-4 lawn fertilizer contains 20 pounds of *actual nitrogen* (the percentage of nitrogen multiplied by the weight of the bag); 4 pounds of phosphate; and 4 pounds of potash. Fertilizer labels are required by law to list the percentages of N, P, and K. Fertilizer labels that contain secondary nutrients (calcium, magnesium, and sulfur) and micronutrients usually list those on the label.

The weight of the nutrients doesn't add up to the total weight of the bag (just 28 pounds of the 100-pound bag in the preceding example), so clearly there are other materials in the bag. These are usually inert ingredients, such as clay granules that make it easier to spread the fertilizer.

The label has a wealth of other information, including exactly what type of nitrogen (slow release or quick release) is in the fertilizer. Most lawn fertilizers contain a higher percentage of nitrogen compared to phosphorus and potassium because that's the nutrient lawns need the most.

**WARNING** Fertilizers that contain all three macronutrients, nitrogen, phosphorus, and potassium, are *complete fertilizers* — and for most lawns, that's usually what you need. If your soil test says otherwise, you have several choices. Some fertilizers, including ammonium sulfate (21-0-0) and ammonium nitrate (33-0-0) contain only nitrogen and are sold for use on lawns. Just beware that they're also quick-release forms of nitrogen and can burn your lawn if used improperly. Ammonium sulfate also tends to increase the acidity of the soil, so if you live in an area where soils generally have a low pH, you may want to avoid using it. Superphosphate contains only phosphate, but your best bet is to work it into the soil at planting time. Potassium sulfate supplies potassium and sulfur.

Guaranteed Analysis:

Total Nitrogen (N) .......................................................... 22%
4.5% ammoniacal nitrogen
13.5% urea nitrogen
4.0% water insoluable nitrogen
Available Phosphoric
Acid ($P_2O_5$) .......................................................... 3%
Soluble Potash ($K_2O$) .......................................................... 7%
Primary nutrients from urea,
ureaform, ammonium phosphate, and muriate of potash

**FIGURE 12-1:** An example of a lawn fertilizer label.

# Using Organic Fertilizers

If you compare the labels on conventional and organic fertilizer bags, you'll see that the mounts of N, P, and K (representing nitrogen, phosphorus, and potassium) are usually lower on the organic formulas. This is because most organic products derived from naturally occurring materials don't have the high concentrations of nutrients that can be achieved during the manufacture of synthetic products. In addition to N, P, and K, most organic fertilizers also contain a range of micronutrients.

TIP

It's possible to have a healthy and beautiful a lawn using organic fertilizers. That said, you'll need to be patient. With organic fertilizer, you won't see the immediate green-up effect that you get with quick-release nitrogen fertilizers, for example.

Organic lawn fertilizers are increasingly available in garden centers and home improvement stores. They can also be ordered online if you can't find what you need locally. (See Appendix A for sources.) The ingredients vary and may include compost; worm castings; aged manures; seed meals such as alfalfa, cottonseed, and soybean; fish emulsion; seaweed; byproducts such as feather meal and bone meal; and rock powders such as greensand (a slow-release form of potassium). Leaving grass clippings on the lawn (more on that in Chapter 13), topdressing with compost, and incorporating clover into your grass mix are important ways to boost nutrients, too.

Organic fertilizers often contain humus (sometimes listed as humic acid or humates). Humus is the stable end product when organic matter is fully decomposed. On its own, humus doesn't add much in the way of nutrients; however, it helps plants take up the fertilizers you apply by supporting soil microbes that break down nutrients into forms plants can use. These beneficial microbes also play important roles in suppressing disease organisms and improving plants' resilience to environmental stressors. Any compost you apply will likely contain humus. Learn more about nurturing soil health in Chapter 6.

**TIP**

If you're looking for organic lawn care products, check the labels for the OMRI Listed seal. If present, it means the product has been approved by the Organic Materials Review Institute (OMRI), a nonprofit organization that verifies whether fertilizers, pesticides, and other farm- and garden-related inputs meet the standards of the USDA National Organic Program or the Canadian Organic Regime for use in certified organic production and processing.

**TIP**

If you're interested in making the switch to organic but are hesitant to dive in, consider changing to an organic fertilizer for one or two of your fertilizer applications. If you're growing warm-season grasses, for example, you can give your lawn a boost in spring with a synthetic fertilizer to help it green up and then switch to organic fertilizers for later applications. Applying a thin layer of compost over your lawn once a year (called topdressing) adds organic matter and builds soil health.

# Determining How Much Fertilizer to Apply

**REMEMBER**

Fertilizer recommendations are based on the amount of actual nitrogen a lawn needs in a year. Although all these precise numbers make it sound like your lawn is one big chemistry lab, in truth, grasses (and the soil they grow in) are alive and are part of the larger ecosystem that is subject to all kinds of variables (temperature, rainfall, and so on) that you don't find in a lab. Keep in mind that leaving grass clippings on the lawn and incorporating clover into your grass mix contribute nitrogen, helping to offset fertilizer needs.

Therefore, while you want to follow the guidelines in this section and on fertilizer packaging, don't sweat the details too much. If your lawn is growing well, you're doing something right. If it's struggling, it could be due to factors other than nutrient levels (see Part 4).

In the next sections, I discuss some of the factors that influence how much fertilizer your lawn needs.

## The type of grass

Different types of grasses need different amounts of nitrogen to keep them vigorous and healthy. Table 12-1 lists the yearly nitrogen requirements for 1,000 square feet of the most common lawn grasses (see the section "Length of growing season," later in this chapter for more information).

**TABLE 12-1**

## Yearly Nitrogen Requirements

| Grass Type | Pounds of Nitrogen per 1,000 Square Feet |
| --- | --- |
| Bahiagrass | 2 to 4 |
| Bentgrass | 4 to 6 |
| Bermudagrass, common | 2 to 5 |
| Bermudagrass, hybrid | 2 to 6 |
| Blue grama | 1 to 2 |
| Buffalograss | 0 to 2 |
| Centipedegrass | 1 to 2 |
| Fine fescue | 2 to 3 |
| Kentucky bluegrass | 4 to 6 |
| Ryegrass | 2 to 4 |
| St. Augustinegrass | 2 to 4 |
| Tall fescue | 2 to 6 |
| Zoysiagrass | 2 to 4 |

# Actual nitrogen in the fertilizer

Now you can see how important nitrogen is. Notice that the numbers in Table 12-1 are based on a lawn's requirement for an entire year. You need to break the total amount into several applications, applying about ½ to 1 pound of nitrogen each time. Apply any more than that, and you may burn the lawn. Any less, and you don't get much effect. You can add some slow-release fertilizers in larger amounts.

The amount of a fertilizer you have to apply to achieve that 1 pound of actual nitrogen per 1,000 square feet, naturally, varies by the percentage of nitrogen in the product. Table 12-2 shows you some application rates.

If you wonder why I stopped at 46, that's the percentage of nitrogen in urea, the most potent fertilizer you can buy.

TIP

This chapter concentrates on dry fertilizers because that's the form most often used on lawns. Liquid or water-soluble fertilizers, which you usually apply through hose-end sprayers, are also available for lawns. Liquid fertilizers are more difficult to apply evenly, and you need to repeatedly refill the hose-end sprayer. The best advice for using liquid fertilizers is to follow the directions on the label.

**TABLE 12-2**    **Nitrogen Application Rates**

| Percentage of Nitrogen in the Fertilizer Bag | Pounds of Fertilizer to Apply to 1,000 Square Feet | Percentage of Nitrogen in the Fertilizer Bag | Pounds of Fertilizer to Apply to 1,000 Square Feet |
|---|---|---|---|
| 1 | 100.0 | 24 | 4.2 |
| 2 | 50.0 | 25 | 4.0 |
| 3 | 33.3 | 26 | 3.8 |
| 4 | 25.0 | 27 | 3.7 |
| 5 | 20.0 | 28 | 3.6 |
| 6 | 16.7 | 29 | 3.4 |
| 7 | 14.3 | 30 | 3.3 |
| 8 | 12.5 | 31 | 3.2 |
| 9 | 11.1 | 32 | 3.1 |
| 10 | 10.0 | 33 | 3.0 |
| 11 | 9.1 | 34 | 2.9 |
| 12 | 8.3 | 35 | 2.9 |
| 13 | 7.7 | 36 | 2.8 |
| 14 | 7.1 | 37 | 2.7 |
| 15 | 6.7 | 38 | 2.6 |
| 16 | 6.3 | 39 | 2.6 |
| 17 | 5.9 | 40 | 2.5 |
| 18 | 5.6 | 41 | 2.4 |
| 19 | 5.3 | 42 | 2.4 |
| 20 | 5.0 | 43 | 2.4 |
| 21 | 4.8 | 44 | 2.3 |
| 22 | 4.5 | 45 | 2.2 |
| 23 | 4.3 | 46 | 2.2 |

## Size of the lawn

All recommendations are based on 1,000 square feet of lawn. For help in figuring out the size of your lawn, see Chapter 6. To find out the total amount of fertilizer you need for one application, divide the square footage by 1,000 and multiply that by the appropriate number in Column 2 of Table 12-2.

For example, say that you have a bag of fertilizer with 30 percent nitrogen (the first number in the analysis) and your lawn is 2,500 square feet. Divide 2,500 by 1,000 (the number the recommendations are based on), and you get 2.5. Now go to Table 12-2, and you see that for a fertilizer that has 30 percent nitrogen, you need to add 3.3 pounds of fertilizer per 1,000 square feet. Multiply 3.3 by 2.5, and you find you need a total of about 8.3 pounds of fertilizer for one application. Bingo.

## Length of growing season

If you look at Table 12-1, you see that the recommended nitrogen for each type of grass is in a range, sometimes quite a wide one. That range has to do with the length of the growing season. If you live in a cold-winter climate where the seasons are short, you use the lower end of the range. If, on the other hand, you live in an area where the summers are long and the winters are mild, you use the upper range. Basically, the longer the growing season, the more nitrogen the grass needs.

## Lawn goals and usage

If you're merely hoping to cover bare soil with a bit of grass, you can get by with less fertilizing than if your goal is a lush carpet of green that will be the envy of your neighbors. Similarly, if your lawn gets only occasional light foot traffic, it will require fewer nutrients than if it gets lots of wear and tear and you need to promote vigorous growth to help it recover from heavy use.

## Soil type and health

Nitrogen leaches through sandy soils very quickly. If you have sandy soil, you can increase fertilizer efficiency by applying less with each application but applying it more often. Or, use only slow-release fertilizers. Healthy soil that is rich in organic matter acts as a reservoir of nutrients; as soil microorganisms break down the organic matter, they transform these nutrients into forms plants can use. (See Chapter 6 for more information about soil types and tips for building healthy soil.)

## What you do with lawn clippings

Leaving the clippings on the lawn adds nitrogen to the soil; you can cut the amount of fertilizer you apply by 25 percent, maybe more (see Chapter 13). As they break down, the clippings also contribute to soil organic matter, which, in turn, improves soil health. And, no, lawn clippings don't cause thatch. Learn more about lawn clippings in Chapter 13.

# When to Fertilize

When and how often you should apply fertilizer depends on the type of grass you grow. Grasses need nitrogen and other nutrients during their seasons of active growth, and they grow best with an even supply. Fertilize grasses when they're naturally dormant, and you're wasting fertilizer. Space your applications too far apart, and your grass grows fine for a while, slows down, and then speeds up again with the next application. Applying slow-release fertilizers, which release nutrients over time, avoids this cycle.

**WARNING**

Warm-season grasses, like bermudagrass and St. Augustinegrass, grow rapidly in warm weather. Generally, you need to feed warm-season grasses from late spring to early fall. If you feed too early in spring, the nitrogen promotes rapid growth of cool-season weeds, and much of the nitrogen may have been lost by the time the grass is actively growing and able to take it up. You don't want that. If you fertilize too late in fall, the grass is likely to be less hardy as it enters cold weather and more susceptible to winter injury.

**WARNING**

Cool-season grasses, such as Kentucky bluegrass and tall fescue, grow most vigorously in the cooler months of fall and spring. In mild-winter climates, such as the deep South and southern California, cool-season grasses can grow throughout winter. So the most important time to feed cool-season grasses is in fall and spring, and sometimes in winter. Fall, in particular, is a very important time to feed cool-season grasses; keeping them growing longer into cool weather and providing the reserves needed for quick green-up in spring. Avoid fertilizing cool-season grasses too early in spring. You end up with overly lush top growth at the expense of root growth, and that can mean trouble.

**WARNING**

Even though cool-season grasses stay green, avoid fertilizing during the heat of midsummer. Growth naturally slows down in very hot weather, and applying fertilizer at that time can weaken the lawn. The exceptions are those lawns growing in far northern or high-elevation climates where the weather stays relatively cool all summer. You can feed lawns in those areas throughout the growing season. For specific fertilizing times, see the lawn care tips for your area in Chapter 2.

For maximum appearance, fertilize your lawn about once every eight weeks during their active-growth period if you're using a fast-release fertilizer. Simply break up the yearly requirement of nitrogen into the appropriate number of applications, say one or two in spring and one or two in fall for cool-season grasses, three (late spring, mid-summer, and early to mid-fall) for warm-season grasses.

If you're not up for the higher-maintenance lawn (that is, frequent mowing), fertilizing once in spring and once in fall for cool-season grasses, and once in late spring and once in late summer for warm-season grasses, gives you a pretty nice lawn.

TIP

Got even less time? Fertilize cool-season grasses in fall and warm-season grasses in late spring. Just remember, no more than 1 pound of nitrogen per 1,000 square feet with each application.

# How to Apply Fertilizer

You can apply dry lawn fertilizers with one of two types of spreaders.

>> **Drop spreaders** apply the fertilizer to a narrow band of grass directly below the spreader, as shown in Figure 12-2.

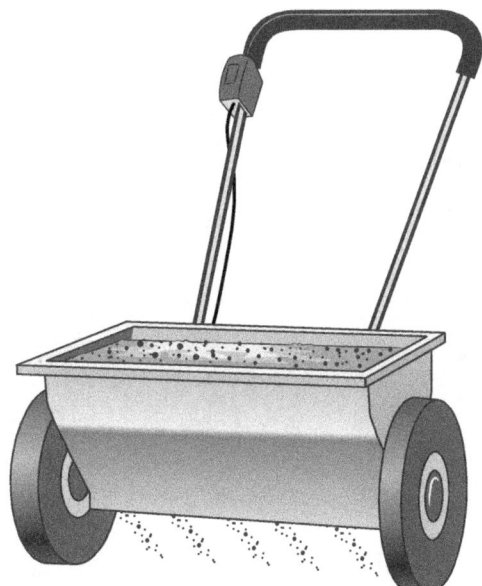

**FIGURE 12-2:**
Drop spreader.

>> **Broadcast spreaders** throw fertilizer over a wider area and are particularly useful for large lawns. This type of spreader comes in handheld (see Figure 12-3) or wheeled models (see Figure 12-4).

To use a broadcast spreader properly, you need to know how wide a band the spreader covers. If the directions that came with the spreader don't indicate the width, put some fertilizer in the spreader and run the spreader over a short stretch of lawn to find out.

**FIGURE 12-3:** Handheld broadcast spreader.

**FIGURE 12-4:** Wheeled broadcast spreader.

Applying dry fertilizers evenly by hand is very difficult and getting anywhere close to even coverage is nearly impossible. If you have no other option, then use this method to apply the fertilizer very carefully and only on small lawns. Wear gloves and walk backward across the lawn as you throw the fertilizer as evenly as possible with a sweeping motion.

You can apply liquid or water-soluble fertilizers with handheld, hose-end applicators, shown in Figure 12-5. Liquids are more difficult than dry fertilizers to apply evenly because it's done by hand, and the handheld sprayers require frequent refilling for large lawns. When using liquid fertilizers and handheld sprayers, follow the label instructions precisely.

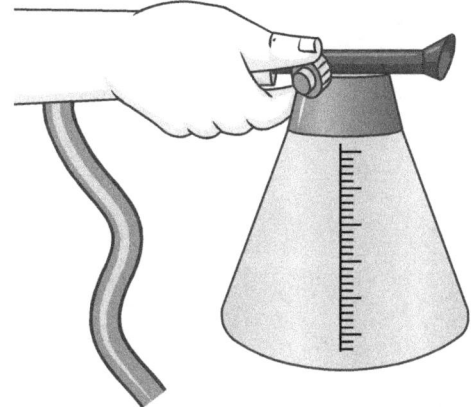

**FIGURE 12-5:**
Hose-end
sprayer.

## How to apply fertilizer evenly

**TIP**

The key to applying fertilizer evenly is to use the spreader properly. Uneven fertilizer application leads to uneven greening or burning of the grass. Take the following steps to achieve a well-nourished, attractive lawn:

1. **Set the spreader settings to correspond to the amount of fertilizer you want to apply.**

   You can find the information you need on the fertilizer label or spreader instructions. If not, you need to calibrate the spreader (see the section later in this chapter called "How to calibrate a spreader").

2. **Place the spreader over a hard surface (like a driveway or walkway) and fill it with fertilizer.**

   Sweep up any fertilizer that spills during filling. Filling the spreader on a hard surface prevents the fertilizer from spilling onto the turf, where it's difficult to clean up and excess left behind can burn the grass.

**3.** Moving at your normal walking speed, spread fertilizer over the edges of the lawn first, as shown in Figures 12-6 and 12-7.

FIGURE 12-6:
Applying fertilizer to rectangular lawns.

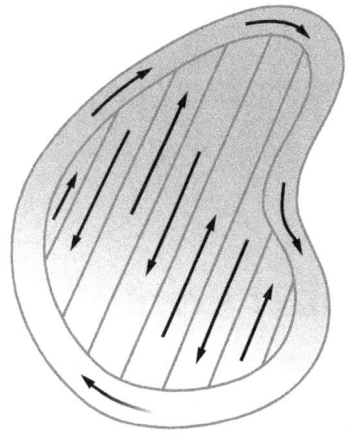

FIGURE 12-7:
Applying fertilizer to irregularly shaped lawns.

Then move back and forth between the edges. To avoid missing strips, make sure to overlap the path of the wheels when using a drop spreader. You should have a little overlap at the edges of broadcast spreaders.

Turn the spreader off when you reach the end strips, when you come to a stop, or when you're turning around to avoid uneven application.

TIP

For the most uniform coverage, you can apply fertilizer in two batches. Apply half of the fertilizer in one direction (such as north-south) and the other in the perpendicular direction (such as east-west). After the first application, check the amount that you've applied to the area. If it's significantly more or less than half, adjust the spreader accordingly.

Water the lawn thoroughly after fertilizing. Watering in the fertilizer washes the nutrients into the soil where lawn roots can use them and where they won't be washed away by a heavy rain. Watering also gets the fertilizer off the leaves, which may cause burning.

**WARNING**

When you finish, clean the empty spreader with a hose. If you skip the cleaning, the spreader can slowly corrode. Wash out the spreader on the lawn. Let the spreader dry before storing.

**WARNING**

If you spill a fertilizer with fast-release forms of nitrogen, clean up the fertilizer as best as you can (you may want to try a vacuum cleaner) and flood the area with water. This will prevent the nitrogen from burning the grass. Organic fertilizers and those with slow-release nitrogen won't burn grass.

To apply liquid fertilizers, start in a corner or edge of the lawn and walk backward in a straight line as you spray. Turn the sprayer off at the end of each row.

## How to calibrate a spreader

The manufacturer presets a new spreader to apply fertilizers at specific rates according to the amount of nitrogen needed per 1,000 square feet. As the spreader gets older, these settings can get out of whack and not apply the proper amount. You also may find that the spreader doesn't have a specific setting for the type of fertilizer you're using. In either case, calibrating a spreader can tell you exactly how much fertilizer you're applying and whether you need to make any adjustments. Calibrating your spreader every year or two is a good idea.

To calibrate a drop-type spreader, follow these steps:

1.  **Make a V-shaped or box-shaped trough out of heavy cardboard or a piece of aluminum gutter.**

2.  **Attach the trough with baling wire beneath the output area of your spreader to catch the fertilizer as it comes out.**

3.  **Set the spreader at the manufacturer's suggested number, put fertilizer into the spreader, and push the spreader over a 100-square-foot area.**

    To cover exactly 100 square feet, if your spreader is

    1.5 feet wide, go forward 66.6 feet

    2 feet wide, go forward 50 feet

    3 feet wide, go forward 33.3 feet

4. **Pour the material that fell into the trough or gutter, weigh it, and multiply the weight by 10.**

   This gives you the amount of fertilizer that you would apply for 1,000 square feet.

   Most fertilizer recommendations are given on a 1,000-square foot basis (or you can go to Table 12-2 to find out how many pounds should be applied for 1 pound of actual nitrogen). If you applied the incorrect amount, too much or too little, adjust the setting number appropriately and try again. When you get the correct amount of fertilizer pouring through the spreader, record the setting number so that you don't forget it next time. Keep in mind that if you change the brand or type of fertilizer, you'll need to recalibrate your spreader because the particle sizes of different formulations can vary widely.

A broadcast spreader is more difficult to calibrate because you can't catch the fertilizer as it's being thrown out. Take the following steps to calibrate a broadcast spreader.

1. **Weigh out an amount of fertilizer to cover a specific size test area — for example, enough for a 200-square-foot area (⅕ of 1,000 square feet).**

   For example, if you're using a fertilizer with 29 percent nitrogen, Table 12-2 shows you need 3.4 pounds of fertilizer for 1,000 square feet. Divide 3.4 by 5 (roughly 0.7 pounds) to get the amount needed for 200 square feet.

2. **Mark a starting point and then push the spreader several feet to measure the width over which the fertilizer is effectively spread.**

3. **Calculate and mark off a 200-square-foot area from the original starting point.**

   For example, if your spreader throws out a 10-foot effective width, mark off a total of 20 feet (10 x 20 = 200 square feet) and complete spreading the fertilizer over 200 square feet.

4. **Increase the setting number if there is still fertilizer in the hopper.**

   If you ran out of fertilizer before finishing, close down the setting. When you have an accurate setting, record the number for future use.

**REMEMBER**

Calibrate the spreader over the lawn area, not on the driveway or street. Not only are you wasting money, but the fertilizer will be washed into storm drains or creeks and other water systems. Find more information about minimizing pollution in the next section, "Fertilizing without Polluting."

# Fertilizing without Polluting

Lawn grasses need a steady supply of nutrients, and fertilizers can supply those nutrients. But fertilizers can also pollute groundwater, lakes, streams, and oceans if used improperly. Act responsibly and take the following steps to help preserve the health of the environment.

>> **Test your soil.** Knowing the type of soil you have and nutrient levels in it keeps you from applying unnecessary nutrients.

>> **Choose a proper fertilizer.** Get one that matches the nutritional needs determined by your soil test. If the test reveals that you don't need phosphorus, don't apply it.

>> **Use slow-release forms of nitrogen.** They're less likely to leach through the soil into ground water.

>> **Correctly time your fertilizer applications.** Don't apply fertilizers when grasses don't need them or can't use them. Never apply fertilizer on frozen ground. Don't apply fertilizer if heavy rain is expected.

>> **Calibrate fertilizer spreaders properly.** Correct calibration ensures that you're not overfertilizing unknowingly.

>> **Prevent misapplications of fertilizer.** Shut off spreaders when crossing driveways and sidewalks and sweep up any spills. Also, be careful when applying fertilizers around drains and sewers.

>> **Rinse off the spreader over the lawn area.** This way the fertilizer doesn't wash into drains and sewers.

>> **Use a mulching mower or leave clippings on the lawn.** You can reduce your lawn's nitrogen needs by as much as 25 percent, maybe more.

>> **Maintain healthy turf.** A healthy, deep-rooted lawn uses most of the fertilizer applied without runoff.

# Fertilizing Precautions

**WARNING**

Follow the instructions on the fertilizing packaging, including all safety recommendations, such as gloves and dust masks, and wash up thoroughly after use. Here are some other guidelines:

>> Avoid fertilizing during drought conditions or during very hot weather, especially if you're using quick-release forms of nitrogen.

>> If, after fertilizing, your lawn turns green unevenly or has dark green stripes in it, you didn't apply the fertilizer uniformly.

>> Store fertilizer in its original packaging in a dry place out of the reach of children and pets. Seal the packaging tightly or place it in an airtight container to prevent the fertilizer from absorbing moisture from the air, which can make it difficult to spread. Keep products containing herbicides or pesticides in locked cabinets.

>> Follow the label instructions regarding re-entry time — the time required between applying a product and allowing people and pets into the area. Liquid products may require waiting until the product has dried. Granular products may require waiting until the dust settles or the product has been watered in and allowed to dry.

IN THIS CHAPTER

» **Choosing a mower**

» **Determining mowing height**

» **Knowing when to mow**

» **Handling lawn clippings and fall leaves**

» **Using lawn mowers safely**

Chapter **13**

# Lawn Mowing

Ahh, that smell of fresh-cut grass . . . the memories it stirs of summers past. After all, for many people, lawn mowing marked the rite of passage from child to young adult — from the "you're too young to use the mower" phase to the weekly "get out there and mow the lawn!" phase.

While a freshly mown lawn transforms a yard into a more inviting version of itself, what you may not realize is that lawn mowing is more than just a Saturday morning ritual that makes the lawn look better. Proper mowing is one of the most important practices in keeping your lawn healthy. Specifics, such as how high and how often you mow, and what you do with the clippings, influence the density of your lawn, amount of water and fertilizer your lawn will need, and how serious insect, disease, and weed problems become.

In this chapter, you discover how to mow your way to a healthier lawn.

## Mowing Turns Grass into Lawn

To understand why mowing is so important to the health of your lawn, you need to take a grass-eye view. Get down to lawn level and see what mowing really does.

What would happen if you didn't mow? Your yard would look more like a prairie than a lawn. You'd have a bumpy surface composed of mounding or spongy grasses, separated by open spaces. Those open spaces would invite other, nongrass plants to fill in.

Mowing changes all that. Few plants besides grasses will tolerate getting repeatedly cut back to just a few inches every week. Because grasses form new growth near the soil line, they're able not only to withstand cutting back, but they actually thrive with it. Mowing turns the individual grass plants into the tightly woven turf we call a lawn.

That said, cutting your lawn is also stressful for the grass. When you mow, you remove the top parts of leaves — the parts that make food for the grass plant. So the mere act of mowing isn't what makes a lawn look good. How you mow, including the mowing height and mowing frequency, determine how healthy and attractive your lawn looks.

These days, you have a fabulous choice of lawn mowers, from small riding tractors to walk-behind mowers powered by gasoline or batteries to robotic mowers. (Hey, in some places you can even rent goats to munch down your grass.)

**WARNING**

Gas-powered mowers are significant sources of air pollution. In many states and municipalities, restrictions are in effect (or efforts are underway) that ban the use of gas-powered lawn care equipment. Areas without outright bans may have restrictions on the use of gas-powered equipment, such as limiting the hours or days of operation.

# Which Is Better: Rotary or Reel?

Basically, you can choose from two types of mowers, rotary and reel, with a number of variations of each.

## Rotary mowers

Rotary mowers, shown in Figure 13-1, are by far the most popular type of lawn mower. This type of mower cuts grass with a circulating blade beneath a metal, plastic, or fiberglass housing called a deck. Rotary mowers are easy to operate and maintain. They're also generally less expensive than reel mowers. You can sharpen the blades at home.

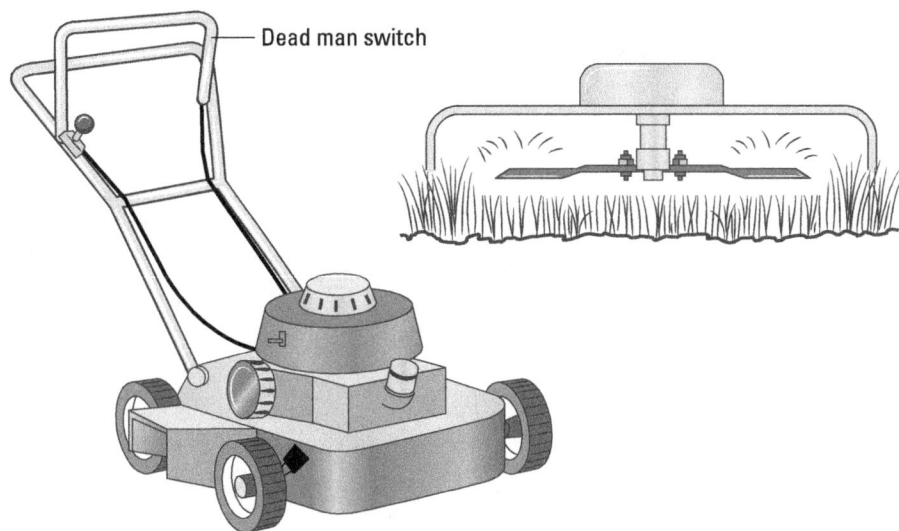

**FIGURE 13-1:**
A rotary mower.

This type of mower has a few downsides, though. They don't cut as cleanly as a reel mower, particularly when used on stiff, wiry grasses like bermudagrass or zoysiagrass. This type of mower also is more likely to scalp a bumpy or uneven lawn unless the mower deck has a "floating" or "oscillating" feature that allows it to move with the ground's contours. This feature generally is necessary but offered only on larger mower decks. If you have a backyard putting green, know that rotary mowers can't cut effectively lower than 1 inch; for that you'll need a reel mower.

There are lots of options for gas-powered and battery-powered rotary mowers; skip to the "Choosing a Rotary Mower" section later in this chapter for help in deciding which type is right for you. (Although corded electric mowers are still available, their popularity has waned. While they avoid messy refueling or breaks for battery recharging, they require a long outdoor-rated extension cord, which limits the amount of ground they can cover.)

## Reel mowers

The original teenager's nightmare, reel mowers have been rediscovered and improved. A reel mower, shown in Figure 13-2, cuts with the scissorlike action of spinning, curved blades passing over a fixed bed-knife. Grass blades get thrown to the front or rear. The most familiar type is the old push model, which sometimes seems to be more common in antique shops than home lawns. The truth is, these old beauties and their new, improved counterparts are still sold and are a great way to cut the lawn and get exercise at the same time. These push mowers are also quiet and nonpolluting. If your lawn is 1,000 square feet or less and composed of mostly soft grasses such as fescue, Kentucky bluegrass, or ryegrass, a push-type reel mower might be right for you.

FIGURE 13-2:
A reel mower.

There are also gas- and battery-powered reel mowers. The mowers that spin counterclockwise throw the cut grass to the rear; those that spin clockwise throw cut grass to the front. Reel mowers are heavier, more expensive than rotary mowers, and require periodic sharpening at an equipped shop. The advantage of reel mowers is that they cut cleaner and are less likely to leave ragged-edged grass blades. You can also adjust the blades to cut lower than a rotary mower, so you can create that putting-green look with bermudagrass or bentgrass lawns. Golf course superintendents use only front-throw reel mowers on the greens.

## Choosing a Rotary Mower

Powered by gas or batteries, rotary mowers are available in push-style or wheel-driven (self-propelled) models. Most riding mowers for home lawn use have rotary blades.

### Push rotary mowers

Push rotary power mowers may come with either side- or rear-bagging units to catch clippings. Side-baggers may be less expensive than rear-baggers. When

Curved lines in the landscape create visual interest and mimic the shapes found in nature.

Grass is the perfect play surface — it's soft and forgiving, yet tough and durable.

Mowing strips reduce maintenance time by allowing you to run the wheels of your lawn mower right up to the edge of the grass, eliminating the need for further trimming.

Taking the time to properly prepare soil prior to sowing seeds or laying sod will improve the overall results and prevent problems down the road.

Laying sod involves rolling out strips or laying pieces of grass over well-prepared soil. After a few weeks of care to help the grass get established, the lawn is ready to enjoy.

Edging not only gives your lawn a finished look, but it also helps prevent grass from migrating into flower beds, gravel walkways, and mulched areas.

Keep a grass-free zone around trees with a circle of mulch, which helps soil retain moisture and protects trunks from mowers and trimmers.

Robotic lawn mowers are compact mower decks that move around your lawn on their own using rechargeable battery packs. Many connect to an app on your phone.

Use a programmable timer or smart controller to automate your irrigation system, ensuring your lawn gets the water it needs while conserving this precious resource.

Aerating is the process of punching small holes all over the lawn. This opens up pathways for air, water, and fertilizer to get into the soil where roots can access them.

A broadcast spreader throws material over a wide area and is perfect for sowing seeds and spreading fertilizer.

A peat spreader (also called a compost spreader) has a cylindrical wire cage that throws down a thin layer of compost to protect freshly sown seeds. It's also ideal for top-dressing an established lawn with compost.

Wildflower meadows are an attractive, long-blooming alternative to a traditional grass lawn. This meadow was grown with Northeast Wildflower Seed, a mix that includes seeds for wildflowers that are well adapted to the region.

Creeping thyme is a low-growing herb with aromatic foliage and flowers that attract pollinators. It can withstand light foot traffic, making it a popular lawn alternative.

Although considered by many to be a weed, dandelions are sources of nectar and pollen for pollinators, and the leaves can be eaten as a salad green.

Microclover has tiny leaves, grows just 4 to 6 inches tall, stands up to light foot traffic, and needs minimal fertilizer, making it ideal for lawns, either on its own or in seed blends.

Planted with an eco-lawn seed mixture that contains turf-type tall fescues, perennial ryegrass, and Microclover, this lawn has excellent wear resistance and drought tolerance, and it has the added benefit of nitrogen-fixing clover.

Adding clovers to lawns reduces the need for nitrogen fertilizers because they "fix" nitrogen — that is, they convert nitrogen in the air into a form that plants can use. The flowers also feed pollinators.

Wildflower meadows are an attractive, long-blooming alternative to a traditional grass lawn. This meadow was grown with Northeast Wildflower Seed, a mix that includes seeds for wildflowers that are well adapted to the region.

Creeping thyme is a low-growing herb with aromatic foliage and flowers that attract pollinators. It can withstand light foot traffic, making it a popular lawn alternative.

Although considered by many to be a weed, dandelions are sources of nectar and pollen for pollinators, and the leaves can be eaten as a salad green.

Microclover has tiny leaves, grows just 4 to 6 inches tall, stands up to light foot traffic, and needs minimal fertilizer, making it ideal for lawns, either on its own or in seed blends.

Planted with an eco-lawn seed mixture that contains turf-type tall fescues, perennial ryegrass, and Microclover, this lawn has excellent wear resistance and drought tolerance, and it has the added benefit of nitrogen-fixing clover.

Adding clovers to lawns reduces the need for nitrogen fertilizers because they "fix" nitrogen — that is, they convert nitrogen in the air into a form that plants can use. The flowers also feed pollinators.

Xeriscaping refers to a style of landscaping that is focused on water conservation while still maintaining an attractive landscape. It often involves replacing thirsty turfgrass with drought-tolerant native plants.

Replacing some areas of lawn with low-growing herbs and perennials reduces maintenance chores, saves money on water and fertilizer, and creates wildlife habitat.

Drought-tolerant, low-maintenance native plants that are well-adapted to the local climate and support your region's wildlife are ideal choices to replace lawns along sidewalks.

Lawns are inviting spots for recreation and relaxation, and yet they're often some of the most labor- and resource-intensive parts of a landscape. It makes sense to carefully consider how much lawn you need and want.

A healthy, lush lawn is a welcoming place where you and your family can spend time outdoors, and it also creates an attractive setting for perennial gardens and other ornamental plantings.

By creating a beautiful, low-maintenance lawn and landscape, you'll spend less time mowing and more time relaxing in the hammock.

choosing a push rotary power mower, test maneuverability and the position of the bagging unit as it relates to your yard's landscape features and check to see how easily the bags come off. (Although it's usually best to leave clippings on the lawn to decompose, there are times when you may need to bag them.) Also, make sure that you can easily adjust mowing height to the proper height for your lawn.

**WARNING**

Most mowers include a blade brake system, colorfully termed as a dead man switch. This device makes the spinning blade stop within seconds after the operator releases a lever on the handle. Older models as well as some specialty mowers may not have this feature. The blade brake system makes power mowers more complicated (and expensive) but has reduced the number of mower injuries. Look for this safety feature and don't try to bypass it in any way.

### Self-propelled rotary mowers

Self-propelled rotary mowers are basically the same as the push rotary power mower but have added features. Naturally, the price is steeper than push rotary models. The self-propelled feature is plain enough: Pulleys and gears link the engine to the front or rear wheels.

## MULCHING MOWERS

Some mowers are "dedicated" mulching mowers, meaning that they mulch all the time. Other mowers may come equipped with mulching "packages" that can convert a traditional rotary mower to a mulching mower. The components of the mulching package generally change the configuration of the mower deck, block off the discharge chute, and include a blade with more "lift" to help circulate the cut blades of grass.

A mulching mower basically is the same as a typical rotary mower. However, the design of the cutting blade and deck keep the cut grass blades circulating within the deck longer. The clippings circulate in the blade housing and get cut and recut until very small. This type of mower usually has a flap that blocks the chute on the side or rear. The pieces drop to the lawn where they break down and disappear, returning both nitrogen and organic matter to your lawn. You can fertilize less if your leave your clippings, and you don't have to bag up and dispose of the clippings.

Even if you use a mulching mower, you still have to cut the lawn at the correct height. Grass that's too long or wet can more quickly clog a mulching mower.

# Battery-Powered Electric Mowers

Battery-powered electric mowers have come a long way since their early days, when their power and run time were lacking. There are now long-running electric mowers with plenty of power to suit nearly every lawn type. Battery-powered mowers offer many benefits compared to gasoline-powered models. They don't require trips to the gas station, messy refueling, or draining the gas tank at the end of a mowing season. They don't produce noxious fumes. They're quieter. They start with a switch, not a pull-cord (though electric-start gas-powered mowers are also available). Finally, because they can be stored in an upright position, they take up less room in storage compared to gas mowers.

**TIP**

Battery technology is rapidly changing, with advancements in solid-state batteries, faster charging, and more sustainable materials are on the horizon.

**TIP**

When idling, battery-powered mowers are much quieter than gas-powered models; however, once you turn on the mower blades their noise levels starts to approach those of gas-powered mowers.

If you're thinking about buying a battery-powered mower, consider the following.

>> **Voltage:** Voltage is the force that drives electrical current; the higher the voltage, the more power the battery can provide. Most residential lawn mowers have batteries in the 36V to 80V range. Higher voltage batteries generally provide more power for tackling tough situations like tall grass, but they also weigh more.

>> **Capacity:** Measured in amp-hours (Ah), this designation indicates the battery's storage capacity. The higher the Ah number, the longer the time between recharges.

>> **Run time:** Manufacturers' run time numbers are only estimates. How long a machine runs depends on the height and texture of the grass, moisture levels, and the terrain. Cutting relatively dry lawns takes a lot less energy than cutting lush, wet turf. The average run time is about 45 minutes between battery charges, with some mowers boasting an hour or more of run time. Some mowers include multiple battery slots; when one battery is spent, another can take over, effectively doubling the run time.

>> **Area mowed:** Rather than giving a run time (how long a machine runs on a fully charged battery), some manufacturers list the amount of lawn, in square feet, that can be mowed on a full charge.

>> **Versatility:** Some manufacturers design lawn equipment so that the batteries are interchangeable.

>> **Cutting swath:** Walk-behind mower decks generally range between 14 and 36 inches. Riding mowers and zero-turn mowers have wider decks, averaging about 42 inches.

# Lawn Mowers That You Can Sit On

This category is broad, and the mowers can be quite expensive. They're best for medium to large lawns.

>> **Riding mowers:** The simplest are correctly called riding mowers, and they do nothing else but cut grass. Riding mowers have comfortable seats and are ideal for large expanses of lawn. Zero-turn mowers, a type of riding mower, are valued for their better speed and maneuverability around obstacles. On zero-turn mowers, the engine is typically in the rear, the mowing deck out in front, and you sit somewhere in between. (There are also zero-turn mowers that you operate from a standing position.)

>> **Lawn-and-garden tractors:** Somewhat larger than sit-down lawn mowers, these look a bit more like farm tractors. You sit and look out over a hood that covers the engine, and the mowing deck is right below the seat. Some models take attachments such as snow-moving blades, and snowblowers or snow throwers.

>> **Garden tractors:** These are scaled-down versions of farm tractors. Equally heavy-duty as their full-size brethren, their frames are heavy 10-gauge steel, and both front and rear axles are cast iron. The benefit of a garden tractor over a lawn-and-garden tractor is that the garden tractor can accept a larger variety of attachments, such as tillers, chippers, or earth-moving blades. A garden tractor is a good tool for weekend farmers who need to do lots of chores.

When shopping for riding mowers, compare mowing widths. The wider the cutting area, the faster you can mow your lawn. However, your mower may be less maneuverable. Also, be sure to check the turning radius — some mowers can turn on a dime, making it easy to go around sharp corners and trees; ease of blade adjustment; and whether you can easily remove the mower deck. (The mower deck may get in the way when you're doing jobs other than mowing.) Don't forget, you have to store this piece of equipment indoors, so make sure you have room for it in the garage, tool shed, or barn.

# Robotic Mowers

Robotic mower decks move around your lawn on their own using rechargeable battery packs, and many connect to an app on your phone. High-end features include all-wheel drive, rain sensors, and anti-theft mechanisms. GPS-enabled models create digital maps of the different areas of your lawn; some have sensors to detect and avoid obstacles. Anti-theft mechanisms include PIN codes for operation, built-in alarms, and real-time GPS tracking so you can pinpoint the location of the unit if it's removed from your property.

# The Safety Factor

Every year, hundreds, maybe even thousands, of people get injured using lawn mowers. Power lawn mowers can be dangerous even when used properly.

**WARNING**

Be proactive when it comes to safety and follow these tips to avoid injuries.

>> **Know the equipment.** Read the owner's manual. Become familiar with all the safety features and how to properly operate and maintain the mower. Don't disconnect any of the safety features. Keep all the nuts and bolts properly tightened.

>> **Check the lawn before mowing.** Pick up any rocks or debris that may become a missile when you hit them with the lawn mower.

>> **Keep pets and children away from the lawn as you mow.** You never know when an object may go flying.

>> **Be careful when fueling.** Stop the mower and let the engine cool for 10 minutes before fueling. To avoid spills, always use a gas can with an adequate pouring spout.

>> **Turn off the mower.** Never leave the mower running unattended. Turn off the power when you cross nongrass areas; otherwise, you turn gravel or debris into flying bullets. When you work on a mower, turn it off and disconnect the spark plug; remove the battery or unplug an electric mower.

>> **Be careful on hills.** Steep slopes are always dangerous because a mower can flip over or go out of control. You should plant such areas with a ground cover other than turf grasses. On gentle slopes, mow across the slope, not up and down. Use a walk-behind mower. A riding mower is more likely to flip, and when it does, it can land on top of you. If you're using a ride-on mower that comes equipped with roll-over protection (ROP) "bars," always wear your seatbelt. If the

machine does flip over, the seatbelt keeps you within the protection of the ROP bars. If the tractor doesn't have ROP bars, do not use a seat belt.

>> **Wear proper clothing.** Heavy shoes and long pants provide the best protection from flying debris. If you're using a reel mower, don't wear loose clothing that may get caught in the blades.

>> **Operate the mower properly.** Don't pull walking mowers. They are designed for pushing.

>> **Supervise youngsters.** Don't let children operate a lawn mower unless they are strong enough and responsible and understand all the operating and safety features. Even then, supervise them.

>> **Never give a young child a ride on a ride-on mower.** A sudden stop can cause a fall that puts the child under the blades. Also, that child can come running toward you unseen, looking for a ride, and find danger instead.

# How High Do I Mow?

Different types of grasses grow best when mowed within their recommended range of mowing heights. (See "Setting mower height" later in this chapter.) For the healthiest, most water-thrifty lawn, mow at the upper end of the appropriate mowing height range for your species of turfgrass. (Table 13-1 shows suggested mowing heights for different grass types.) By allowing grasses to grow to the high end of the range, they have more capacity for photosynthesis, which benefits turf in shady areas, and will develop deeper roots and a thicker, denser turf that helps keep weeds at bay. Taller grass also shades the soil, keeping it cooler and conserving moisture. It's especially important to mow at the upper end of that range when the lawn is under stressful conditions, such as hot weather or drought.

Table 13-1 shows suggested mowing heights for different grass types.

**TIP**

If you don't know what type of grass you have, dig up or pull up a little piece near an unseen edge, place it in a plastic bag, and take it to your local nursery. They should be able to identify it for you.

**WARNING**

If you cut a grass too low for the grass type, the roots also will be too shallow. A shallow-rooted lawn dries out quickly and needs more water and is less likely to spring back from drought or a missed watering. Short-cut lawns are harder to care for and less likely to stay healthy. Also, low cutting exposes weed seeds and seedlings to just enough light to give them a foothold. If you mow too low — bingo — you get more weeds and weak grass.

**TABLE 13-1**

## Ideal Mowing Heights

| Grass Type | Height |
| --- | --- |
| Bahiagrass | 2 to 3 inches |
| Bentgrass | ¼ to 1 inch |
| Bermudagrass, common | 1½ to 3 inches |
| Bermudagrass, hybrid | 1 to 2½ inches |
| Blue grama | 2 to 3 inches |
| Buffalograss | 2 inches to unmowed |
| Centipedegrass | 1½ to 2 inches |
| Fescue, fine | 2½ to 4 inches |
| Fescue, tall | 2½ to 4 inches |
| Kentucky bluegrass | 2½ to 3½ inches |
| Ryegrass, perennial | 2½ to 4 inches |
| St. Augustinegrass | 2½ to 4 inches |
| Zoysiagrass | 1 to 2½ inches |

**WARNING**

If you mow some types of warm-season grasses too high, the grass blades can lean over, resulting in an uneven turf. (See Chapter 14 for more information on thatch.)

## The one-third rule

Follow the one-third rule. For a thriving lawn, never cut away more than one-third of the grass blade in any one mowing (see Figure 13-3). For example, if you usually cut your lawn to 3 inches high, mow when the grass is no more than 4½ inches high. If you usually cut it to 2 inches high, mow when the grass is 3 inches high.

If the grass gets ahead of you because of wet weather or your busy schedule, move up the cutting height of your mower to the highest possible setting and mow. If clippings are too long and heavy, even at that cutting height, catch them with the bagging unit or clean them up after mowing with a leaf rake. Then move the cutting height back to your normal range and cut the lawn again a few days after that first mowing.

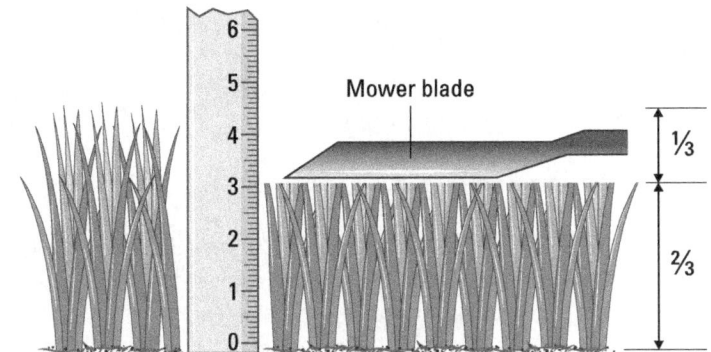

**FIGURE 13-3:**
Remove no more than ⅓ of the grass blades with each mowing.

# Setting mower height

Setting the blade height is pretty easy on most mowers — usually by just pushing a lever or raising or lowering wheels to move the mower deck up or down. The manufacturer's instructions will show you how to adjust the height.

To get a more precise measurement of the blade height, place the mower on a hard surface like a driveway and remove the spark plug on a gas-powered mower or the battery on a cordless electric mower (or unplug a corded electric mower). Then use a ruler to measure the distance from the mower blades to the ground, as shown in Figure 13-4. Adjust accordingly. You can double-check the mowing height by making a couple of passes over the lawn with the mower. Then, using the ruler, measure the height of the grass blades and readjust the blade height if needed.

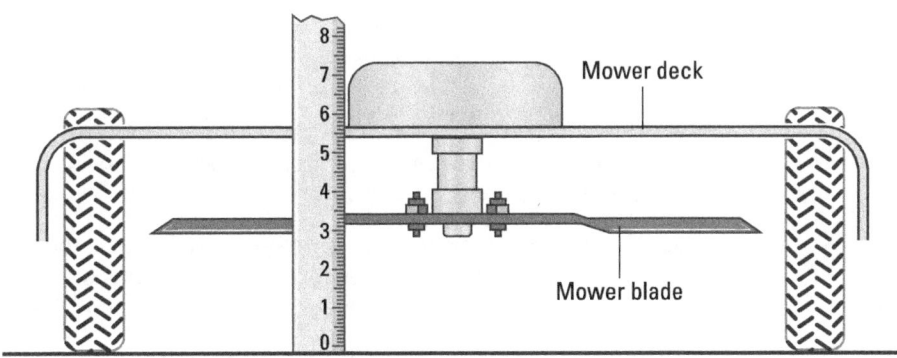

**FIGURE 13-4:**
Use a ruler to measure the distance between rotary lawn mower blades and a hard, flat surface.

## NO MOW MAY

"No Mow May" is a campaign that encourages people to temporarily stop mowing their lawns during the month of May as a way to support beneficial insects and other lawn denizens that together create a healthy landscape ecosystem.

Conventionally maintained lawns do little to support wildlife, especially bees and other invertebrates. Frequent mowing, for example, removes the flowers on clovers, dandelions, and other nongrass lawn plants before they can provide visiting bees with nectar and pollen. Mowing also destroys potential nesting sites for many beneficial insects.

Why No Mow *May*? Spring is an important time for native bees and other pollinators. By allowing lawns to grow taller and letting flowers bloom, your lawn can provide habitat and food at a critical time in their life cycles. (In regions where spring arrives earlier, the campaign is sometimes called No Mow April, or just No Mow Spring.)

The campaign isn't just about skipping a few weeks of mowing, however. It's also raising awareness of how we can take small but important steps to support biodiversity in our landscapes. Letting some flowers bloom in our lawn may seem inconsequential; however, if entire neighborhoods and communities take small steps like these, the cumulative effects can be transformative. If you can't forego mowing your entire lawn, even leaving just a section of your lawn unmowed for a few weeks can make a difference.

# How Often Do I Mow?

How often you need to mow your lawn depends on how quickly it grows. Of course, how quickly your lawn grows depends on a number of conditions:

>> **How much you fertilize:** The more nitrogen fertilizer you apply, the faster the lawn grows, and the more you have to mow. You can find out more about fertilizing lawns in Chapter 12.

>> **The time of year:** Cool-season grasses grow fastest in the cool months of fall and spring. Warm-season grasses grow faster during the hot months of summer. During those periods, you have to mow more often.

>> **How you water:** Obviously, if you stop watering, or at least cut way back, the grass grows less and you don't need to cut as often. More water usually means more mowing. For more on watering, see Chapter 11.

**TIP**

How do you know when to mow? Here's the rule: Mow your lawn when the grass reaches about one-third higher than the recommended mowing height (refer to Table 13-1). For example, if you usually cut your lawn to 2 inches high, you need to mow your lawn when the grass is about 3 inches high.

If you let your lawn grow too high and then mow it all the way down in one pass, it's no big deal, right? Wrong. Cutting really long grass shocks the roots. The height of the grass relates directly to the depth of the roots. If you whack off a large portion of the top, you're cutting off the food, and you hurt the roots.

Mowing tall grass also makes a mess. You have to clean up all those clippings because if you don't, the extra-long clippings can smother the grass. Besides, those clumps of clippings look terrible.

**REMEMBER**

The bottom line is to mow as often as needed to maintain your lawn at the top of the recommended range for your type of grass while removing no more than one third of the grass blades at each mowing. On the (hopefully) rare occasion that the lawn grows extra tall, refer to the section "How High Do I Mow?" earlier in this chapter for tips.

# What to Do with Lawn Clippings

How should you handle lawn clippings? Send them off to the landfill? No! Landfills are too full already, and in some areas, sending grass clippings to them is illegal. Besides, grass clippings are valuable organic matter and chock-full of nitrogen and other nutrients. Use them!

As long as you mow often enough to remove no more than one-third of the grass blade, the easiest thing to do is just to leave clippings on the lawn. The pieces break down quickly and reduce the amount of fertilizer you have to use by as much as 30 percent. Leaving clippings on the lawn doesn't cause thatch to build up.

Lawn clippings break down quickly, thanks to two factors:

>> A variety of hard-working microorganisms love the nitrogen in lawn clippings.

>> Clippings consist of 85 percent to 90 percent water.

The clippings can break down in a matter of days — especially if you use a mulching mower, which chops the grass into small pieces that scatter evenly and decompose quickly. If you see clumps in your lawn, you can scatter them by hand. Don't leave large clumps of clippings; these are slow to break down and can smother the grass underneath.

# REDUCING WEED SEEDS IN YOUR CLIPPINGS

If your lawn has a lot of weeds, you may have weed seeds in your clippings. You can reduce weed seeds in your clippings by doing the following:

- **Mowing often:** If you mow often, weed seeds don't have time to mature between mowings.

- **Composting:** The heat generated during the composting process kills many weed seeds. So compost the clippings instead of spreading them around. For more information on composting, see the section "Compost clippings," later in this chapter.

- **Minimizing weed growth:** Reduce the weeds in the lawn. See Chapter 15 for tactics in battling weeds.

**WARNING**

If you've treated your lawn with weed-and-feed products, herbicides, insecticides, or fungicides, it's best to leave the clippings on the lawn, where they can break down. You also can spread clippings in an out-of-the-way place where they can decompose without affecting nearby plants.

If you're the type who just can't stand the sight of clippings on your lawn, even for a day, here are a few other options.

## Compost the clippings

Turn your clippings into nutrient-rich compost. Use fresh grass clippings as the "green" component in your compost bin, alternating them with dry (brown) materials, such as dried leaves or straw. (Find tips for making compost in Chapter 6.) Don't compost clippings that have been treated with lawn chemicals.

Clippings and other moist materials like kitchen scraps need air to break down to earthy compost. A pile consisting solely of fresh clippings will stay too wet and won't get enough air, resulting in a slimy mess with a sour smell. If your pile starts to smell, add in some dry materials and fluff the pile with a garden fork every few days to aerate it.

## Use clippings as mulch

Mulches made from dried grass clippings, shredded leaves, bark mulch, pine straw, and other organic materials reduce soil temperatures and slow evaporation from the soil, conserving water in the process. As the mulches break down, they improve the soil and add nutrients. Mulches also reduce weeds by smothering weed seeds and preventing them from germinating. Weeds that do germinate and grow are easier to pull out of the loose mulch.

Spread a thin layer of fresh or dry clippings around the base of perennials, vegetable plants, trees, and shrubs, keeping it an inch or two away from stems. (Don't use clippings from a lawn that has been treated with chemicals.)

### See if your municipality has a composting program

Ask if they accept grass clippings. (If your lawn has been treated with lawn chemicals, ask if the treated clippings are accepted.) Your waste disposal company might also have their own composting program and might pick them as long as you separate them from your regular trash as instructed.

REMEMBER

Don't use clippings from treated lawns around garden plants and keep them out of compost that you may spread around garden plants.

# Tips from the Pros

Here are some guidelines for getting the cleanest cut and best-looking lawn:

>> **Keep the blades sharp.** Dull blades leave a ragged edge on the top of the grass blade, giving the whole lawn a browned-out look a day after mowing. You need to take reel mowers to a lawn mower shop for a professional sharpening. You can bring your rotary mower (or just the blades) to a shop for sharpening or sharpen them yourself following the manufacturer's instructions. How often your blades need to be sharpened mostly depends on how large your lawn is, the type of grass you have. If you have a small, cool-season lawn you may need to sharpen the blade only once a year. More wiry grasses, such as bermudagrass or zoysiagrass, may dull blades faster.

You should sharpen your mower blades before your lawn shows any damage, and few blades should go a full season of mowing without sharpening, even on small lawns. Also, you need to periodically examine mower blades for damage that may occur, such as nicks from hitting a rock.

>> **Alternate mowing directions.** Alternate mowing direction every time you mow. Doing so helps avoid compacting soil, and it helps keep grass growing

upright, which makes for a more even cut. Try mowing at a 45-degree or 90-degree angle to your last pattern. You may find you even like the looks of a pattern better.

>> **Don't cut wet grass.** Wet grass cuts unevenly, and the clippings settle in big globs, smothering the grass. Cutting wet grass also promotes the growth and spread of disease organisms.

>> **Avoid sharp turns.** You scalp the grass by turning sharply. Make wide turns or use sidewalks or driveways to swing around.

>> **Level uneven spots.** If you constantly scalp a part of the lawn, that spot is probably uneven or bumpy. For help leveling parts of your lawn, see Chapter 14.

>> **Keep the mower deck clean.** On rotary mowers, the mower deck design and the spinning action of the blade combine for maximum air flow to help the grass stand up straight as the blade passes over and cuts it and to circulate the clippings to the discharge chute (or in recycling mowers, back into the blade to be cut smaller). On both rotary and reel mowers, the blades need adequate room to move freely. Debris caked within the mower deck messes up all the hard work of the design engineers and cuts down on the operating efficiency of your mower. So clean the underside of the deck (following the manufacturer's recommendations) before you put the mower away after cutting the grass.

>> **Maintain your mower.** Follow the manufacturer's instructions to keep everything running shipshape. Good maintenance includes adding or changing oil and the oil filter on a regular basis, keeping mower blades sharp, and occasionally tightening nuts and bolts. Drain the gas tank before you store the mower over the winter.

>> **Wait to mow a newly sodded lawn until the sod is firmly rooted in the soil.** The pieces of sod should stay in place when you give them a gentle tug.

# Edging and Trimming

Edging and trimming are the finishing touches of mowing. They accentuate the lines of the lawn and planting beds and gives the whole picture a well-manicured look.

Most mowers do a relatively poor job of cutting grass along the edges of the lawn. The grass just grows too sideways in that area for the blades to get at it, or you can't get the wheels into planting beds nearby. So to add the final touch, you'll probably need to do some edging or trimming along the perimeter of the lawn. Installing a mowing strip or edging greatly simplifies trimming; see Chapter 7 for more on installing edging.

Some tools are called edgers because they're designed to trim the lawn along a hard surface like a driveway or sidewalk. Edgers cut a nice clean edge but leave some dirt and grass debris that you need to clean up. Trimmers, on the other hand, can be used anywhere — along a hard surface, in tight spaces, next to planting beds, and so on. Trimmers also leave some clippings on paths and driveways that you need to sweep up.

Edgers and trimmers come in a number of different types (shown in Figure 13-5), from simple handheld clippers to gas or electric models. The classic push-pull, handheld rotary edger does a clean job along walks and driveways. Simply place the wheel on the hard surface with the blade just over the edge, and push and pull. Power models, with rotating blades, make the job easier, especially if you have a large area to cover. Take care, though — power models can be dangerous, so follow all the manufacturer's safety precautions. You can also use gas or electric string trimmers, which cut with rotating nylon filament.

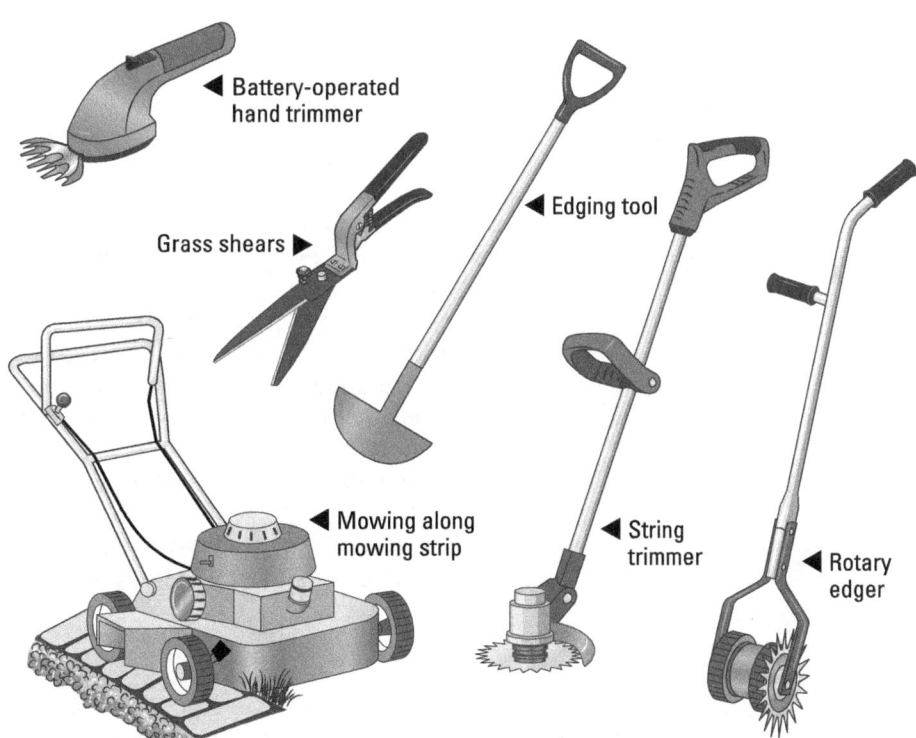

Battery-operated hand trimmer

Grass shears ►

◄ Edging tool

◄ Mowing along mowing strip

◄ String trimmer

◄ Rotary edger

**FIGURE 13-5:** Edging and trimming tools.

**WARNING**

# MOWERS AND TRIMMERS — A TREE'S WORST ENEMIES

Arborists battle an enemy they've named "lawn-mower disease" that kills thousands of trees, particularly young ones, each year.

Here's how the damage starts. You have a tree in your lawn. To cut the grass near the trunk you circle around with a mower or weed whip, hitting the trunk once in a while. Gradually, the tree starts to grow poorly. Branches die. Maybe the tree falls over in a windy storm.

Repeatedly banging a mower against a tree trunk or whipping it senseless with a string trimmer can seriously damage the bark and the sensitive tissues underneath. The damage can restrict the growth of young trees to the point where the base of the trunk is so weak and girdled that the tree just snaps off in the slightest wind.

To protect the tree, leave a ring of grassless soil at least 3 feet wide around the trunk and cover the open soil with a 2- to 3-inch layer of organic mulch such as shredded bark or pine straw. (Keep the mulch a few inches away from the base of the tree.)

Some trimmers use a section of plastic or plastic chain instead of a string filament, and some even use metal rather than plastic. Generally, these machines cut off the top portion of long grass or slice off weeds close to ground level. You can even use the filament types to edge a portion of the yard by turning them at the proper angle and holding them in place long enough to cut into the soil. You can use hand-powered grass shears to cut away (trim) part of the grass blade. Battery-operated models do the same thing, only faster and easier.

After mowers, string trimmers are the most widely used power tool used in landscape maintenance. Some trimmers are electric (using a power cord or battery), and some are gas-powered. Most of the gas-powered models use two-stroke engines, which require you to mix special oil into the gasoline. Quieter, four-stroke engines that run on regular unleaded gasoline are also available.

**REMEMBER**

Gas-powered lawn tools are significant sources of air pollution. In many states and municipalities, restrictions are in effect (or efforts are underway) that ban their use. Areas without outright bans may have restrictions, such as limiting the hours or days you can use gas-powered equipment.

Choose a trimmer with an automatic or semiautomatic feed system for the nylon whip. Some trimmers force you to stop the engine and lengthen the cutting string by hand every time it wears down.

# Lawn and Leaf Blowers

These do just what they say — they put out a steady blast of air that you can use to blow leaves and grass trimmings off paving and sidewalks or to gather fallen leaves in autumn. These machines are noisy monsters. How many times have your Saturday and Sunday mornings been disturbed with the constant noise they create throughout your neighborhood? Many cities are outlawing blowers for just that reason. Buy a broom and a rake. If you opt for a blower, do be considerate of others as you use it.

# Dealing with Leaves on the Lawn

Although fallen leaves are a source of organic matter and plant nutrients, a thick layer of leaves can smother a lawn, preventing light from reaching the grass. Wet leaves are especially problematic because they can form a slimy cover that prevents air from circulating through the turf, which promotes disease. So let's face it — you may need to get leaves off the lawn. Here are some ways to deal with fallen leaves:

» **Mow over them and leave them:** If the leaves are dry and not too thick or heavy, a mulching mower should be able to chop them into fine enough pieces so that they filter down harmlessly into the lawn.

» **Mow over them and pick them up:** If the leaves are too thick to leave in place after mowing, mow over them and collect them in the grass collector of your lawn mower. Empty the grass collector into your compost pile.

» **Rake them up:** Get out the old leaf rake and get some exercise. Or hire the neighbor's kid to rake them up. Then put the leaves in the compost pile or use them as mulch.

» **Compost them:** They'll break down faster if you run them through a shredder first. Or simply mow over them a few times to shred them. Pile up the leaves near your compost bin. Alternate layers of dried leaves (the "browns" with kitchen scraps and other fresh material (the "greens"). See Chapter 6 for composting tips.

» **Use a chipper vac:** This machine sucks up the leaves, shreds them into small pieces, and then shoots them into a collection bag. You can then use the ground-up leaves as mulch or compost them.

» **Use chopped leaves as mulch:** Leaves make a great mulch, especially under shrubs and trees. They slowly break down and improve the soil.

>> **Make leaf mold:** Composed of decomposed leaves, leaf mold is a valuable soil amendment. Shred the leaves and pile them up in an out-of-the-way spot. Moisten them periodically and turn the pile occasionally. The leaves will break down slowly into a rich, earthy material that's ideal for enriching garden soil.

>> **Use them to insulate plants:** Pile up dried leaves around tender plants as a protection against cold and to insulate soil from alternating freeze/thaw cycles that can harm perennials. Or use them to cover carrots, beets, and other root crops to prevent the ground from freezing, so you can harvest them into winter.

However you collect fallen leaves, be sure to put them to good use. Don't send leaves to the dump! And don't burn them! Leaves are a great source of organic matter and some nutrients for your garden.

If you're unable to use the leaves in your landscape, call your local disposal company and see whether they have programs to pick up organic debris. Many communities also have community composting programs. The municipal waste district collects leaves and grass clippings, composts them, and uses the compost in parks and playgrounds or sells it to landscapers and gardeners. Check with your solid waste district office to see whether you have such a program in your town.

Chapter **14**

# Aerating, Dethatching, and Renovating

D espite your best-laid plans, something probably will go wrong with your lawn sooner or later. It may start with something simple — maybe it'll be the kids taking the same path back and forth to the swing set, compacting the soil just a little each time they go. Or you may find that you just can't seem to keep a section of your lawn wet so that weeds start to creep in — and before you know it, you've got trouble.

A troublesome lawn (or section of your lawn) can start in a lot of ways, or perhaps you just inherited a lousy lawn when you bought a new house. In any case, you may want to do something about it, and, fortunately, the solution may not be all that hard.

## Is Something Wrong?

The first rule for any new detective is to not make assumptions. Observe, ask questions, and look at the evidence. In the case of lawns, don't assume that a struggling area has a pest problem or needs more fertilizer. There may be other factors in play, and if you just dump pesticides or fertilizers, they won't help, and they may actually hurt your grass. Here are some questions to help you figure out the problem.

>> When did the problem start? Is it new this year? Did it start a few weeks ago? A few days?

>> Is the problem occurring over your entire lawn or just in one or a few sections?

>> What are the characteristics of the problem spot? Is it an area that gets a lot of foot traffic? Is it in shade? Does it stay wet after a rainstorm?

>> Have you checked your irrigation system to ensure it's working properly and there's complete coverage?

>> Did you apply anything to the lawn (fertilizer, herbicide, pesticide, and so on) recently? If so, did the problem start after that? (It's always a good idea to keep a calendar of what you apply to your lawn and when.)

TIP

Sometimes, the best solution for an area that struggles is to consider doing something else with it. Create a walkway along a well-worn path through the lawn. Mulch the area under a tree or plant a shade-tolerant ground cover instead of trying to get grass to grow. Plant a rain garden in a wet spot. Fighting to have every part of your landscape covered in a perfect carpet of green grass simply isn't practical for most of us. Give yourself permission to have a few rough spots or get creative with alternatives. (See Chapter 19 for lawn alternatives.)

That said, most lawns benefit from some simple yet often overlooked maintenance practices. Aerating is one of them.

## Why Aerating Matters

Years of walking on a lawn or driving heavy equipment on it during construction can compact soil, smashing the particles tightly together and forcing all the air out. You got it: No air is bad for roots. You can identify the compacted areas because that's where the water always puddles up. Eventually, the grass declines and starts turning brown because the roots receive no air, and water can't get to them either.

Compaction is particularly troublesome where soils are heavy clay. In fact, clay soil can have poor aeration and be slow to absorb water without your help. Walk all over clay soil, especially when soggy, and you really have problems. For more information on clay soil and other soil types, see Chapter 6.

You can help compacted and clay soils by aerating them. Aerating is the process of punching small holes all over your lawn. This opens up pathways for air and water to get into the soil where roots can access them (Figure 14-1).

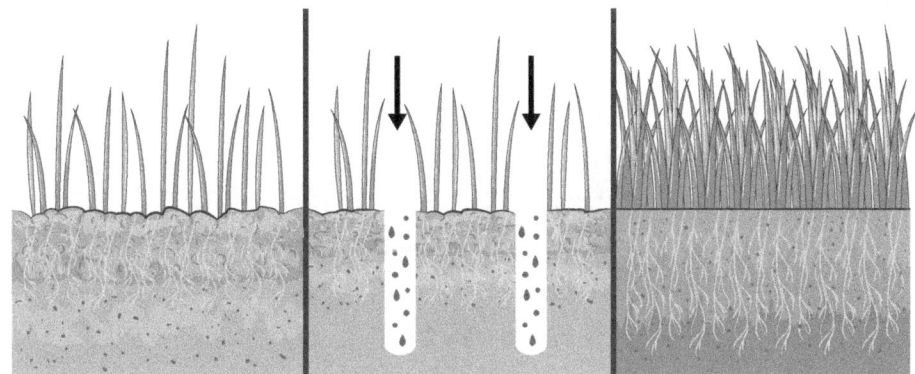

**FIGURE 14-1:** Aerating creates holes that allow air and water to reach roots. Roots respond by growing deeper and stronger so the grass can form a thick, healthy turf.

Signs that your lawn needs to be aerated include

>> Worn areas where people walk often.

>> Water puddles after irrigating.

>> Water runs off the lawn after only a few minutes of watering.

>> Parts of the lawn that just can't seem to keep moist.

Aerating helps create a dense turf that is more resistant to weeds and pests.

## Types of aerators

There are several types of lawn aerators.

### Core aerators

The most effective aerators are core aerators that use hollow tines to pull out small plugs (cores) of grass and soil. The cores are about ½- to ¾-inch in diameter and 2 to 4 inches long. Here are some options for core aerators:

>> **Gas-powered core aerators** can be purchased or rented from a rental center. They're the best choice for large or heavily compacted lawns.

>> **Battery-powered core aerators** are good for medium-sized lawns and soils that aren't too compacted.

>> **Hand core aerators** (Figure 14-2) are good for small lawns or sections of lawns.

**FIGURE 14-2:**
Hand core aerator.

### Spike aerators

Spike aerators use short tines to punch holes in the turf. Some are designed to be pushed by hand and others to be pulled behind a lawn tractor. There also aerators with 2-inch spikes that you strap onto your shoes. Spike aerating is not nearly as effective as core aerating.

## Where and when to aerate

Most lawns benefit from aeration. If your area has clay soil or gets lots of foot traffic, you may want to aerate your entire lawn at least once a year. Otherwise, aerating every few years, or aerating only in spots where soil is compacted, are options. Sandy soils are the exception; they generally don't need aeration.

Aerate your lawn at the beginning of their season of active growth. The goal is to give your desired grasses — not weeds — the chance fill in and create a dense turf. Aerate cool-season grasses in early fall. (In many regions, soils are too wet in spring.) Warm-season grasses benefit from aeration in mid-spring to early summer. Don't aerate a dormant lawn, and don't aerate during hot, dry weather.

Aerate when the soil is moist but not saturated. If necessary, irrigate a few days before aerating.

TIP

When you aerate, strive for an even 3- to 4-inch spacing between holes throughout the lawn. To do so, you must make two passes in different directions. Make sure that the soil is slightly moist — not too wet or too dry. Set the aerator to pull out cores about 3 inches long.

## After aeration

**TIP**

After you core aerate your lawn, you'll end up with loads of little soil plugs strewn all over the lawn. It's best to leave them there. They'll break down over the course of a few weeks, disappearing as they return the organic matter and nutrients in them to the soil. Yes, they look like goose droppings, but resist the temptation to rake them up.

Post-aeration is the ideal time to top-dress your lawn with high-quality, sifted compost. Use a peat moss spreader to spread a thin scattering of compost over your entire lawn. The compost will get washed down into the soil by rain or irrigation, where it can do its good work of improving soil health. (Learn more about building healthy soil in Chapter 6.)

For a few weeks after aerating, keep a close eye on irrigation, since newly aerated lawns can dry out quickly until the grass fills in. Maintain your fertilizer schedule (see Chapter 12) to promote vigorous growth.

## Aerating helps prevent thatch

In addition to enabling roots to breathe and improving water penetration, aerating your lawn helps control thatch, that layer of stems and surface roots that can form between grass blades and the soil line. Aerating improves the habitat for soil microorganisms that break down organic matter, including thatch. Aerating thatch-prone grasses annually is one of the best things you can do to both prevent thatch buildup and control it when it starts to build up.

# How Much Thatch Is Too Much?

Excessive thatch is a common problem in many lawns. Thatch is a layer of organic matter that forms between the grass blades and the soil line. The organic matter consists of tightly woven, living and dead grass stems, roots, and crowns. These parts of the grass plants are high in lignin, an organic material that breaks down slowly. However, in most healthy lawns, thatch breaks down on its own and doesn't build up.

A little bit of thatch — less than ½ inch —is natural for many types of turf. The thin layer cushions the turf, reduces soil compaction, and helps conserve moisture. But if the layer gets more than a ½ inch, then thatch starts to cause problems. Left unchecked, thatch can get several inches thick. Fortunately, good mowing and fertilizing practices can keep it in check and help lawns recover.

# The problem with thatch

A thick layer of thatch (shown in Figure 14-3) between grass blades and soil blocks the movement of air, water, and nutrients to grass roots. This condition results in a shallow-rooted lawn. Such lawns are sensitive to drought, heat, and cold. They dry out quickly, and because thatch can repel water, getting moisture to the root is difficult. Thatch also can result in a spongy, bumpy lawn that you can easily scalp when you mow. Lawns with excessive thatch are also more susceptible to insects and disease.

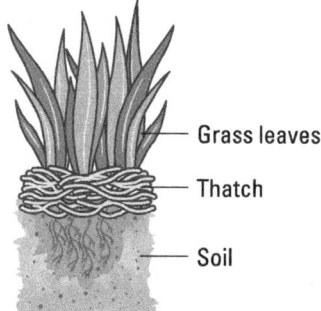

**FIGURE 14-3:** Thatch buildup prevents air, water, and nutrients from reaching grass roots.

Grass leaves

Thatch

Soil

# What causes thatch

Usually, the most common causes of excessive thatch buildup are incorrect or inconsistent lawn maintenance techniques. These, in turn, compromise the ability of the microbes to break down thatch and keep it in check.

The causes of thatch include

>> **Frequent, shallow watering:** It causes roots to concentrate near the soil surface. Watering deeply and less often encourages deep roots.

>> **Overfertilization:** Excessive fertilizing, especially with fast-release, high-nitrogen fertilizers, makes grass grow too quickly for the natural decomposition cycles to keep up.

>> **Infrequent mowing:** Leaving grass clippings on the lawn generally doesn't contribute to thatch buildup. However, if you wait until your lawn gets tall and then cut it all down in one mowing, you'll end up with a thick layer of clippings. These add to the organic matter that microbes are already trying to break down to keep thatch in check. (Find techniques for mowing when grass gets too tall in Chapter 13.)

>> **Excessive use of lawn chemicals:** Pesticides, herbicides, and fungicides can harm or kill the organisms that normally break down thatch. Use lawn chemicals judiciously; learn more in Part 4.

>> **Improper soil pH:** Test your soil to make sure that the pH level is correct. If not, see Chapter 6 for tips on how to correct it. Healthy soil with the proper pH supports robust populations of beneficial microbes that are responsible for breaking down thatch.

>> **Soil compaction:** Compacted soil is poorly aerated, leading to shallow roots and fewer beneficial soil microbes, slowing down the decomposition of thatch.

>> **Grass's tendency to develop thatch:** This factor is beyond your control. Some types of turf grass are more likely to develop thatch than others. No matter how much effort you put into your lawn, you end with some thatch buildup on lawns with a high thatch tendency. Table 14-1 shows which grasses are more vulnerable to thatch.

**TABLE 14-1**

## Tendency of Lawn Grasses to Develop Thatch

| Lawn Grass | Tendency |
|---|---|
| Bentgrass | Medium to high |
| Bermudagrass | High |
| Centipedegrass | Medium |
| Chewings fescue | Medium |
| Creeping red fescue | Medium |
| Hard fescue | Medium |
| Kentucky bluegrass* | Medium to high |
| Perennial ryegrass | Low |
| St. Augustinegrass | Medium |
| Tall fescue | Low |
| Zoysiagrass | Medium to high |

*Can vary by variety

## When thatch gets too thick

TIP

You can start to tell you're getting a thick layer of thatch if the lawn feels spongy when you walk on it. To check, remove a small wedge of the lawn (go deep enough to get some soil) with a knife or shovel. You can see the thatch when you examine the turf. The thatch is the spongy layer of brownish, stuff below the grass blades and above the soil. Measure the thatch layer; if it's more than ½ inch thick, it's time to take steps to remedy the situation.

You have a few basic choices: aerate, dethatch, or verticut. Aerating helps reduce a thin layer of thatch, about an inch or so deep. Compared to dethatching, which can pulverize a lawn, aerating leaves the lawn in pretty good shape. Consequently, if you have a minor thatch problem, aerating once a year probably solves the problem. (Read more about aerating earlier in this chapter in the "Why Aerating Matters" section.) Verticutting slices through the thatch to the soil surface and is the preferred technique for thatch buildup on warm-season turf species.

If you have thatch buildup that's thicker than ½ inch, you need to dethatch. For cool-season lawns, the best time to dethatch is in late summer or early fall. Dethatch warm-season lawns in early to midsummer.

**TIP**

Before you dethatch, make sure that you have the soil tested so that you know how to correct pH and nutrient problems that may be contributing to the problem.

**WARNING**

The power equipment used in dethatching and aerating can be dangerous and requires careful handling. If you're renting the equipment, make sure that you get proper instructions from the people at the rental center and follow their advice. Follow all instructions in the manual as well as safety warnings in the manual and on the equipment. Before getting started, flag all the permanent sprinkler heads, if any. (Underground pipes should be deep enough not to be threatened by aerators or dethatchers.)

# Dethatching the Patch

Dethatching involves cutting through the thatch with knifelike blades and then removing the debris. Debris removal involves a combing operation in which you comb out the debris. You can buy a thatching rake (see Figure 14-4), which has knifelike blades rather than normal tines. You vigorously rake the lawn to remove the thatch, but it's hard work and really only practical for small lawns.

The more practical and effective method is to rent a gas-powered machine called a dethatcher, verticutter (also called a vertical mower), or power rake. A dethatcher cuts through the thatch with rotating blades or stiff wire tines. For warm-season grasses like bermudagrass and zoysiagrass, use a verticutter (see Figure 14-5), which creates vertical slices that cause less damage to the grasses' stolons (horizontal stems).

**FIGURE 14-4:**
Thatching rake.

**FIGURE 14-5:**
Vertical mower
with steel blades.

A dethatcher works best when the lawn is lightly moist — not too wet or too dry. Here's how to do it:

1. **Mow the lawn a little lower than normal right before you dethatch.**

2. **Make at least two passes over the lawn with the dethatcher to get all the thatch. Make the second pass at a 90-degree angle to the first.**

3. **Rake up all the debris. If you haven't used any pesticides on the lawn and it's not a weedy grass like bermudagrass, you can compost the debris or use it for mulch.**

4. **Water and fertilize the lawn (according to your soil test results). See Chapter 12 for specifics on fertilizing.**

TIP

Dethatching is pretty stressful on a lawn, and it can be on you, too. The lawn ends up looking pretty ratty, but if you dethatch at the right time, the lawn recovers quickly and fills in.

For a quicker fill-in, some people prefer to reseed the lawn right after dethatching. You simply spread the seed, rake the lawn so the seed gets down to the soil surface, cover with a light mulch, rake lightly again, and keep everything moist. Reseeding is not recommended for bermudagrass, zoysiagrass, centipedegrass, or St. Augustinegrass lawns. For more information on planting a lawn from seed, see Chapter 8.

TIP

If you don't want to reseed but worry that weed seedlings may take over before the grass recovers, apply a pre-emergent herbicide (it prevents weed seeds from germinating) after dethatching. (See Chapter 15 for details on battling weeds.) If you really have a bad weed problem, don't do anything until you read the section "Renovating Your Lawn," later in this chapter.

# Renovating Your Lawn

Renovating a lawn can be simple or complex, depending on the problems you have. Simple renovation may include just aerating and dethatching to solve thatch problems. Then, if you pay careful attention to how you water, fertilize, and mow, your lawn may recover and grow into the lush lawn of your dreams.

If weeds are starting to get the upper hand, march on over to Chapter 15 for a full debriefing on tackling weeds. If your lawn is more weeds than grass, you might be better off just starting all over again. Ditto if you just don't like the kind of lawn you have, and you want to start over with something new. A more thorough renovation may involve killing the existing grass plants and then replanting. Learn more in Chapter 7.

## Patching a dead patch

Small dead spots are a fact of life for most lawn owners. A number of things can cause the spots, including spilled gas or fertilizer, insect damage, or dog urine. Whatever the cause, patching a dead spot is relatively easy (see Figure 14-6).

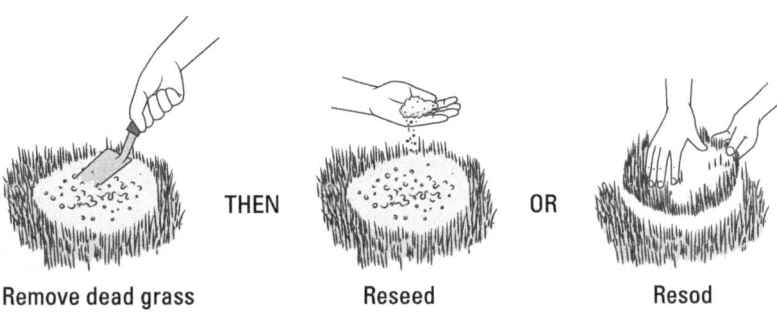

**FIGURE 14-6:**
Patching a
dead spot.

THEN     OR

**Remove dead grass
and amend soil**     **Reseed**     **Resod**

You'll find lawn patch kits at most nurseries and garden centers. They usually combine grass seed with a biodegradable paperlike material that acts like a mulch and helps keep the new seed moist until it's firmly rooted. If you want to match the patch to the rest of your lawn, plant the same grass species or seed mix, if you know it. You can also patch a lawn using a piece of sod of the same type of grass. Here are the basic steps to patching a lawn:

1. **Dig out the dead spot.**

   Use a small shovel or spade to remove the dead grass. Remove everything right up to the edge of the healthy grass, taking the top inch or two of soil.

2. **Water the spot.**

   Make sure the cause of the dead spot has been solved. For information on controlling insects and diseases, see Chapters 16 and 17. If you think a spill caused the damage, flood the spot with water several times to leach out the material.

3. **Amend the soil.**

   Add a few inches of organic matter such as compost and work it into the soil with the shovel.

4. **Level the soil.**

   Smooth out the soil and level it with your hand or a rake. If you are going to reseed the spot, the soil should be level with the surrounding soil. If you use sod, the soil needs to be an inch or so lower, so the new sod will be level with the surrounding grass.

5. **Replant.**

   If you're planting seeds, sprinkle them over the spot, making sure not to overdo it. Cover the seed with a thin layer of organic matter (a scattering of compost or straw work well) and water thoroughly. If you plant sod, cut a piece the size of the patch and lay it in. Put a little organic matter around the edges to prevent them from drying out and water.

6. **Keep it moist.**

You need to treat the new patch just like a new lawn and that means watering at least once a day (more in hot weather) until the grass is established. See Chapters 8 and 9 on starting new lawns from seed and sod.

# Overseeding: Turning brown grass green

If you live in a hot-summer, mild-winter area where warm-season grasses predominate, you don't have to put up with brown grass in winter. (Some warm-season grasses go dormant and turn brown in winter.) You can overseed the lawn with cool-season grasses, which keep the lawn green all winter. Because annual ryegrass fills in so quickly, it's usually used for overseeding, but you can also use perennial ryegrass or a mixture of the two. Wait until nighttime temperatures drop consistently below 65°F and your existing warm-season lawn slows and begins to lose color.

**WARNING**

If you overseed with cool-season grasses, they'll compete with your warm-season turfgrasses for sunlight, water, and nutrients during the important spring green-up period. Your warm-season lawn will be stronger if you don't overseed, so consider skipping it if you can tolerate the winter browning.

One way to overseed is to aerate the lawn first. Then sow the seeds and top-dress with a thin layer of compost. When the weather starts to warm the following spring, the warm-season grass comes back by itself.

If your lawn doesn't need aerating and dethatching, here's a simpler method of overseeding.

1. **Mow your lawn extra short.**

In fall, use a heavy-duty reel-type mower (see Chapter 13). Rent or borrow the reel mower if you don't own one. Set the cutting height very low so that it is just above the soil line, and mow to remove most of the grass blades, called scalping.

2. **Rake up the debris.**

Use metal thatch rake to rake up the grass clippings and other debris. The goal is to expose and loosen the soil surface so the grass seeds can make contact with it.

3. **Sow cool-season seed.**

Put it down heavier than normal (up to 10 pounds per 1,000 square feet for annual ryegrass; see Chapter 8 for other seeding rates).

4. **Top-dress, water, and fertilize.**

   Apply a thin layer of organic matter, such as compost, and then fertilize and water like you would for a newly seeded lawn. You can find out all about that in Chapter 8.

5. **When the cool-season grass becomes established, mow it at the proper height (see Chapter 13) over the winter.**

   As the weather warms up in spring, fertilize and start cutting the lawn at the lower height for the warm-season grass. Soon, the warm-season grass again predominates and the winter grass disappears.

# Leveling and fixing uneven spots

If you have a high or low spot in your lawn that wreaks havoc with your mower, here's how to fix it:

1. **Strip off the grass.**

   To do so, take a spade and outline the uneven area by pushing the spade in a few inches around the perimeter. If it's a large area, cut across the middle with the spade so that you create 18- to 24-inch wide strips of sod. Then push the spade about 2 inches underneath the sod and gently pry it up so that the roots separate from the soil.

2. **Roll up the sod and keep it moist.**

   If the weather is hot, put the sod in a wheelbarrow and move it to a shady spot.

3. **Level the soil.**

   Turn the soil with the spade and add or remove enough soil to bring the area to the proper level. (Don't forget to consider the thickness of the sod.) Water the area to settle the soil.

4. **Replace the sod.**

   Unroll the sod in the same order in which it was removed. Because the bottom of the sod probably won't be smooth, shave off a little or remove some soil so that it sets evenly.

5. **Keep the area irrigated.**

   Water the leveled area just as you would newly planted sod (see Chapter 9 for more information). You may need to water more than once a day in hot weather.

TIP

If you have a small low spot, you can often raise it simply by gradually spreading good topsoil over the area, no more than an inch at a time. Eventually the grass grows through the soil, and the area will be higher.

In cold-winter climates, where freezing and thawing causes soil to heave and become bumpy and uneven, or in areas where earthworms leave castings on soil surface, you can level your lawn in spring with a water-filled roller (see Chapter 8 for more information). The soil should be moist, but not saturated. Fill the roller about a third full of water and go back and forth over the lawn. If the surface hasn't evened out, add a little more water to the roller to increase its weight and repeat the process until you get a level surface. However, be careful that you don't overdo it, or you'll compact the soil and cause other problems.

# 4

# Tackling Lawn Problems

Chapter **15**

# Managing Weeds

A completely weed-free lawn is impractical, if not impossible. A beautiful lawn that includes a few weeds is both practical and possible — and acceptable. That said, weeds can get out of control and ruin the look of a lawn. After all, if you wanted weeds, you wouldn't have planted a lawn in the first place.

The first step in controlling weeds — and the most important one — is to build dense, robust turf by using proper watering, fertilizing, mowing, and other lawn care techniques (see Part 3). Healthy grass that is well adapted to your region will outcompete most weeds for sunlight, water, and nutrients, making it difficult for weeds to gain a foothold.

This chapter offers an overview of lawn weeds and strategies for tackling them.

## Understanding Weed Terminology

Following are some weed words and categories:

» **Broadleaf weeds** is a term that describes most nongrass weeds, such as dandelions, dollarweed, and oxalis. Features of broadleaf weeds include wide leaves with veins that have a netlike pattern, in contrast to the parallel veins of grasses. Broadleaf weeds, shown in Figure 15-1, often have showy flowers.

**FIGURE 15-1:**
Dandelion, a
broadleaf weed.

>> **Narrowleaf weeds** include grasses such as "devil" grass (which, by the way, is the same as bermudagrass, shown in Figure 15-2), crabgrass, and annual bluegrass. These grasses have narrow leaves with parallel veins. Other narrowleaf weeds include sedges and wild onions.

**FIGURE 15-2:**
Devil grass (aka
bermudagrass), a
narrowleaf weed.

>> **Sedges** comprise the third type of plant that occasionally can be a troublesome weed. Sedges look like grasses, except they have stems that are triangular in cross-section. For more on sedges, head to the section called "Profiles of 16 Common Lawn Weeds" later in this chapter.

## WHAT'S IN A NAME?

In the case of a rose, not much perhaps. But when it comes to bermudagrass, the name says volumes. If you planted bermudagrass, chances are you like it and admire its virtues and refer to it respectfully by its proper name. If, on the other hand, you planted another type of grass and are constantly pulling the creeping, wiry stems of an invading grass, you call that invader devil grass.

>> **Annual weeds** grow for one season, produce seed, and die. The next year the seeds sprout, and the cycle repeats itself. The most common annual weeds are crabgrass and annual bluegrass.

>> **Perennial weeds** include dandelions, plantains, and other plants that live on from year to year, although some become dormant or stop growing for part of the year. Perennial weeds are especially hard to control because, not only do the plants live year to year, but they also produce seeds that help the weed spread.

>> **Growing seasons** also delineate weed categories. Like lawn grasses, you can consider most weeds as either cool-season or warm-season plants. In other words, the weed's principal season of growth is either in cool weather or warm weather.

# Giving Your Lawn the Upper Hand

In nature, plants are continuously jockeying for position, and this happens in your lawn, too. Lawn grasses are constantly competing with weeds, and the winners determine the weediness of your lawn. Like many competitive situations, the healthiest, most vigorous competitor wins. If you take all the steps necessary to keep your lawn in tiptop shape, the grass usually wins.

Good cultural practices give lawn grasses the best shot at outcompeting weeds:

>> **Mow at the right height,** and the grass will shade out weed seeds and seedlings. Mow too low and the grass will get weak, and the weeds will take advantage of the opportunity to take over.

>> **Mow regularly,** and you will build the lawn's density and reduce mowing stress. Regular mowing can remove new flowers on weeds, so the seeds never get a chance to mature and scatter near and far. If you don't mow often enough, the weed seeds will have a field day.

>> **Remedy overly wet, dry, or compacted soils** to create the best growing environment for your lawn grass. Water properly, build healthy soil, and aerate as needed. Weeds are experts at colonizing areas where other plants are struggling, but they can't compete with lush, healthy turf.

>> **Fertilize properly to give your lawn the nutrients it needs.** Unlike lawn grasses, weeds are remarkable in their ability to adapt to infertile soil. (For proof, just look at the weeds growing in roadside gravel.)

Keep an eye out for pest problems and take steps to remedy them. When lawn grass is weakened by diseases or insect pests, the turf thins out, creating open spaces for weeds to get established.

## WORDS OF APPRECIATION FOR WEEDS

Many so-called weeds provide habitat, food, and shelter for butterflies, bees, birds, and many other members of a healthy ecosystem. Clover, dandelions, and violets, for example, are sources of nectar and pollen for pollinators.

Also, many of the plants we call weeds have long histories of medicinal and culinary use. Here are a few examples; this list is included to spark interest in, and appreciation for, lawn "weeds."

No plant should be eaten or used for medicinal purposes without consulting experts. Never eat or otherwise use plants from lawns that have been treated with chemicals.

- **Broadleaf plantain** (*Plantago major*) has been used as an anti-inflammatory, to support digestive health, and in wound healing.

- **Dandelion** (*Taraxacum officinale*) leaves are popular salad greens in many European and Middle Eastern cuisines.

- **Dock** (*Rumex* species) has been used as an anti-inflammatory, to treat stomach ailments and parasites, and to soothe skin irritation.

# Techniques for Dealing with Lawn Weeds

There are several techniques for keeping lawn weeds to a minimum. Usually, a combination of the techniques in the following sections works best:

## Eliminate weeds before you plant

If you're planting a new lawn, you can eliminate many weeds and greatly reduce future problems before you even plant. Check out Chapter 7, which shows you how to get rid of weeds before you lay sod or plant grass seed.

**TIP**

One of the best ways to start with a weed-free lawn is by planting sod. Sod lawns are delivered to you virtually weedless. When the carpet of sod gets placed on your soil, many of the most common weeds are buried and never seen again. There are exceptions: Bermudagrass and similar tough spreading grasses can, and often do, invade new sod lawns.

Make sure the lawn grasses you plant are well adapted to your region as well as the conditions in your yard. Learn more about the types of lawn grasses in Chapters 3 through 5. Consult with your local cooperative extension office for advice about the best grass species and varieties for your locale.

## Outcompete the weeds

If you water, mow, and fertilize your lawn properly and aerate to reduce thatch and compacted soil, you'll encourage vigorous, dense turf that can outcompete weeds for light, nutrients, and water. On the other hand, if you're neglectful and give the weeds just the slightest edge, they'll start to gain a foothold. The more the lawn grasses struggle, the more the weeds will dominate.

## Pull weeds by hand

Hand-pulling weeds can really help keep their populations in check. This is especially true if you have a young lawn, but it can also go a long way to controlling weeds in an established lawn. Spend a few minutes every day or two pulling a handful of weeds at a time. Make this a regular habit, and you'll be surprised at how well the weeds are controlled. Alternatively, you can really go over the lawn and get as many as you can all at once. Plan to do this every few weeks.

Try to pull the weeds, root and all, before they flower and set seed. Watering the lawn a few days before your weeding session will soften the soil and make the weeds easier to pull by hand. Once you get started, you might actually find this task satisfying, and even therapeutic. Figure 15-3 shows an example of one hand tool that can make the job easier. There are also long-handled, ergonomic weed pullers that save you from having to bend.

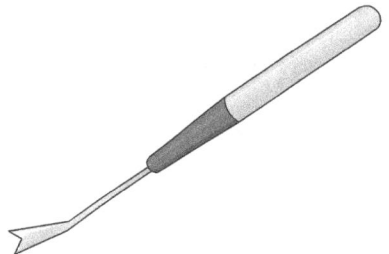

**FIGURE 15-3:**
Weed puller.

## Renovate your lawn, if needed

If the weeds really have the upper hand, consider a complete renovation by replacing your lawn as described in Chapter 7. By renovating, you can kill all the weeds, repair the soil conditions that may have favored the invaders, and possibly replant with a tougher turfgrass.

## Learn to live with a few weeds

Maybe you can learn to live with the weeds. They really don't get in the way of the kids playing on the lawn, do they? If the lawn looks reasonably good from the street, does it matter if you have a few weeds?

### USING A LAWN CARE COMPANY

Lawn care companies are a popular and convenient way to care for your lawn. Most companies can do everything from mowing to fertilizing and pest control. But before you sign up with a lawn care company, you should ask some questions about the type of chemicals that they use and how often they use them.

Unfortunately, some lawn care companies apply herbicides, insecticides, and fungicides as a matter of routine rather than necessity. If you're concerned about the company using lawn chemicals in your yard, ask these questions:

>> Which chemicals and treatments do they use and how often?

>> What criteria do they use in determining their treatment plan?

>> Will they notify you when they use lawn chemicals?

>> Will they flag the lawn after applications?

>> Do they offer organic pest control alternatives?

# Using Herbicides: A Last Resort

Before applying herbicides, also called weed killers, to your lawn, picture the nearest river, lake, or even the ocean. All land drains to a body of water some-where, either above or below ground. Some of whatever you apply to your lawn may end up there, especially if you misuse the herbicide. Use herbicides only as a last resort, when cultural methods of control have failed or are impractical.

**WARNING**

There are no magic herbicide bullets. No single herbicide controls all lawn weeds, and not all herbicides can be used on all types of lawn grass. Identify problematic weed(s) and know your turfgrass species before deciding on an herbicide.

**REMEMBER**

Using an herbicide may kill the weeds in your lawn, but if the soil or water or nutrient conditions that promote the growth of that weed aren't remedied, the fix is only temporary. You can easily become dependent on annual applications of herbicides and never really fix the true cause of your weed problem.

Herbicides pose other risks to the health of your lawn. Overusing herbicides can take your lawn out of its natural balance, intensifying other problems, especially thatch (see Chapter 14).

**WARNING**

An herbicide label is a legal document that provides important information about the herbicide. It lists all the weeds it can be used to control, so always check this list against the list of weeds you're trying to control. (If you're unsure which weed you have, take a sample to a local garden center or cooperative extension office for identification.) The label also includes weather restrictions, steps you'll need to take to avoid damage to nontarget plants and the precautions needed to protect people, pets, and the environment. You are obligated, by law, to follow the label instructions.

# The types of herbicides

Nursery shelves are chock-full of various kinds of herbicides. New ones come along from time to time, and sometimes ingredients fall out of favor or get banned outright. If you have questions about the herbicides you see (or don't see) on store shelves, contact your local cooperative extension office for the latest information.

## Pre-emergence herbicides

Pre-emergence herbicides (sometimes called pre-emergent herbicides or weed preventers) disrupt the germination process by inhibiting the growth of roots and/or shoots, preventing the weed seeds from becoming weed plants! These herbicides do nothing to control existing weeds. To be effective, most pre-emergence herbicides must be applied before the weed seeds germinate. Follow the label instructions for details on when and how to apply the product.

WARNING

Pre-emergence herbicides act on all types of seeds, so don't use them before planting a lawn from seed or on newly seeded lawns. Also, avoid using them if you plan to overseed your lawn. In addition, because the products inhibit root formation, avoid using them on newly sodded lawns, too.

TIP

Corn gluten meal, a by-product of corn syrup production, is an effective pre-emergence herbicide against some weed species, and is particularly useful against crabgrass. As an added benefit, it's also a natural, slow-release nitrogen-rich fertilizer.

## Post-emergence herbicides

Post-emergence herbicides kill weeds that are already growing. They fall into two categories:

>> **Broad-spectrum herbicides:** Also called nonselective herbicides, these herbicides damage or kill any other plant they touch. Be very careful not to apply this type of herbicide to your desired plants.

>> **Selective herbicides:** These target certain types of plants, such as broadleaf weeds or grasses.

Post-emergence herbicides are further classified as either contact herbicides or systemic herbicides:

>> **Contact herbicides:** These kill only the part of the plant they come into contact with.

>> **Systemic herbicides:** These travel through the plant, often down into the roots, so they kill more completely.

**TIP**

It's important to use the type of herbicide that's most appropriate to your weeds and your situation. Using inappropriate herbicides won't have the effects you're looking for; this wastes money and adds unnecessary chemicals to the environment.

**WARNING**

For both effectiveness and, in some cases, safety, it's important to read the label carefully and follow it explicitly. Timing is often critically important; some products are effective only within a limited temperature range, or in specific weather conditions, or at a certain time of year. Most product labels provide information on when you can use the herbicide, but you may want to get more specific information for your area from your local cooperative extension office.

## Herbicide safety

**WARNING**

It goes without saying that it's important to follow directions, especially when it comes to your own safety. If the herbicide label says to wear a mask, do it. If it says to wear gloves, wear them. Wear a long-sleeved shirt, long pants, rubber boots, and safety goggles. Always follow instructions on the product label exactly. Doing otherwise is against the law.

**WARNING**

You must use herbicides carefully. Most of these products kill desirable plants as well as weeds. For example, trees and shrubs growing near the lawn can absorb some herbicides, so follow the instructions on product labels exactly. Make sure that the package label lists the weed you're trying to control. Here are some additional guidelines:

- **Avoid spraying on windy days.** You want to minimize the chance that herbicide drift could fall on desirable plants. Close the doors and windows to your home.

- **Cordon off areas you'll be spraying with tape, streamers, or some type of barrier.** Make sure kids, pets, and anyone nonessential to the application are off the lawn and away from the yard before mixing and applying herbicides. Make sure herbicides don't get tracked into the house.

- **Mix herbicides and fill sprayers outdoors or in a well-ventilated area.** Mix only what you need for the current application so you don't need to dispose of any excess.

- **Apply as directed; more is not better.** Dilute according to the label instructions. Apply at the recommended frequency and not more often.

- **Follow herbicide label instructions for the reentry time**. This is the period of time after application you need to wait before allowing people and pets to enter the treated area.

>> **Store herbicides in their original containers out of the reach of children and pets.** A locked cabinet is best. Even relatively safe herbicides can be dangerous in concentrated forms.

>> **Dispose of empty herbicide containers as described on the label** or contact your local waste disposal company for appropriate disposal sites. If you're disposing of partially full containers, they may need to go to a site that handles hazardous waste.

>> **Wash your clothing after application.** Wash your hands thoroughly before eating or smoking.

Other tips on using herbicides:

>> **If you're using a dry herbicide applied by a drop spreader, make sure that your spreader is properly calibrated and adjusted.** (Head over to Chapter 12 for tips on calibrating a spreader.)

>> **If all your lawn needs is fertilizer, don't apply a weed-and-feed product just because you have some around.** Conversely, if you just fertilized, don't follow up with a weed-and-feed product to control weeds. In general, don't apply anything to your lawn unless you're sure the lawn needs it.

>> **If weeds are a problem in only part of the lawn, treat that area separately.** If needed, you can spot-treat really troublesome patches. For information on patching lawns, see Chapter 14.

## Organic herbicide options

One of the key benefits of organic herbicides is that they break down quickly in the environment so there's minimal risk of long-term soil contamination.

**WARNING**

Note that organic herbicides are still potent and can cause eye, skin, and respiratory irritation; always wear goggles or a face shield as well as waterproof gloves, long sleeves, and long pants when handling and spraying them.

Organic herbicides fall into the broad-spectrum, contact herbicide categories. Spray them on foliage and within a day or so, the foliage will brown and wither. For best results, apply these products during warm, sunny weather. These products don't travel through the plants, so roots remain alive and will likely resprout. Repeated applications are needed: Apply the product, wait a few days or a week to allow weeds to resprout, apply again, and repeat until plants don't resprout, indicating that the food reserves in the roots are depleted. Once it looks like the herbicide has done its work, you can rake off any debris.

Here are a few active ingredients found in organic herbicides:

>> **Vinegar:** While supermarket-variety vinegar (5 percent acetic acid) will knock back young weed growth, horticultural-grade vinegar (20 percent acetic acid) is four times stronger and much more effective.

>> **Essential oils:** Products containing certain essential oils, notably citrus, clove, and cinnamon, kill plants by disrupting their cell membranes.

>> **Caprylic acid and capric acid:** These plant extracts are derived from coconut oil and palm seed kernel. Herbicide formulations containing these ingredients cause plants to dry out and wither.

Note that pelargonic acid (also known as nonanoic acid) is an ingredient found in some herbicides labeled as organic. A naturally occurring fatty acid found in many plants, notably pelargoniums, pelargonic acid is manufactured using a synthetic process, making it ineligible for use in certified organic agriculture.

## Non-organic (synthetic) herbicide options

While garden center shelves are usually well stocked with a variety of synthetic herbicides, the availability of specific products can change for a variety of reasons. For example, as new and improved formulations are introduced, others fall out of favor. Sometimes, active ingredients are subject to new regulations or bans. Also, states may have laws that are stricter than federal regulations; an herbicide available to your cousin living in the next state over may not be for sale at your garden center. Your local cooperative extension office will have the latest information and can help you decide which herbicide is best for your needs.

**WARNING**

It's critical to read the product labels to determine the active ingredients. For example, "Roundup" was once synonymous with "glyphosate," but this is no longer the case. There are other formulations of Roundup herbicide, some of which contain no glyphosate but rather a variety of other herbicides.

Like organic herbicides, synthetic herbicides may require multiple applications to fully kill existing vegetation. Apply the product and wait to see if weeds return. If they do, then apply again, and repeat until plants don't resprout, indicating that the food reserves in the roots are depleted. Once it looks like the herbicide has done its work, you can rake off any debris.

# Applying Different Herbicide Formulations

Herbicides are applied in different ways, depending on the formulation of the product.

>> **Granular formulations** are generally confined to pre-emergence types. The active ingredient is impregnated into small granules which are applied using a drop spreader or rotary spreader.

>> **Ready-to-use (RTU) liquid formulations** are sprayed directly from the bottle onto weeds, according to the label directions.

>> **Liquid concentrates** must be diluted according to the label instructions. These are applied over a large area using a sprayer.

**TIP**

Wick applicators can be used to spot-treat weeds with liquid herbicides. The liquid is carried by gravity from a reservoir to a sponge or rope wick, which is then wiped on the weed, leaving a thin film of the herbicide. They are ideal for applying herbicides around trees and shrubs and near gardens.

>> **Wettable powders** are formulated so that the active ingredient is carried on dustlike particles. The material is mixed with water and sprayed, according to the directions on the label. Because the particles don't dissolve in the water but are simply held in suspension, it's important to agitate the spray tank often to keep the powder suspended.

>> **Aerosol sprays and foams** are also available for spot treating weeds.

# Profiles of 16 Common Lawn Weeds

The following sections describe 16 troublesome weeds, with information to help you identify them and tips for controlling them. In general, applying a preemergence herbicide prior to weed germination and/or applying a postemergence broadleaf herbicide to weeds already growing in the lawn are options to achieve control of many common lawn weeds.

Your local cooperative extension office may have information to help you identify weeds in your region, as well as the best options for controlling them. You can find a link to your state extension office at https://extension.org/find-cooperative-extension-in-your-state.

## Annual bluegrass

**What it looks like:** Annual bluegrass is a bright green annual grass with grainlike seedheads that give the lawn a whitish, speckled look. Annual bluegrass is sometimes called *winter grass* in mild-winter climates where it shows up in lawns. (The dormant grass is brown.)

**How it grows:** This narrowleaf annual, shown in Figure 15-4, grows in cool weather. Seeds sprout in fall. Grass grows in fall, winter (in mild climates), and spring. Annual bluegrass sets seeds in spring and then dies out in hot weather, leaving irregular, yellow areas in the lawn. This plant thrives in moist, compacted soil.

**What to do about it:** Aerate compacted soil. Mow higher to shade out seedlings. Mow more frequently, so seedheads don't mature. Water only when necessary. Apply pre-emergence herbicide in late summer to early to mid-fall. Spot-treat with a selective herbicide in dormant bermudagrass lawns.

**FIGURE 15-4:** Annual bluegrass.

## Bermudagrass

**What it looks like:** Bermudagrass, shown in Figure 15-5, is a light green, perennial grass with fine textured leaves. It spreads rapidly by seed, stolons (creeping, above-ground stems), and rhizomes (below-ground stems). Seedheads are arranged like helicopter blades.

**How it grows:** This narrowleaf perennial grows quickly in warm weather and turns brown in winter. Bermudagrass is an invasive weed in turfgrass growing in mild winter climates. The plant makes a tough lawn in the same areas.

**What to do about it:** This grass is tough to control without herbicides, and it eventually takes over and becomes the lawn in many mild winter areas. Pre-emergences can prevent seeds from germinating. You can spot-treat existing plants with herbicide when the bermudagrass is not dormant or drought-stressed, or you can renovate the entire lawn. Otherwise, if you're trying to keep your cool-season grass, make sure that it grows vigorously by caring for it properly.

**FIGURE 15-5:** Bermudagrass.

# Broadleaf plantain

**What it looks like:** Broadleaf plantain has bright green leaves that are often scalloped.

**How it grows:** The broadleaf perennial, shown in Figure 15-6, has broad leaves and 4- to 12-inch, wiry flower stalks in summer and fall. Broadleaf plantain spreads by seed and thrives in moist, compacted soil.

**What to do about it:** Aerate compacted soil. Avoid overwatering. This weed is easy to pull by hand when the plant is young.

# Burclover

**What it looks like:** Burclover is easy to identify by its light green, cloverlike leaves, yellow flowers, and spiny seed pod (the bur).

**FIGURE 15-6:**
Broadleaf plantain.

**How it grows:** This plant, shown in Figure 15-7, is a broadleaf annual that grows vigorously in spring and fall. It thrives in dry, infertile soils and poorly growing lawns.

**FIGURE 15-7:**
Burclover.

**What to do about it:** Use cultural controls to improve the health of the lawn. Aerate soil to increase water penetration. Water more efficiently and fertilize at recommended levels.

## Crabgrass

**What it looks like:** Crabgrass leaves are blue-green and form a tight, compact, crablike circle (hence the name). Stems are spreading. Seedheads form in summer and fall and can reach several feet high if not mowed.

**How it grows:** Crabgrass, shown in Figure 15-8, is an annual, narrowleaf weed that thrives in hot weather and thin, overwatered lawns.

FIGURE 15-8:
Crabgrass.

**What to do about it:** Growing a dense, healthy lawn is the best prevention. So step up your maintenance and water, fertilize, and mow properly. Hand pull individual plants before they set seed.

# Dallisgrass

**What it looks like:** Leaves are light green and seedheads look a little like the tail of a rattlesnake.

**How it grows:** This narrowleaf perennial, shown in Figure 15-9, forms spreading clumps in the lawn. Dallisgrass grows vigorously in summer and thrives in wet, infertile soils (especially low spots in the lawn). The weed is most common in southern climates. Dallisgrass can reach up to 5 feet high if left unmowed and spreads by seeds and underground rhizomes.

FIGURE 15-9:
Dallisgrass.

**What to do about it:** Dallisgrass is difficult to control. Aerate to improve drainage. Adjust sprinklers to allow wet areas to dry partially between waterings. Dig out individual plants (make sure that you get as many of the short rhizomes as possible) and reseed or plant plugs to fill in the spots.

# Dandelion

**What it looks like:** The perennial broadleaf weed (refer to Figure 15-1) with familiar yellow flowers and puffball seedheads has leaves that are dark green and scalloped.

**How it grows:** This plant grows throughout the year in mild winter climates. Dandelions spread by seed. The weed is most troublesome in thin, poorly cared-for lawns.

**What to do about it:** Pull individual plants whenever you see them. Cut off flowers before they form seeds.

# Dock

**What it looks like:** Dock grows as a tight rosette of dark green leaves with a tall flower stalk that turns rusty brown as it dries.

**How it grows:** Dock is a broadleaf perennial weed, shown in Figure 15-10, that grows in spring and fall; it flowers in summer. Dock thrives in wet, shady areas.

**What to do about it:** Aerate to improve drainage. Allow the lawn to dry out between waterings. Dig out individual plants by hand. Reduce shade by pruning trees. Cut off any seed heads that form.

**FIGURE 15-10:**
Dock.

# English daisy

**What it looks like:** This low-growing broadleaf perennial sports daisylike white flowers with a yellow centers and dark green leaves.

**How it grows:** The English daisy, shown in Figure 15-11, grows in spring and fall in most climates; all seasons in cool-summer climates. It thrives in moist, underfertilized lawns.

**What to do about it:** Some people just leave this weed alone — they like the flowers. Otherwise, pull by hand and water and fertilize more efficiently.

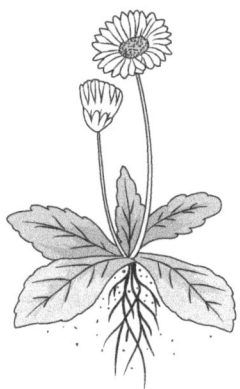

**FIGURE 15-11:**
English daisy.

# Ground ivy

**What it looks like:** Leaves are dark green, round with scalloped edges. Small, purplish flowers appear in spring.

**How it grows:** Ground ivy, shown in Figure 15-12, is a broadleaf perennial that spreads by seed and creeping stems, forming a dense mat among the grasses. The plant thrives in thin, poorly cared-for lawns.

**What to do about it:** Improve lawn health with appropriate watering and fertilizer. Pull young plants out by hand.

# Henbit

**What it looks like:** Small, roundish, scalloped leaves appear in pairs along square stems and are hairy. Pink to purple flowers form on the top of upright stems in fall and spring.

**How it grows:** This annual broadleaf weed, shown in Figure 15-13, thrives in cool weather. Henbit has a spreading growth habit, with stems that take root as the plant grows. Henbit thrives in moist, fertile soil.

**What to do about it:** This weed is easy to pull by hand. Keep the lawn growing vigorously and mow properly.

## Mallow

**What it looks like:** Mallow has dark green, roundish, heavily crinkled, leaves.

**How it grows:** This tenacious broadleaf annual weed, shown in Figure 15-14, usually shows up in new or thin lawns. The weed is long-lived, thriving through most of the season.

**What to do about it:** Mallow is hard to control. Hand-pull in new lawns. Keep the lawn growing vigorously and mow at the proper height.

FIGURE 15-14:
Mallow.

# Oxalis

**What it looks like:** Oxalis has bright green cloverlike leaves and small, yellow flowers.

**How it grows:** This broadleaf weed, shown in Figure 15-15, is annual or perennial depending on the species and climate. It thrives in the cool weather of spring and fall, and spreads by creeping stems and seed.

FIGURE 15-15:
Oxalis.

**What to do about it:** Oxalis is hard to control. Keep the lawn growing vigorously with appropriate water and fertilizer.

# Prostrate knotweed

**What it looks like:** Prostrate knotweed has small, pointed, blue-green leaves. Tiny, white to yellow flowers form on stems during summer to fall.

**How it grows:** Prostrate knotweed, shown in Figure 15-16, is a creeping, annual, broadleaf weed. The plant forms a wiry mat among the grass and thrives in compacted, heavy traffic areas.

FIGURE 15-16: Prostrate knotweed.

**What to do about it:** Pull individual plants by hand, making sure that you get the crown and roots. Aerate compacted areas.

## Spotted spurge

**What it looks like:** Spotted spurge has tiny green leaves, each with a red spot.

**How it grows:** Spotted spurge, shown in Figure 15-17, is a broadleaf annual weed that thrives in hot weather. The weed forms a ground-hugging, circular mat. Milky sap exudes from broken branches. Spotted spurge reseeds heavily.

FIGURE 15-17: Spotted spurge.

**What to do about it:** Keep the lawn growing vigorously and mow at the correct height. Pull individual plants.

# Yellow nutsedge

**What it looks like:** This perennial sedge has three-sided stems and yellow-green, grasslike leaves. A tall, brownish-yellow flower spike appears in summer.

**How it grows:** Yellow nutsedge, shown in Figure 15-18, spreads by seeds and small nutlets that form on the roots. The weed thrives in wet soils.

**FIGURE 15-18:**
Yellow nutsedge.

**What to do about it:** This weed is hard to control. Aerate to improve drainage. Let the lawn dry out partially between waterings. Pull weeds by hand when very young.

IN THIS CHAPTER

» **Understanding integrated pest management**

» **Preventing insect problems**

» **Choosing the best controls**

» **Controlling seven serious lawn insects**

Chapter **16**

# Addressing Insect Problems

Many types of insects find lawns ideal homes. However, most of those insects don't damage the grass. The bugs, worms, and creepy crawlies just go about their daily business without chewing roots, nibbling grass blades, or causing any kind of havoc at all. In fact, many insects that inhabit a lawn do good work, fending off bad bugs and keeping the lawn environment in pleasant harmony.

Alas, some bad bugs occasionally cause problems. A few can even be a real head-ache. What do you do about those? You go after them, but maybe not in the way you think. You can control many insects simply by altering the way you care for your lawn — watering or fertilizing appropriately, mowing higher, or reducing thatch.

You also can choose pest-control products and techniques that are safer to use and have a limited impact on the environment. After all, you want to get rid of bad bugs, not birds. If your lawn problems really get out of hand, you may have to take more drastic measures. However, take that extreme step only if you know exactly which bug is causing the problem and you exhaust all other alternatives.

In this chapter, I show you how to tackle the bad bugs. Keep in mind that the goal is to manage pests, not annihilate them.

# Employing Integrated Pest Management

The term integrated pest management (IPM) describes a comprehensive, commonsense approach to keeping plants healthy. IPM outlines logical steps with a focus on long-term pest prevention, but it also offers options for dealing with pest infestations.

**WARNING**

Spraying pesticides at the first sign of a pest might be satisfying in the moment, but the long-term effects of this approach can be harmful. Overuse of pesticides not only wastes money, but it can also harm beneficial organisms like butterflies and bees, pollute water resources, and expose you, your family, and your pets to unnecessary toxins.

There are five basic steps to IPM: prevent, monitor, identify, decide if control is necessary, and then choose the least harmful, yet effective, control method.

## TYPES OF PESTICIDES

*Pesticide* is a catch-all term that describes materials used to kill pests. The most common pesticides used by gardeners are

- **Insecticides**, which are used to kill insects

- **Fungicides**, which are used to control fungal diseases

- **Herbicides**, which are used to kill plants

It may seem like stating the obvious, but it's critical that you choose the right type of pesticide for the problem. An insecticide won't control a disease and vice versa.

# Preventing problems

Watering, fertilizing, and mowing properly will go a long way toward creating dense, vigorous turf that is resistant to pest infestations. Building healthy soil is another important step to creating a resilient lawn. Here are a few other prevention tips.

>> **Start with pest-resistant varieties:** Plant breeders work tirelessly to create plants that are resistant to common insects and diseases. If you're starting a new lawn, find out what pests are common in your locale and look for resistant varieties and types of turf. If a particular insect gives you problems over and over again, maybe you have the wrong type of grass. (Learn more about choosing grasses in Chapters 4 and 5.) Also, match the variety to the conditions in your yard. For example, plant shade-tolerant varieties in shady spots.

>> **Keep time on your side:** Many pests are especially attracted to young, vulnerable plant tissues. As plants mature, the tissues get tougher and more fibrous.

>> **Don't overfertilize:** Excess nutrients, especially nitrogen, cause weak, rapid growth that is a magnet for pests and diseases.

>> **Aerate:** In addition to promoting deeper roots, aerating allows water and oxygen to penetrate, reducing standing water and promoting strong root growth.

>> **Remove excess thatch:** Thatch is a layer of organic matter that forms between the grass blades and the soil line. A thin layer (up to a half inch thick) is fine. However, when thatch builds up, it creates an ideal spot for pests to eat, reproduce, and live (see Chapter 14).

The goal isn't to eliminate all pests, because if all the pests disappear, so will the birds and other beneficial creatures in your landscape that feed on them. Tolerating a small number of pests means predators will stick around to help keep them in check.

# Monitoring your lawn

Getting to know what your lawn looks like when it's healthy is an important step in knowing when something is wrong. Stroll through your yard on a regular basis, noting areas where grass is growing well along with areas of concern. This practice isn't just good for pest control; it's also helpful in determining if your sprinkler system is working properly, if some areas of lawn are getting scalped during mowing, if thatch is building up, and so on.

**TIP**

# MAKE FRIENDS WITH NATURAL PREDATORS

Birds are one of your biggest allies; they consume a wide variety of insects and larvae. Put out the welcome mat with feeders and birdbaths. Toads and lizards eat loads of insect pests, grubs, and slugs. Opossums devour common lawn pests, including insects, slugs, and snails, as well as disease-carrying ticks.

Beneficial insects to welcome into your garden include these:

- **Lacewings:** The larvae of these delicate-winged insects are called "aphid lions" for good reason — they consume large numbers of aphids as well as thrips and spider mites.

- **Ladybugs:** The adults and larvae eat aphids, thrips, mites, and insect eggs. Get familiar with their larvae, which look like tiny, orange-and-black alligators.

- **Ground beetles:** There are thousands of species, many of which are dark in color with grooves or ridges along their wing covers. The adults and larvae spend most of their time on or near the soil surface, where they feed on grubs, cutworms, and armyworms.

- **Parasitic wasps:** These small insects lay their eggs inside other insects, such as caterpillars; the eggs hatch and the developing larvae devour the host. They are helpful in controlling lawn pests, and they don't bite or sting people.

- **Rove beetles:** These beetles also spend most of their time at ground level, feeding on seeds and insects. Note that, if handled, a few species of these beetles can release a toxin that causes skin irritation.

Attract beneficial insects by planting a variety of flowering plants to provide a food source (nectar and pollen) and habitat. Native wildflowers are good choices, as are flowers in the carrot family, such as dill and fennel. The flowers of sweet alyssum, and thyme are also magnets for many of these beneficials.

Some low-growing lawn "weeds," such as violets, dandelions, and clover, support beneficial insects. In addition, leave some of your landscape unmown to provide overwintering sites. Always be judicious in your use of pesticides or avoid using them altogether. Pesticides can harm beneficial insects along with pests.

The earlier you catch problems, the easier and less costly they are to remedy. If something seems amiss but you aren't sure, check the area every day for the next week or two to see if the problem progresses.

## Identifying the culprits

Once you decide there's a problem with your lawn, which often looks like brown spots or dead patches, it's time to figure out what's causing the problem. Many things can kill grass, from spilled gas to dog urine to fungal diseases — and, of course, bugs. Until you properly identify the problem, how can you find a solution?

**REMEMBER**

Just because you see an insect in your lawn doesn't mean that it's a pest. There are loads of insects milling about on plants and in the soil, and most are either benign or beneficial.

**TIP**

Pinpointing the culprit isn't always easy — you need to do some homework. You may even have to get down on your hands and knees to get a close look. Scan through all of Part 4 — not only this chapter but Chapters 17 and 18, which are about solving other types of lawn problems, like diseases. Try to find symptoms that match what you see in your lawn. Most of the descriptions in those chapters provide ways to confirm your diagnosis or, at least, start to confirm it.

**TIP**

Your local cooperative extension service will have loads of resources with information on what pests are most common in your area and when they're likely to show up, new pests that may just be making an appearance, and control options best suited for your region.

If you think the problem is an insect, consider the following factors on your way to making a final determination.

>> **Life cycle:** Many insects are problems only during certain phases of their life cycles. With night-flying moths, for example, it's their soil-dwelling larvae

(usually the dreaded sod webworm) that damage the lawn. However, the adult forms (the moths) often are more apparent; seeing the moth may indicate that the pest is present. (You still need to confirm that there are larvae feeding on the grass blades and in sufficient numbers to be a problem.) Even more important, many pests are easiest to control, or can be controlled, only during specific times of their lives. You need to time your control measures to when an insect is most vulnerable. You can find out more about that in the section called "Seven Serious Lawn Invaders and What to Do about Them," later in this chapter. But for really precise information for your area, you have to contact your cooperative extension office.

>> **The insects' geographic range:** Not all insects occur everywhere. If you live in Montana and your suspect bug lives only in the deep South, you need to do a little more research.

>> **The type of lawn you have:** Many pests occur only on specific types of grass. So make sure that you know what type of lawn you have and if your suspect bug attacks it.

>> **Physical proof:** You can confirm most insects with your eyes. If the critters live below ground, you may have to coax them to the soil surface by applying soapy water to a small area or doing a little digging. If the insects are night-feeders, you may have to spend some time on your hands and knees with a flashlight. (What will the neighbors think?) Learn how to do that sleuthing in the section called "Seven Serious Lawn Invaders and What to Do about Them," later in this chapter. The point is to always try to make a visual identification to confirm your suspicions about a particular insect.

Once you think you've identified the culprit, or at least narrowed it down, your next step is to enlist the help of an expert to confirm your suspicions. Gather all the evidence you can. Collect insects in jars or bags. Dig up small samples of sod (both affected grass and adjacent healthy grass), including leaves, roots, and soil, sealing them tightly in plastic bags. Call around to local nurseries or your cooperative extension office and ask if you can bring the samples by for help with identifying the insect or other cause of the problem. Also, your cooperative extension office may be able to direct you to a local university's pest diagnostic lab that will help with diagnosis for a small fee.

**REMEMBER**

There really is no substitute for getting a local expert's advice to make sure that you cover any location-specific influences or problems. Just a distance of a few hundred miles can make a difference in which insects are troublesome. More importantly, your location can greatly affect the timing for using various control measures.

TIP

Don't assume that all problems are caused by insects or other pests. Environmental conditions may be at fault. Excessive heat, not enough or too much sun, not enough or too much moisture, freezing temperatures, and hail can also cause damage. Plants that are stressed by these factors are, however, also more vulnerable to attack by disease and insects. Sometimes, once the environmental stress is gone, so is the pest problem.

## Deciding if control is necessary

One of the most challenging — and important — steps in IPM is determining whether taking action is really necessary. Resist the temptation to react immediately with an insecticide or fungicide. If damage is minor, control measures may not be warranted.

WARNING

In IPM, this is called *establishing damage thresholds*, and it's fundamental to ecologically friendly pest control. Small populations of some pests may not warrant control, and they provide food for the beneficial organisms that keep them in check. In other words, kill all the pests, and their predators will leave. Then, when the next pest outbreak occurs, all the predators will be gone.

For example, during one of your monitoring walks, you notice some brown spots where the turf is thin. You probe the soil a bit and see a grub or two. How do you know if you need to treat for them? Examine the roots under a one-foot-square patch of grass in the affected area (instructions for doing this in the "White grubs" section later in this chapter). If you find fewer than seven grubs, control may not be warranted, though you'll want to keep monitoring the area. Most lawns can tolerate this level of grubs. If you find eight or more, you may need to think about treatment, depending on the health of your lawn.

# Choosing an Insect Control Option

REMEMBER

A healthy vigorous lawn has fewer problems. Take a look at the recommendations for watering, fertilizing, and mowing in Part 3. Make any necessary alterations in the way you're handling these tasks, and you may find that your problem goes away. For example, you can often reduce chinch bugs by watering more efficiently. Many insects are more troublesome in lawns that have a thick layer of thatch, so aerate your lawn as described in Chapter 14.

Pinpointing your insect problem is the first step. The list of insects in the "Seven Lawn Invaders and What to do about Them" section later in this chapter includes tips on how to identify the pest, how to determine if control is warranted and, finally, recommended controls.

## ORGANIC MATERIALS REVIEW INSTITUTE

The nonprofit Organic Materials Review Institute (OMRI) provides an independent review of inputs, such as herbicides, fertilizers, and pest controls, that are intended for use in certified organic production, including turfgrass management, under the USDA National Organic Program. Acceptable products are OMRI Listed and can feature the OMRI logo on their labels. Visit their website, *www.omri.org*, to learn what products and ingredients are OMRI-listed.

Fortunately, for most pests, there are control options that don't rely on strong insecticides and have a low impact on the environment. Don't forget — lawns are where kids play and where birds feed. Lawns should be safe places to be.

**WARNING**

When choosing pest control products, make sure the label lists the pest(s) you're targeting and that it includes your specific type of lawn grass (or lawn grasses in general). Not all products work on all types of insect pests, and not all products are safe to use on all types of plants.

Following are some choices for controlling lawn insects:

## Biological controls

This method involves pitting one living thing against another. You can choose from several useful biological-control methods for controlling lawn insects or use a combination of several methods. All those mentioned here are harmless to humans and pets:

» **Parasitic nematodes:** These microscopic worms attack the soil-dwelling larvae of several common lawn pests, including May/June beetle grubs, Japanese beetle grubs, mole crickets, sod webworm, and cutworms. You simply mix the nematodes with water, sprinkle them on a moist lawn, or water them into the soil if grubs are the target pest, and let them do their stuff.

» ***Bacillus thuringiensis:*** Also known as Bt, this bacterium attacks a wide range of insects, including caterpillars (the larvae of moths and butterflies) and grubs, and it can control sod webworms and similar pests. Different strains of Bt target different pests.

» **Milky spore:** This soil-dwelling bacterium can help suppress populations of Japanese beetle larvae (grubs). However, milky spore takes time to work (it takes many years to build up levels in the soil to the point where it can be effective) and must be sprayed repeatedly. While effective in many parts of the country, it has not been effective against the most common grubs in the South.

>> **Spinosad:** Spinosad is derived from a naturally occurring bacterium, *Saccharopolyspora spinosa* and is effective against cutworms, armyworms, sod webworms, and fire ants.

>> **Endophytes:** These microscopic fungi grow inside the blades and leaf stalks of grasses. Endophytes are harmless to humans but toxic to many lawn pests, including sod webworms, chinch bugs, and billbugs. Recently, scientists have found a way to inoculate seeds of some types of lawn grasses (mostly tall fescues and perennial ryegrass). When you grow the inoculated grass, the endophytes help keep the bad bugs away. Note that some endophytes are harmful to grazing livestock.

## Botanical insecticides

As the name implies, botanical insecticides are derived from plants. They break down quickly in the environment and are relatively nontoxic to mammals, including humans, though some are toxic to aquatic life. Two botanical insecticides are particularly useful against insects that infest lawns:

>> **Neem** comes from the tropical tree *Azadirachta indica*. This insecticide kills young feeding insects, including aphids. (Greenbugs, a lawn pest in the midwestern United States, are aphids.) Neem also repels Japanese beetles, which may prevent the beetles from visiting your lawn, laying eggs, and giving you a white grub problem. Make sure to use the azadirachtin form of neem rather than neem oil for these turf pests.

>> **Pyrethrin** derives from the pyrethrum daisy, *Chrysanthemum cinerariifolium*. Pyrethrin is a broad-spectrum insecticide, which means it kills a wide range of insects — both good and bad. However, this insecticide is useful for spot-treating areas of the lawn infested with cutworms, armyworms, sod webworms, billbugs, chinch bugs, and aphids.

## Conventional (synthetic) insecticides

You'll find an array of synthetic insecticides in the pest control section of your local garden center or big box store. They fall into two categories:

>> **Contact insecticides** kill an insect when the insect comes in direct contact with the insecticide or its active residues.

>> **Systemic insecticides** are taken in by the plant and distributed throughout the plant tissues.

Because they're taken up by the plant, systemic insecticides are longer acting than contact insecticides. However, they also pose more risks to bees and other beneficial insects, due to both the material's long-acting nature and its presence in pollen and nectar.

**WARNING**

Use synthetic insecticides only as a last resort. Using these chemicals can have a negative impact on your lawn, killing beneficial organisms that live there. Don't forget, treating a lawn is not like treating one sick shrub. You usually have to treat a large area and use a significant amount of insecticide. Remember, too, the other creatures — kids, birds, bees, and pets — that visit your lawn.

# Understanding Pesticide Safety

Insecticides applied to your lawn can inadvertently drift or leach and contaminate neighboring property and water sources. No matter which pesticide (insecticides, fungicides, herbicides, and other products used to control pests or plants) you decide to use, you must use it safely. Even pesticides that have a relatively low impact on your garden environment can be dangerous to use and toxic to humans.

Follow these safety guidelines when working with insecticides to protect yourself, your family, your neighbors, pets, and the environment:

>> **Always follow instructions on the product label exactly.** Doing otherwise is against the law.

>> **Make sure the label lists both the pest(s) you're targeting and the plant you're spraying.** Look for your specific type of lawn grass (or turfgrasses in general) on the label. (Sometimes, the label lists plants as groups, such as landscape shrubs or lawn grasses.)

>> **Apply as directed; more is not better.** Dilute according to the label instructions. Apply at the recommended rate and frequency and not more often; insecticides take time to work, and you may not see immediate results. The recommended treatment intervals are generally based on the target insects' lifespan. Applying too much of a product can actually harm your lawn.

>> **Make sure kids, pets, and anyone nonessential to the application are out of the area before mixing and applying pesticides.** If necessary, cordon off the area with tape, streamers, or some type of barrier.

>> **Mix pesticides and fill sprayers outdoors or in a well-ventilated area.** Mix only what you need for the current application so you don't need to dispose of any excess.

>> **Wear all recommended personal protective equipment (PPE) when mixing and applying pesticides.** Rubber gloves, long pants, a long-sleeved shirt, closed-toed shoes, and eye protection are advisable. Many of the chemicals in pesticides can be absorbed through the skin, so cover up as much as possible.

>> **Spray when winds are calm.** You want to take every precaution to ensure that pesticides end up only where they're needed. A strong breeze can blow pesticide mist onto nearby plants, pets, and people. Close the doors and windows to your home.

>> **Don't spray if rain is in the forecast.** The water may wash the chemicals off the grass blades, where it's needed to be effective. Also, the chemicals can be washed into storm gutters and storm drains. This is hazardous to the environment and wastes money. (When used to control soil insects, a light rain or irrigation after application can help move the insecticide into the soil where the insects are feeding.)

>> **Store chemicals in their original containers out of the reach of children and pets.** A locked cabinet is best. Even relatively safe pesticides can be dangerous in concentrated forms.

>> **Dispose of empty pesticide containers as described on the label** or contact your local waste disposal company for appropriate disposal sites. If you're disposing of partially full containers, they may need to go to a site that handles hazardous waste.

>> **Wash your clothing after application in a load separate from other laundry.** Wash your hands thoroughly before eating or smoking.

>> **Follow label instructions for the reentry time**. This is the period of time after application you need to wait before allowing people and pets to enter the treated area.

WARNING

>> **Be prepared in case of emergency.** Prior to using a product, read the label for directions on first aid for that product. If someone has swallowed or inhaled a pesticide or gotten it in the eyes or on the skin and is exhibiting symptoms, call 911. Call the Poison Control Center at 800-222-1222 if you have a question about a possible poisoning.

TIP

The National Pesticide Information Center (NPIC) provides science-based information about pesticides and pesticide-related topics to enable people to make informed decisions about pesticides and their use. NPIC is a cooperative agreement between Oregon State University and the U.S. Environmental Protection Agency. Its website (https://npic.orst.edu) has a wealth of information on individual pesticides, guidelines for use, and safety information.

Neonicotinoids (often shortened to neonics) are a class of synthetic, systemic insecticides that are widely used on lawns. They are chemically similar to nicotine. Although effective against pest insects, they are also extremely toxic to beneficial insects, including bees, so much so that some states have restricted their use or banned them outright.

# Seven Lawn Invaders and What to Do about Them

Following are seven of the most troublesome and common lawn insect pests with tips on how to identify them, how to determine if control is warranted, and, finally, some control options.

REMEMBER Your best source of information for your region is your local cooperative extension office. They'll have the latest information on pest activity and outbreaks and the control options available to you in your area.

## Armyworms and cutworms

Armyworms and cutworms are common lawn pests in all but the coldest regions. They can raise havoc with your lawn but will also raid your vegetables and flowers. Cutworms are usually solitary feeders, while armyworms are usually present in larger numbers and feed as a group.

**What they look like:** Armyworms and cutworms (shown in Figure 16-1) are both moth larvae (caterpillars). Armyworms are light green to greenish brown caterpillars with three lighter colored stripes down the back and sides. The middle stripe ends up as an inverted Y on the head. They often look greasy. Cutworms are almost always curled into a tight circle when you find them. They are plump, usually brown to black, and sometimes with lighter colored stripes or spots.

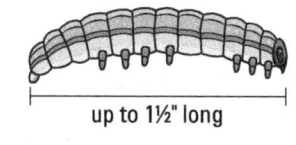

up to 1½" long

**FIGURE 16-1:**
Control
armyworms (top)
and cutworms
the same way.

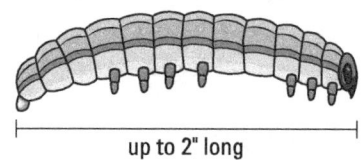

up to 2" long

**The damage they do:** Both armyworms and cutworms feed on grass blades at night or on cloudy days, causing circular or irregular dead spots. In a really bad infestation, armyworms can strip a lawn of foliage in just a few days.

**How you know you have them:** Armyworms are most common in cool, moist spring weather, but they can also be troublesome in fall. Cutworms prefer new lawns. You can often detect armyworms during the day, but it's best to look at night; examine the lawn with a flashlight. To see whether you have cutworms, bring them to the surface: Drench the soil in an areas with living turf that is declining with a soapy water solution (2 tablespoons of lemon-scented dish soap in a gallon of water) slowly applied over a 3' × 3' area using a sprinkling can. Watch the area for five minutes to see if any caterpillars appear. Treat if you find five or more armyworms or cutworms per square yard.

**What to do about them:** Control armyworms and cutworms the same way. *Bacillus thuringiensis* is an effective control. Beneficial nematodes and pyrethrin sprays are also effective. You also can reseed with grass varieties that include endophytes. Some synthetic insecticides are labeled for control of armyworms and cutworms.

# Billbugs

Billbugs are a problem across the United States.

**What they look like:** Billbug adults, shown in Figure 16-2, and larvae feed on lawns. You can recognize the ¼- to ¾-inch, brown to black adult weevils by their long snouts. Adult billbugs feed on grass stems. The small, white larvae look like a gooey piece of rice with an orangish-brown head. The larvae feed on plant crowns and roots. The larvae's feeding is usually most destructive.

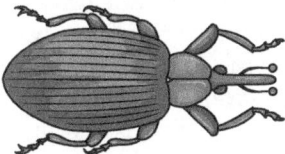

**FIGURE 16-2:**
Billbug adults, along with larvae, feed on lawns.

**The damage they do:** Adults cause irregular dead spots that look like the lawn has burns from spilled fertilizer. Larvae cause the grass to wilt and die in irregular patches. Overall, the lawn looks as if it's dried out.

**How you know you have them:** In southern climates, bermudagrass and zoysiagrass are favorite targets. Billbugs prefer bluegrass lawns farther north. Look for the pest at the edges of dead spots and a little into the healthy turf as well. You also can see a sawdustlike frass (debris) near where the insects feed. If the dead grass pulls up easily, that's another good sign you have billbugs.

**What to do about them:** Aerate the lawn and reseed with endophytic grass varieties. Some synthetic insecticides are labeled for control of billbugs.

## Chinch bugs

Chinch bugs are tiny, hard-to-see insects whose damage is usually confused with drought stress. They can occur almost anywhere.

**What they look like:** Chinch bugs are small, red (young) or black (mature) insects with a white spot or markings on their back. The bugs, shown in Figure 16-3, grow to about ¼ inch long at maturity.

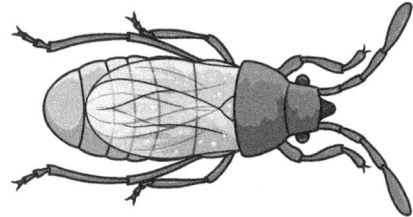

**FIGURE 16-3:** Chinch bugs suck juices from grass blades.

**The damage they do:** Chinch bugs suck the juices from grass blades. Irregular patches of the lawn first look drought-stressed and gradually turn yellow and then brown.

**How to know you have them:** Chinch bugs are most common on St. Augustine-grass lawns during hot, dry weather. Infestations can also affect bentgrass, Kentucky bluegrass, and fine fescue lawns. You can often see chinch bugs by examining the grass near the soil surface. Look for the pest at the edges of dead spots and a little into the healthy turf as well. To be sure, push a bottomless metal can several inches into the ground in an area where the grass is just turning yellow. Fill the can with water, and the chinch bugs will float to the surface (see Figure 16-4). Repeat the procedure in several locations around the lawn. Or drench the soil in an area with living turf that is declining with a soapy water solution (2 tablespoons of lemon-scented dish soap in a gallon of water) slowly applied over a 3′ × 3′ area using a sprinkling can. Watch the area for five minutes to see if the pests appear. If you estimate more than 15 chinch bugs per square yard, you probably need to do something.

**What to do about them:** Chinch bugs thrive in neglected lawns, especially those with a buildup of thatch. Aerate and dethatch the lawn to improve water and fertilizer penetration (see details in Chapter 14) and follow good cultural practices. *Beauveria bassiana* is a fungus that can effectively attack chinch bugs under the proper condition. Endophytic lawn varieties also resist chinch bugs.

**FIGURE 16-4:** Test for chinch bugs with a can and warm water.

# Greenbugs (aphids)

Greenbugs are particularly troublesome on northern lawns growing in shady conditions.

**What it looks like:** Greenbugs, shown in Figure 16-5, are aphids — small ($\frac{1}{16}$ inch), egg-shaped, long-legged, almost transparent insects that congregate on grass blades.

**FIGURE 16-5:** Green bugs are especially troublesome on Kentucky bluegrass in the Midwest.

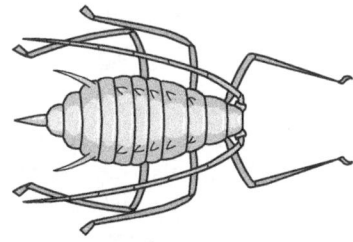

**They damage they do:** Greenbugs suck plant juices, turning the grass blades yellow to burnt orange and finally brown.

**How you know you have them:** These pests are particularly troublesome on Kentucky bluegrass lawns in the midwestern United States. Visual examination is the best way to confirm their presence — get down on your knees and look carefully. Greenbugs are most common in shaded areas during the hottest part of summer.

**What to do about them:** Most of the time, naturally occurring beneficial insects like ladybugs and lacewings keep greenbugs under control. Other times, try spraying the lawn with insecticidal soap, trying to wet as many aphids as you can with the spray.

# Sod webworm

Sod webworms can occur almost anywhere.

**What they look like:** Sod webworms, shown in Figure 16-6, are the larvae of a buff-colored, night-flying moth. The larvae are about ½ to 1 inch long gray or light tan caterpillars with black spots on their back. However, you may notice the adult moth first. They flutter over the lawn at night, flying just above the lawn in a crazy zigzag pattern for a short distance, dropping eggs as they go. If you see a lot of the moths in late spring, you can figure the caterpillars are about ten days to two weeks behind.

**FIGURE 16-6:**
Sod webworms
thrive in dry or
thatchy lawns.

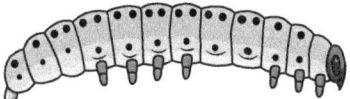

**The damage they do:** Sod webworms feed on grass blades, causing small irregular dead patches that gradually expand into larger dead patches. The damage is often most severe in drier parts of the lawn or areas with heavy thatch. Sod webworms attack any type of grass.

**How you know you have them:** Examine the lawn at night with a flashlight (during the day, worms hide in silky, weblined tunnels in the ground, hence the name). You can see the webworms feeding. Small, greenish-tan pelletlike droppings and flocks of feeding birds are other signs. You can also examine the thatch layer with a small shovel. Look for the webworms in their silken tunnels where they hide during the day. To confirm their presence, soak a small section of lawn (about 2 × 2 feet) with soapy water (2 tablespoons of dish soap in a gallon of water). The soap brings the worms to the surface in about five to ten minutes. Treat the lawn if you find more than two or three webworms per square foot.

**What to do about them:** First, aerate the lawn to reduce thatch and improve water penetration. *Bacillus thuringiensis* is the preferred biological control of sod webworms. Parasitic nematodes, insecticidal soaps, and pyrethrins are also effective.

If problems are really severe, consider reseeding bluegrass, perennial ryegrass, or fescue lawns with endophytic-treated lawn seed.

## White grubs

One or another type of white grub (a general name for the larvae of scarab beetles) can occur almost anywhere.

**What they look like:** White grubs are the larvae of various types of scarab (or *chafer*) beetles. These include Japanese beetle grubs, May/June beetle grubs, and masked chafer beetle grubs. The type of grub that infests your lawn depends on where you live, but the grubs all look pretty much alike and do the same damage. The larvae, shown in Figure 16-7, are milky-white with brown heads and three sets of small legs. They are usually about ½ to 1½ inches long and curled into a C-shape.

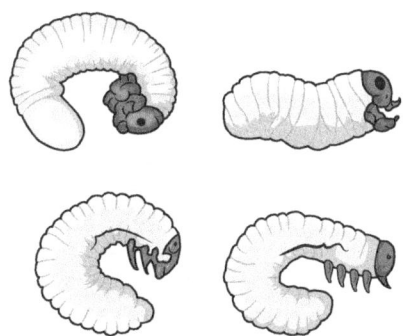

**FIGURE 16-7:**
White grubs are milky-white, C-shaped pests.

**The damage they do:** The grubs feed on grass roots, causing the lawn to turn brown in large, irregular patches. The most serious damage appears in summer to fall. Grubs can attack almost any type of lawn. The adult beetles usually feed on trees, shrubs, and other landscape plants.

**How you know you have them:** If dead sections of the grass pull up like a piece of carpet revealing severed roots, you probably have grubs. Birds, moles, raccoons, and skunks like to feed on grubs, so if your lawn looks like a zoo, that can be another sign.

**What to do about them:** Use a shovel to cut three sides of a one-foot-square section of turf near the edge of an area of dying turf. Peel back the turf and dislodge the soil around the roots. Count the number of grubs. If there are five to ten grubs (or more) per square foot, treatment may be warranted. (After you're finished, flip the piece of turf back into place to facilitate recovery.) Timing is very important because most control measures work best when the larvae are small. If you see a lot of beetles flying around your back porch light at night, it probably means there's some mating going on. That means eggs and small grubs are not far behind. But to find out exactly the best time to control grubs, contact your local cooperative extension service.

Parasitic nematodes effectively control many types of grubs. A product containing the strain Bt 'galleriae' is effective for controlling May/June beetle and Japanese beetle grubs. If you live in an area where Japanese beetles are common, such as the northeastern United States, treat the lawn with milky spore, a biological control that is specific to that beetle's larvae. It may provide some control, though it takes time to work.

# Chapter **17**

# Tackling Lawn Diseases

L awn diseases often are very hard to identify, and they can do serious damage to a lawn in short order. They can easily be confused with other issues, such as drought, nutrient deficiencies, shady conditions, and even insect damage. The good news is that you can cure or prevent most lawn diseases by properly caring for your lawn. Dense, vigorously growing turf is well-equipped to fend off diseases. Planting the wrong turf species for your region and conditions, mowing too low, watering improperly, under- and overfertilizing, and ignoring a thick layer of thatch all encourage various lawn diseases to develop. Part 3 of this book gives you all the details you need to nurture a healthy lawn.

Even with that knowledge, however, you still need to know how to prevent and control lawn diseases. This chapter covers the bases: how different factors contribute to disease, how to identify common lawn diseases, and, most important, what to do about them.

# Factors Affecting a Lawn's Susceptibility to Disease

Fungi cause many — in fact, almost all — lawn diseases. For a fungal disease to occur, the fungal pathogen must be present, it must have the right plant to infect, and the conditions must be favorable for it to spread. Temperature, moisture, and plant vigor all play a role. A fungus's reproducing spores travel from one place to another, usually through moisture or wind. Spores, however, can also be carried on a lawn mower or on the feet of the person pushing it.

Here are some factors that influence whether or not your lawn gets a disease.

## The type of grass

Any grass that you plant near the edge of or outside its normal range of adaptation is bound to be more subject to disease. The grass just doesn't grow as well, and that weak growth makes the grass more susceptible. Read Chapter 2 for the full scoop on lawn climates and which grasses grow well in each of them.

**TIP**

If you're starting a lawn from seed, purchase seed from a reputable source. Look for grass varieties that are resistant to the turf diseases common in your region and choose certified seed if it's available. Your lawn is a long-term investment, and the quality of seed you purchase directly affects the quality of lawn you end up with.

In addition, make sure the grass species is adapted to the conditions in your yard. You may need to plant different grasses in different areas of your yard. For example, plant shade-tolerant grasses in shady spots. The better suited the grass, the healthier it will be, and therefore the more resistant to diseases. Keep in mind that conditions can change over time. For example, as trees grow, they cast more shade and grass that once thrived underneath them may begin to struggle due to lack of sunlight.

Even when you plant the right grass in the right climate, some grass types are more likely to get a specific disease than others. There are some varieties of grass that resist specific diseases, and plant breeders continue to develop new, even more disease-resistant ones. Your local cooperative extension office will have information on the best grass varieties for your region, as well as details on the newest grass varieties. You can also turn to the National Turfgrass Evaluation Program (https://ntep.org) to find data on the disease resistance of different species and varieties.

## Sunlight and air circulation

Most fungal diseases thrive in dark, moist environments, so do what you can to ensure adequate sunlight and airflow. For example, prune shrubs and remove the lower branches of trees to increase the amount of sunlight reaching the ground. Removing branches so that morning sun can dry the lawn is particularly helpful because most diseases require moist leaf surfaces to spread. Pruning will also increase air circulation, which helps grass blades dry off quickly after rain or irrigation.

In spots with dense shade or very poor air circulation, such as along a fence, consider scrapping the lawn altogether in favor of an alternative, such as a ground cover. (Find lawn alternatives in Chapter 19.)

## How you irrigate

This element is a biggie. Most lawn diseases thrive in moist or humid conditions. If you water in ways that keep the lawn constantly wet or wet for long periods, guess what? Your lawn is more likely to have disease problems. Water in the morning (5 a.m. to 8 a.m.) so that the lawn dries off quickly afterward. Water deeply but infrequently so that the lawn dries out between waterings. Doing so also promotes deeper root systems and more resilient turfgrass plants.

Use extra caution when irrigating during periods of high humidity, which slows evaporation (even in hot weather) so that the lawn stays wet longer. Also, newly seeded lawns that are just getting established are at particular risk of disease, so take extra care to irrigate when conditions favor the quick drying of leaf surfaces. Read Chapter 11 to get the whole picture on lawn watering.

Soil that is compacted often drains poorly, leading to wet spots. Aerating your lawn improves its ability to absorb water and can help reduce disease problems. Learn about aerating in Chapter 14.

## Temperature

The temperature is important for two reasons. The first reason concerns planting the right grass. If you live in the desert and you grow a grass that doesn't like heat, such as rough bluegrass (*Poa pratensis*), you guessed it — diseases lurk in your future. The same is true for cool climates, if you grow heat-loving grasses. The point: Grow grasses that are well-adapted to where you live.

The second reason why temperature is important has to do with the conditions in which the various diseases thrive. Some fungi like the temperature warm; some like it cool. Some, like snow mold, even like it close to freezing. If you know the conditions in which a certain disease thrives, you can better diagnose the disease and predict when it may occur. You find that information in the "Nine Dastardly Diseases" section later in this chapter.

## How you fertilize

Some diseases run rampant in heavily fertilized lawns; others are more problematic in underfertilized lawns. Some diseases even prefer a certain soil pH. The point is to apply the recommended amounts of right fertilizer (see Chapter 12) and then adjust if needed. And don't forget the value of a soil test to determine nutrient levels and soil pH. Learn more about soils in Chapter 6.

## Mowing practices

If you mow your lawn lower than the recommended height (details in Chapter 13), then you're setting yourself up for troublesome lawn diseases. Mowing too low creates the grass conditions that disease organisms love: weakened (getting mowed is the most frequent stress on grass) and wounded (mower cuts are the ideal place for some diseases to enter). After the disease gets started, you can even spread it around via the mower because the disease organisms ride on it. The lower the mowing height, the more effort it takes to maintain your lawn, and this includes preventing and dealing with disease outbreaks. Avoid mowing the lawn when the grass is wet if at all possible. That's just asking for trouble.

## Thatch

Diseases love thatch, that spongy layer of grass stems and debris that forms between the leaves and the roots. Everything about thatch favors fungus growth and development. Thatch holds moisture near the surface of the lawn, blocks water and nutrient penetration, and restricts air. Heck, if you were a fungus, you'd love thatch, too. Overfertilizing is one of the culprits; too much fertilizer can result in a lawn that looks lush and green for a while, but over time it can lead to excess thatch. So do something to reduce thatch, such as aerating, vertical mowing (verticutting), or dethatching; you can find out how in Chapter 14.

## INTEGRATED PEST MANAGEMENT

The term *integrated pest management* (IPM) describes a comprehensive, commonsense approach to keeping plants healthy. IPM requires cultivating observational skills and learning what problems are most common in your region on the turfgrasses you're growing. It outlines logical steps with a focus on good cultural practices (such as mowing and watering properly and not overfertilizing) that help prevent pests and diseases and offers steps for dealing with problems. Learn about IPM in Chapter 16.

## Herbicide and pesticide use

Using some types of insecticides and herbicides can upset the natural balance of a lawn, killing off earthworms and other beneficial organisms. Usually, that imbalance results in a thicker layer of thatch because those organisms contribute to the breakdown of thatch. (Fortunately, some of the worst chemical offenders have been taken off the market.)

Herbicides, both preemergence and postemergence types, can also damage the lawn, especially when overapplied. This results in significant grass stress and even death.

If you want to avoid diseases, plant the right type of lawn and then take good care of it.

# Get Help If You Need It (and You Probably Will)

Here's the cold, hard truth about lawn diseases — most are very difficult to identify properly. Lawn diseases are hard to tell apart and easy to confuse with other problems, such as insect damage and even simple physical maladies like fertilizer burn. If you can't identify the disease, you'll have a hard time fixing it.

Although there are general descriptions of the most common lawn diseases later in this chapter, for most diseases (rust and snow mold may be exceptions), those descriptions may not be enough. You need to look for more help to properly identify the problem. The best place to find that help is through your local cooperative extension office. Cooperative extensions have, or can lead you to, properly trained professionals who can diagnose the problem. Even those pros may have to grow the organism in a laboratory to find out exactly what it is and tell you how to deal with it.

But even before professionals can perform their magic, you need to provide them with a sample and as much information as possible. The more information you offer, the better. Following is the information the professionals can use to help them identify whether or not a disease pathogen is the cause of the problems you are seeing:

>> **A sample of the lawn:** A 4-inch-square, 2-inch-deep piece sod taken from an area where the problem is just starting to show itself is ideal. Take the sample from the right place: Half should be healthy lawn; the other half should be just starting to show symptoms. Make sure the sample doesn't have wet grass blades and place it in a plastic bag to keep it fresh and retain any insects that might be involved. If you must mail the sample somewhere to be checked, ask how to wrap and ship it. There may be an online submission form where you can submit details, too.

>> **Age, variety, and species of grass:** It may be tough to provide this, but if you can tell how old the lawn is and the type of grass it's made of, it helps.

>> **Symptoms:** How does the lawn look overall? Do you see dead patches? Where do they occur? What size, shape, and color are the patches? Do you see mushrooms? What do individual grass blades look like — spotted, melted, wilted? Do the grass blades pull up easily or stay attached to the roots?

Look for patterns. Do the spots run in a straight line? Is there any consistent relation to the location of the sprinkler heads? Do the spots follow the mowing lines? Do they follow the slope like runoff water? Are the spots mostly in shade, sun, or both?

Use your phone's camera to capture a variety of information. For example, close-up images of leaves can show individual lesions, while images taken from 5 to 10 feet away can give an idea of the overall size of the damage area (it's best to include a ruler or something to show scale, such as keys).

>> **How you care for the lawn:** This includes general information about your soil and how you water, fertilize, and mow. Have you applied any pesticides? Herbicides? (Don't forget to include weed-and-feed products.) Note if you've applied any fungicides to address the problem. If so, what product(s) did you use and when were these applications made?

> **»** **History:** When did you notice the problem? What was the weather like? Has there been any construction or painting on your house? Has anything like gasoline, alcohol, fertilizer, or anything else been spilled on the lawn? Write down any dates you can remember.

All this information may seem like overkill, but if you really have a serious problem then you want to figure out for sure if it's a disease problem or something else. And if the problem turns out to be caused by a disease organism, you'll be on the way to a solution.

# About Fungicides

Using chemical controls to tackle weeds and insect pests should be the last resort, and the same holds true for diseases. Fungicides should be considered only after alternative measures have failed.

All lawn chemicals pose some risks, but fungicides have come under increased scrutiny in recent years. Several fungicides are no longer available for use by homeowners and others are now heavily regulated due to their toxicity and their negative effects on the environment. (Professional licensed pesticide applicators are trained to employ best practices for minimizing harm to the environment and risk to nontarget species.)

Add to this the fact that some lawn diseases are so difficult to correctly identify (even for experienced professionals), thereby increasing the chance that you may use the wrong fungicide, and you can see why recommending traditional fungicides is dicey business.

Say you've altered your lawn-care practices, and you still have a problem that you think a disease organism is causing.

There are a few biological control measures approved for use on lawn diseases. Products containing *Bacillus subtilis* and *Bacillus licheniformis*, both naturally occurring beneficial soil bacteria, can help protect against fungal diseases. That said, the efficacy of these materials is inconsistent.

When in doubt, go to a professional to get a correct diagnosis and a recommendation for an appropriate control measure. Use a fungicide specifically labeled to control the disease. Be sure to follow all the safety procedures for using pesticides listed in Chapter 16, which covers insects.

# Nine Dastardly Diseases

This section presents some of the most troublesome lawn diseases, their symptoms, when they're likely to occur, and what to do about them. Your local cooperative extension office may have information to help you identify diseases common in your region, as well as the best options for controlling them. You can find a link to your state extension office at `https://extension.org/find-cooperative-extension-in-your-state`.

## Large patch/brown patch

Large patch/brown patch (caused by *Rhizoctonia solani*, a soil-borne fungus) can occur anywhere where humidity is high, but it is particularly troublesome in the Midwest, Southeast, and transition zone.

**What it looks like:** This disease looks like circular brown patches, shown in Figure 17-1, ranging in size from a few inches to several feet wide. There is often a "smoke ring" of gray to dark gray grass around the edges of the patch. The grass gradually dries out and turns brown as the patch expands. Sometimes the grass inside the patch recovers, leaving a brown ring around green grass. There may be white, cottony, threadlike material on the grass, especially in the morning.

**FIGURE 17-1:** Large patch/brown patch can range from a few inches large to several feet wide.

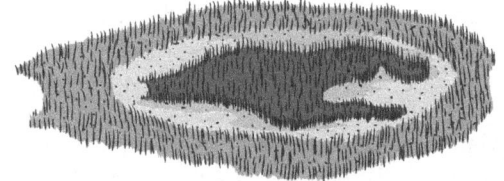

**When it's trouble:** This disease is especially problematic on overly wet, overfertilized lawns with a thick layer of thatch. Brown patch is most troublesome in areas with high summer rainfall. The disease can infect any grass but is particularly problematic on centipedegrass and St. Augustinegrass. The edges of the rings may be burnt orange rather than gray. This disease can become extremely damaging when grass stays wet for extended periods of time and temperatures are in the range of 60°F to 75°F. In the Midwest, the disease can affect tall fescue, especially in the summer as temperatures and humidity increase.

**What to do about it:** Water deeply and infrequently, allowing the grass to dry out between waterings. Aerate to break down thatch. Test soil to check low levels of calcium, phosphorous, and potassium. Imbalances in these nutrients can make the problem worse. If brown patch occurs in shady areas, thin out tree branches. Pruning trees allows more sunlight to come through and increases air circulation so the area dries out faster.

Address areas with poor drainage and if renovating a lawn area, consider planting bermudagrass, which is less affected by this disease.

## Dollar spot

Dollar spot is most troublesome in humid areas of the Midwest, South, and Pacific Northwest.

**What it looks like:** You can identify dollar spot by its round, sunken dead spots in the lawn that measure 2 to 3 inches wide. On close-cut bentgrass, the spots are the size of a silver dollar, hence the name. The color is bleached to straw-colored, as shown in Figure 17-2. Several of the spots may grow together, killing larger areas. Infected blades usually have a tan to purplish streak between the white and green portions of the blades. These white-banded blades are most evident between dead areas and green turf. The turf may also look constricted or have a shape similar to an hourglass around the infected area. You may also see white, cottony, threadlike material on the grass when the disease is actively growing.

**When it's trouble:** Dollar spot is common when a combination of warm days and cool nights produce dew on the lawn in the morning. Overly wet lawns that are underfertilized or overfertilized are more susceptible. Heavy thatch also contributes to dollar spot. It's most troublesome on creeping bentgrass and Kentucky bluegrass lawns, but it can infect others.

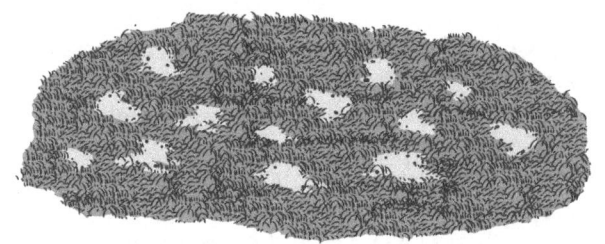

**FIGURE 17-2:**
Dollar spot occurs in overly wet lawns with heavy thatch.

**What to do about it:** Take better care of your lawn. Water deeply but infrequently, allowing the soil to partially dry out between waterings. Water in the morning so that the grass dries out before nightfall. Aerate to reduce thatch. Increase fertilization (actively growing turfgrass can actually grow out of the disease). Mow at the proper height. You can also plant resistant varieties of Kentucky bluegrass, and/or plant a mixture of grasses that includes less susceptible types such as perennial ryegrass or tall fescue.

## Summer patch

This disease is most common in the heat of the summer across parts of the country where wet, humid weather is the norm, such as the Midwest as well eastern to southeastern states.

**What it looks like:** Circular patches of dead grass start out small (4 inches in diameter) and slowly expand to up to 2 feet in diameter, leaving the center green — hence, the nickname "frog eye" (see Figure 17-3). The small patches start out dark-bluish purple and gradually turn straw-colored as the turf dies.

**When it's trouble:** Summer patch is common in hot, dry, windy weather near the end of summer, particularly when soil temperatures climb above 83°F. Drought-stressed shallow-rooted Kentucky bluegrass lawns are most susceptible, though fine fescues can also be affected. The disease often shows up near paving or other parts of the lawn that dry out first. Overuse of nitrogen fertilizers and thatch make problems worse.

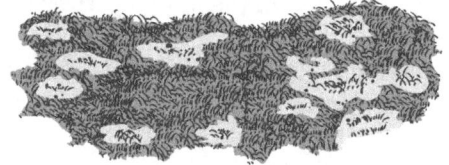

**FIGURE 17-3:**
Summer patch can leave "frog eyes" in your lawn.

**What to do about it:** Plant resistant varieties of Kentucky bluegrass (contact your cooperative extension office for suggested varieties). You can also switch to a less susceptible type of grass, such as tall fescue, perennial ryegrass, or bermudagrass. Studies reveal that simply adding a small percentage of perennial ryegrass to a bluegrass lawn can greatly reduce the problem. Aerate to reduce thatch and improve water penetration. Proper mowing is important in managing this disease (see Chapter 13). Water deeply, making sure to wet the entire root zone. (Don't let the turf dry out.) Apply less nitrogen, particularly in midsummer, on Kentucky bluegrass lawns.

## Fairy ring

This lovely sounding disease can occur anywhere.

**What it looks like:** Fairy ring, shown in Figure 17-4, starts as circular or partial ring bands of especially lush, deep-green grass. The rings range from 3 to 12 feet wide. Sometimes, the lush grass dies. Mushrooms or puffballs often form near the outside of the ring.

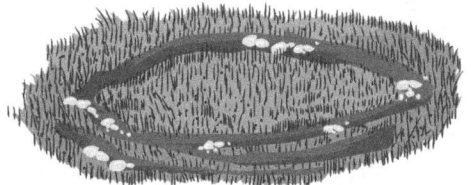

**FIGURE 17-4:**
Fairy ring doesn't actually attack the grass.

**When it's trouble:** The disease can occur on any lawn at any time during the growing season.

**What to do about it:** Fairy ring develops from naturally decaying organic matter in the lawn, usually wood debris or decaying tree roots left in the ground at planting time or heavy thatch. The fungus doesn't actually attack the grass. (If areas of the grass die, it's usually due to moisture stress.) Aerate to reduce thatch. Water and fertilize properly.

## Melting out or leaf spot

This lawn disease is most problematic for Kentucky bluegrass in the northern U.S., though it can also be a problem on bermudagrass in southern parts of the U.S.

**What it looks like:** Early symptoms of melting out, or leaf spot, are elongated circular spots on the grass blades, shown in Figure 17-5. The spots are brown with a blackish or purple edge. Eventually, the entire blade turns brown, and the lawn starts to thin or "melt out."

**When it's trouble:** The disease is most troublesome on Kentucky bluegrass lawns in cool, wet weather. Development is promoted by factors such as inadequate or excessive nitrogen levels, an overabundance of thatch, prolonged leaf wetness, drought conditions, and mowing at low heights.

**FIGURE 17-5:** Melting out begins with elongated circular spots on grass blades.

**What to do about it:** Adjust your mowing height upward, reduce nitrogen fertilizer application, especially in spring, and water more efficiently. Aerate to improve water penetration and reduce thatch. Many newer varieties of Kentucky bluegrass resist melting out.

## Pythium blight or grease spot

This fungus thrives most anywhere. In the United States, it's most common in the Southeast or after summer rains in the West.

**What it looks like:** Pythium blight, shown in Figure 17-6, causes grass blades to turn reddish-brown and die. When wet, the blades look water-soaked and slimy. Dead areas are irregularly shaped but usually elongated and often surrounded by cottony purple-gray to white fungus. Pythium blight spreads easily by equipment or water. It often shows up in a streaky pattern across the lawn matching mower or drainage patterns. The matted patches may have a gray color as well as a slightly moldy smell. The disease affects all turfgrass species.

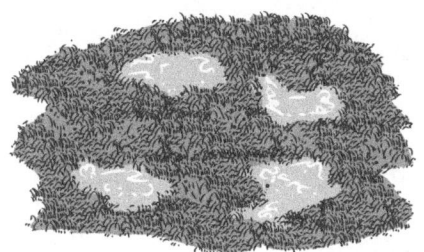

**FIGURE 17-6:**
Pythium blight
makes wet grass
look slimy.

**When it's trouble:** This disease is common in warm, humid weather, especially if nighttime temperatures don't drop below 70°F. High soil pH and compacted soil make problems worse. It's also a common problem on newly seeded areas. If damage is widespread and weather conditions are favorable, this disease is a likely culprit.

**What to do about it:** Have your soil tested to make sure the pH is not overly alkaline, which can make the lawn more susceptible. Aerate to decrease thatch and improve water penetration. Fix drainage problems if necessary. Water properly and don't overfertilize. If possible, mow infected areas separately from unaffected areas to reduce spread of the disease.

## Red thread

This fungus looks just like you'd imagine: red threads. It occurs most anywhere, from perennial ryegrass in the Midwest to fescue lawns in the Pacific Northwest.

**What it looks like:** Red thread, shown in Figure 17-7, causes the grass blades to turn brown. When the grass is wet, you can see small, red to pinkish strands on leaf blades, especially near the ends.

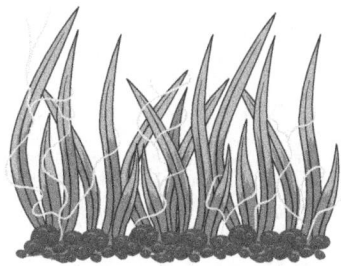

**FIGURE 17-7:**
Red thread is
most visible on
wet grass blades.

**When it's trouble:** This disease occurs commonly in cool, moist weather in lawns of slow-growing, fine fescue and perennial ryegrass. Underfertilization makes the disease worse.

**What to do about it:** Get your soil tested to make sure that all nutrients are in balance and the pH is in the proper range and then take better care of your lawn. Water and fertilize properly, mow at the right height, and reduce thatch. Contact your local cooperative extension office for resistant varieties.

## Rust

This makes for a frustratingly "off-colored lawn" and can occur almost anywhere.

**What it looks like:** You can identify rust by small, rust-colored spores on leaf blades, shown in Figure 17-8. The entire lawn picks up a yellowish-orange cast. You may also notice the rust color on your footwear after walking through the lawn.

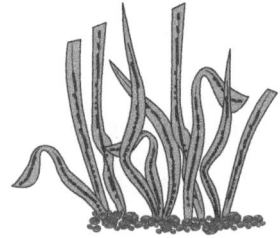

**FIGURE 17-8:**
Rust puts a
yellow-orange
cast on
your lawn.

**When it's trouble:** Rust can appear during moderately warm weather and when the lawn stays wet from dew for long periods. The disease is most common on Kentucky bluegrass and perennial ryegrass lawns that have been stressed by hot summer weather, but it can occur on other grasses.

**What to do about it:** The easiest way to control rust is to fertilize and mow more frequently, and, in general, take better care of your lawn. Rust isn't nearly as apparent or troublesome on a healthy, frequently mowed lawn. If you're planting a new lawn, look for resistant varieties.

## Snow molds

Like you'd expect, this occurs where it snows. But it's especially a problem in shady areas.

**What it looks like:** Snow molds, shown in Figure 17-9, are common to cold-winter climates, especially where the snow cover is long-lasting. You can find two types of snow mold: gray and pink.

Gray snow mold shows itself as gray to brown dead spots near melting snow. It can form circular patches up to 3 feet in diameter and can kill turf. You can usually see fuzzy, gray mold near the edges of the dead spots.

Pink snow mold also causes dead spots near melting snow, but — you guessed it — it produces a pinkish fuzz near the edges. This disease does not always kill the turfgrass but will cause it to mat down somewhat.

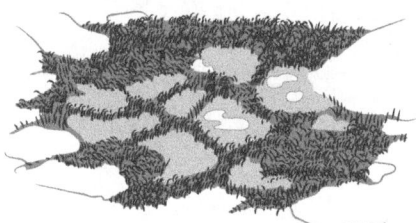

**FIGURE 17-9:**
Snow mold is common in shady areas.

**When it's trouble:** These diseases occur as snow melts on cool-season grasses where winters are cold. Gray snow mold likes temperatures from 32°F to 40°F. Pink snow mold thrives during extended periods of cool (40°F to 55°F), wet, cloudy weather in spring and fall. Compacted soil and overfertilization in fall can make problems worse. Both are common in shady areas where the snow is last to melt.

**What to do about it:** Aerate the soil to reduce thatch and improve water penetration. Don't promote lush growth by fertilizing heavily in fall. Reduce shade if possible. Mow the grass as long as it continues to grow in the fall. If the grass is tall going into winter, it can mat down, making it more susceptible to snow mold.

Chapter **18**

# Diagnosing Other Lawn Problems

S ome interesting things can happen to your lawn. If you live in Texas, you may wake one morning to find armadillos digging up your grass. In Kentucky, the excavators may be raccoons. In other areas, you may see skunks that want to add their singular scent to your lovely lawn environment. Phew!

No critters? Lucky you. However, you may have one dead spot in the lawn where you just can't seem to grow anything no matter how many times you reseed. Or perhaps you have a dry spot that never seems to look right. How do you handle those mysterious lumps, bumps, and bare spots?

Some sleuthing through this chapter on lawn weeds, insects, and diseases may reveal the answer to your problems, but if not, don't give up. This chapter handles some of the other lawn problems that aren't weed, bug, or fungus.

## Creatures That Dig in the Night (Mostly)

You may be surprised by the kinds of animals that can cause lawn problems. Professionals call these "nuisance wildlife" but, in all fairness, the animals are just looking for food. You don't have to live in the country to come across these garden visitors — or at least the damage they cause. They can show up in suburbs and even urban areas.

You might be willing to overlook a few dug-up areas, but when the damage is more severe, you'll want to figure out the culprit. Sometimes you can identify the wildlife visitor by the size, shape, and location of the holes or other damage. You might even get lucky and find some of their tracks in the mud. (If you're so inclined, there are also websites to help you identify garden visitors by their scat, or droppings.)

Some animals are common across the country and in a variety of habitats. Squirrels, for example, have adapted to live just about everywhere. But you won't find armadillos in Vermont.

## Big diggers: Armadillos, skunks, and raccoons

If you keep finding parts of your lawn unexplainably dug up, the reason may one of these mammals looking for food. They all love grubs, those belowground-dwelling larvae of beetles, including Japanese beetles. These mammals generally feed early in the morning and late in the evening, so those are times you want to keep an eye out and try to confirm that one of these is doing the digging. Check out Figure 18-1 for a look at these pests.

If you feel that the damage to your lawn warrants control, start by checking your lawn to see if you have a large population of grubs (learn how to do this in Chapter 16). If you do, you can take steps to control the grubs in the hope that these critters will look elsewhere for food.

**TIP**

Don't assume that you have grubs and reach for a pesticide. Always confirm the presence of any pest, as well as the population level. It is important for the health of your lawn, and of the ecosystem, to be judicious in the use of pesticides. Properly identifying pests and determining if control is warranted are foundational principles of integrated pest management; read more in Chapter 16.

As a last resort, you may want to contact a local pest control company that can come out and set traps. Be sure they use humane methods. It's not wise to trap these animals yourself; they may carry rabies and other diseases. In some areas it's illegal to trap and relocate wildlife.

## Armadillos

These fascinating creatures, whose name means "little armored one" in Spanish, prefer warm, wet climates. They're common in parts of the southern United States from Texas to Florida, though they're expanding their range northward, and a few have even been found as far north as Illinois and Nebraska. Damage is usually worst in the summer months, when irrigation softens soil for easier digging. Armadillos tear up the grass when they dig shallow holes, usually about 6 inches across, as they look for food. (They don't leave mounds next to the holes like woodchucks and moles.) They sometimes root around like pigs, tearing up the grass as they go.

In addition to grubs, their diet includes beetles, cockroaches, wasps, yellow jackets, fire ants, scorpions, spiders, and snails. Armadillos also dig larger holes for burrows, though they prefer to dig these in forested areas.

**TIP**

Monitoring your irrigation can help deter armadillos. Since they prefer loose, moist soil, watering deeply and then allowing the soil to dry out before watering again can make digging more difficult for them. Unfortunately, repellants don't seem to deter armadillos, nor do scare tactics. You can exclude them using a short fence (at least 24 inches high) that is slanted outward at a 40-degree angle, with at least 18 inches buried in the soil to prevent them from burrowing under it.

## Skunks

Skunks create holes by pressing their noses onto the lawn and then using the sharp claws on their front paws to dig. The holes tend to be cone-shaped, almost like a golfer's divot. Although individual holes are only 2 to 4 inches across, there can be so many holes that the area almost looks like it's been tilled. You may smell this odoriferous culprit even before you see the damage to your lawn.

Skunks stick close to the ground; they can't jump or climb. So sturdy fencing made from chicken wire or woven wire can keep them out. Secure it to the ground so the skunks aren't tempted to burrow under it.

Although it's small consolation if you're plagued by skunks, at least you should know that they also eat large quantities of lawn pests. In addition to grubs, they eat cutworms, armyworms, and grasshoppers.

## Raccoons

These masked bandits use their front paws like hands to lift and peel back sod. Raccoons are particularly notorious for rolling up newly laid sod. They don't typically dig holes in the lawn; if you see holes, the culprit is likely a different mammal.

Raccoons are adaptable creatures. Once found mostly in the deciduous and mixed forests of North America, they have extended their range to just about every habitat, including suburban and urban locales.

If raccoons are damaging your lawn, they're probably searching for grubs and worms. It's just about impossible to outwit these clever animals with repellants and scare tactics. Their agility and ability to jump and climb makes fencing them out a challenge; the best option is a two-wire electric fence with wires set 6 inches and 12 inches high.

**FIGURE 18-1:** Armadillos, skunks, and raccoons.

Raccoon

Shunk

Armadillo

## Small diggers: Moles and gophers

People often confuse moles and gophers (see Figure 18-2). They both create underground tunnels, but what they eat and the damage they cause differ. Although they both improve the soil by aerating it, that is small consolation if they're ruining the look of your lawn.

### Moles

Moles are small, 6- to 8-inch-long, furry mammals with distinctively pointed snouts and large, clawed front paws they use for digging. Moles feed on underground insects, not grass, but they become a problem because of the raised ridges they leave in the lawn as they burrow around in the soil. The ridges are unsightly and raise havoc with your lawn mower.

Ever heard the expression "making a mountain out of a molehill"? When moles dig tunnels, they push out the soil at the entrance, creating volcano-shaped mounds — the molehill. These round hills of soil, along with raised ridges in the grass, indicate that a mole is, or was, living nearby. Other small mammals are quick to make use of abandoned mole tunnels.

There are several different species of moles. They're found across much of the United States, though they are less common in dry climates. Accustomed to living underground, their eyesight is poor, but they make up for that with their sensitive snouts and paws. These impressive diggers can tunnel up to 18 feet per hour. To fuel this activity, they consume a remarkable number of grubs, centipedes, millipedes, and earthworms.

Like most diggers, they prefer moist, loose soil. You can tell if a mole tunnel is active by pressing on a section of the ridged area. If it's pushed up again the next morning, a mole has been at work. They are most active in late spring and summer, especially after a warm rain.

**TIP**

Although there are numerous devices advertised to send moles packing, including ultrasonic devices and pinwheel-like noisemakers, their effectiveness is questionable. There are also poison baits, but, really, do you want to poison your landscape? The most effective control is to set a mole trap on their permanent runways (following the instructions on the trap). However, once you catch the culprit another mole will likely move right in. Considering the beneficial role they play in controlling grubs and other pest insects, you might want to make peace with these visitors and tolerate the damage.

**FIGURE 18-2:** Gophers and moles.

Gopher          Mole

## Gophers

There are several species of gophers ranging in size from 5 to 14 inches long. The most widespread species is the plains pocket gopher, which is common from the Great Plains south into Texas and Louisiana. Other species are found in the West and Southeast. The "pocket" in pocket gopher refers to the external cheek pouches, which they use to carry food. They turn these fur-lined pockets inside out for emptying and cleaning.

Unlike grub-eating moles, gophers are vegetarians. Roots, bulbs, tubers, and other fleshy, underground plant parts make up the bulk of their diets, though they'll occasionally eat the aboveground parts of plants. You'll rarely see a gopher because they live most of their lives underground. If you're lucky, you might see one poke its head out to grab a plant, and then pull the whole plant underground, just like in the cartoons.

Gophers push soil to the surface as they dig, leaving large mounds of freshly dug soil on the lawn. These mounds are generally fan-shaped or semicircular, often with a visible soil plug, distinguishing them from the round, volcano-shaped mounds created by moles. Gophers generally burrow deeper than moles and don't leave raised ridges in the lawn.

The common practice of planting tulips and other bulbs in wire cages to prevent gophers from eating them isn't practical for lawns. Fortunately, gophers are usually an occasional nuisance and don't pose long-term problems. That said, they are known to gnaw on plastic irrigation lines, and the mounds are unsightly and interfere with mowing.

The many commonly available gopher-control devices, including electronic gadgets and repellants, are marginally effective, if they have any effect at all. The more effective control methods are lethal ones. Poison baits and fumigation are options but introduce toxins into the environment. The most effective control is to set gopher traps on their permanent runways (following the instructions on the trap). That said, another gopher will likely move into the empty tunnels, and you may find yourself on a never-ending, mind-numbing cycle of trapping. Gophers do play beneficial roles in grassland ecosystems, such as aerating compacted soil (earning them the nickname "ecosystem engineers"), so before going the lethal route, ponder if you can tolerate these pesky visitors and the damage they cause.

# Daytime Marauders

These creatures are active during the day, and sometimes 'round the clock. Overall, they tend to cause less damage to lawns than the nighttime diggers. (They're usually more interested in the fruits and vegetables growing in your gardens.)

## Tunnel-digging voles and groundhogs

These mammals are notorious for their propensity to dig tunnels, and it's this digging that creates unsightly damage to lawns. Though both animals will eat grass and grass roots, they're more interested in other food sources.

## Voles

There are many species of voles, including meadow voles, long-tail voles, and pine voles, and they can be found across much of North America. Also known as meadow mice, voles are about the same size as, or slightly larger than, a house mouse, with small ears and a short tail. They spend their time eating roots, tubers, and bulbs. Their presence is most noticeable in late winter and early spring, when melting snow reveals a crisscrossing network of surface runways and trails of dead grass.

Vole populations vary from season to season and year to year, with populations peaking every two to five years. Although the damage to lawns in unsightly, it's usually temporary, and the lawn quickly recovers. They will also raid vegetable gardens and cause significant damage by gnawing the bark on trees, especially in winter when other food is scarce. In these instances, control is best done by excluding the pests by creating wire cages around the soil in vegetable beds and installing tree guards.

Lethal traps are available and can be used for short-term control in lawns, though more voles will likely move in to fill the vacancy. Poisons and other toxic methods of control are ill-advised because they risk poisoning the many predators that keep vole populations in check, including hawks, owls, foxes, weasels, and snakes.

## Groundhogs

Also known as woodchucks, groundhogs are large rodents common across much of North America. Unlike many mammal visitors, they're active during the day, especially in spring and summer. Being active during the daytime, along with their comfort around human activity, keeps them safe from predators that are most active at dawn and dusk, such as coyotes and bobcats.

Stout and stocky, groundhogs grow up to 20 inches long, with short legs and large front teeth. Although they're usually after vegetables and fruits to eat, these herbivores cause damage to turf by digging their extensive burrows and nesting chambers, leaving lawns feeling soft and spongy and. Worse yet, they leave gaping entrance and exit holes, ready to twist the ankle of a passerby.

These chunky mammals are surprisingly agile. They run fast and climb fences with ease. Their personalities vary. Some will scare easily, others can be aggressive, and they will defend themselves if threatened. Their large front teeth and sharp claws can cause serious bites and scratches. Don't get close to a groundhog or let your dog approach one.

Repellents and scare tactics don't work on groundhogs. Fencing should be at least 3 feet tall; it must be made from heavy wire and buried at least a foot deep. The top part of the fence should be angled outward to prevent these nimble climbers from scaling it. Trapping these animals puts you at risk of getting a nasty bite, so it's best left to a professional pest control company.

## Nuisance diggers: Squirrels and rabbits

Common just about everywhere, these furry visitors can become a nuisance, but the damage they cause is usually minor and lawns quickly recover.

### Squirrels

Although most notorious for raiding bird feeders, squirrels can also damage lawns by digging holes, usually to bury or retrieve a cache of nuts and seeds. The shallow holes are about an inch in diameter. Usually, in the process of hiding their food they refill the hole (how polite of them!), so all you'll see are coin-sized patches of soil. Squirrels are more troublesome when they dig up seedlings and newly planted bulbs and can become a major nuisance if they gnaw their way into your attic to build a nest.

Techniques to protect plants, such as planting bulbs in little wire cages, isn't feasible for lawns. Trapping them is futile; more will move right in to fill the vacancy. You can try to deter them with motion-activated sprinklers, peppermint sprays, and fake predators (such as statues of owls and foxes). Rotate through your arsenal because these clever creatures will quickly figure out that they aren't real hazards. Aside from squirrel-proofing your bird feeders, your best bet is to learn to appreciate their agility and enjoy their antics.

### Rabbits

The occasional rabbit is cute, but when their populations explode, as they sometimes do, they can cause a good deal of damage to turf. When other food sources are scarce, they'll chew grass down to the roots, and their urine leaves unsightly brown spots. Fortunately, rabbits rarely kill the grass roots, so it will likely recover. Rabbits are nearly impossible to control with trapping or repellants. If your lawn is small, you can try fencing them out.

# What's Causing That Dead Spot?

Sooner or later, you may find yourself with some troublesome dead spots that are slow to recover, if they do so at all. The spots may not have any predictable shape or pattern. Some dead spots may show up all of a sudden; others may slowly turn yellow and then die. Still others may have dead centers with rings of dark green grass around them.

Insects and diseases can cause dead spots; see Chapters 16 and 17 for information on those, respectively.

# Common causes of dead spots

It can take some sleuthing to figure out what's causing dead spots. Here are some possibilities.

## Dog urine

If there's a ring of healthy grass surrounding the dead spot, dog urine is one likely culprit. Dog urine contains lots of nitrogen, and it can burn grass in much the same way that improperly applied, fast-acting nitrogen fertilizer can. Female dogs are particularly problematic because they squat and urinate in one place, while male dogs tend to urinate in smaller quantities over a larger area. Spots caused by dog urine are often ringed with bright green grass, offering clear evidence that nitrogen boosts the growth of grass, even if too much is harmful (see Figure 18-3).

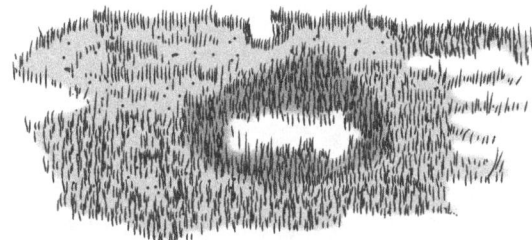

**FIGURE 18-3:**
Damage from dog urine.

If you have a lawn and a dog that needs to urinate on it, there isn't much you can do beyond taking good care of the lawn and repairing dead spots as they occur. If your neighbor's dog is causing the problem, you can ask them politely to walk their dog in their own yard.

Immediately flooding the area with water to dilute the urine will help, but for most of us, following our dog around with a hose isn't a practical long-term solution.

**WARNING**

Although there are medications and supplements that supposed to alter the dog's urine so that it doesn't kill grass, these aren't effective, and they're not recommended by veterinarians.

### Fertilizer spills

If the spot resembles the damage from dog urine (see Figure 18-3) and Rover's not the problem, then the cause might be a fertilizer spill. Take extra care when filling your fertilizer spreader or sprayer. If any fertilizer spills, clean it up right away and flood the area with water to dilute the fertilizer.

### Other causes

**WARNING**

Spilled gasoline and oil can kill grass, as can spills of other chemicals. It goes without saying to be careful when filling your mower or other lawn equipment. Herbicide spills are another common cause of dead spots. Spilled salt (the kind used to melt icy driveways and sidewalks) can also kill grass. Objects left on the lawn too long will kill grass by preventing light from reaching the blades.

## Fixing dead spots

To fix dead spots, dig out the dead grass to a depth of about 4 to 6 inches. Then put a slow-running sprinkler or hose over the hole and let it run long enough to flush the soil clean. You may need to do this over the course of several hours if the problem is spilled gasoline or something similar. Fill the hole with good soil and reseed it or patch it with a piece of sod. Keep the area moist until the roots become established.

# Dealing with Dry Spots

Maybe you notice that part of the lawn never looks quite right. The color is off — sort of gray-blue-green or yellowish. The color change is most apparent late in the day or during really hot weather. You may also see the discoloration on sloping ground or a raised part of the lawn.

It's possible that that particular part of the lawn is drying out before the rest. There are lots of potential causes. Slopes, where water runs off rather than soaks in, are prone to drying out. Areas where soil is compacted by frequent foot traffic often dry out more quickly than surrounding areas. Concrete and asphalt absorb and radiate heat on sunny days, which can dry out the lawn that abuts them. Fences can impede cooling airflow and reflect sunlight onto the lawn, both of which increase drying. Tree roots can suck the water out of areas even if the branches aren't shading it.

TIP

Or maybe your sprinklers are missing part of your lawn; check the sprinkler coverage next time they're running. Put several cans or plastic cups of the same size on the dry spot and on the green areas near it. Run the sprinklers for 10 to 15 minutes. If the sprinkler coverage is good, all the cups or cans will have the same amount of water. If they don't, readjust the spray pattern.

It's possible that some areas just need more water than others. You can apply more water by adjusting or changing the sprinkler heads. On sloping ground, you can install sprinklers that apply water more slowly, so it doesn't run off. Aerating dry spots, especially areas that get compacted from foot traffic, increases water penetration.

Take a look at Part 3 for more information on watering and aerating.

# Lawn Mower Damage

Your trusty lawn mower can cause a number of problems. Improper adjustment (one side cuts lower than the other) may leave uneven ridges in the lawn, scalping strips while leaving other parts fine. If you mow in the same pattern every time, the problem worsens until your lawn sports stripes of dead and alive areas. Just mowing in the same direction every week can leave compacted strips where the wheels have traveled for years. These strips grow poorly. Figure 18-4 shows an example of mower damage.

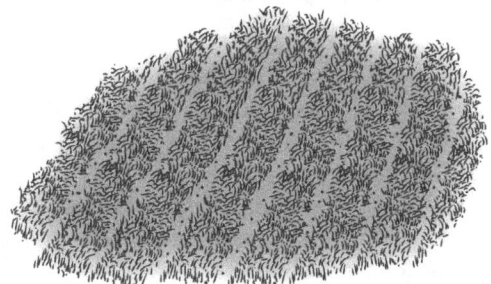

FIGURE 18-4:
Lawn mower
damage.

Your mower also can scalp bumpy or uneven spots, turning them into straw-colored dead spots. If your mower blades are all dull, the lawn looks ragged after cutting.

TIP

Mowing your lawn is stressful to the grass. Even after mowing properly, a lawn can look a little traumatized. Don't confuse mowing's aftereffects with insects or disease. Keep an eye on the lawn to see if it recovers in a few days.

**TIP**

Keep mower blades sharp and adjust the cutting height for your type of lawn grass, as described in Chapter 13. If you have bumpy spots, level them as described in Chapter 14.

# Worn-Out Paths in the Lawn

Let's face it. Any attempts to try to discourage people from taking shortcuts across a section of lawn are likely to fail. Whether it's your kids making a beeline to the jungle gym, your neighbors cutting across the corner of your yard, or the neighborhood kids taking a shortcut home from school, you're unlikely to dissuade them no matter how many signs you put up or areas you cordon off.

Even if you can get people to change their habits in the short-term, the soil underneath the trampled lawn is likely compacted. It will take some effort to loosen it, aerate it, and otherwise return it to lawn-worthy.

Rather than waging a continuous battle that you probably aren't going to win in the long run, consider putting in a path. It can be as simple as a series of flagstones set in the lawn, or as complex as a fancy brick sidewalk. Gravel and mulch are other common path materials; just be sure to keep them contained with edging (learn more about edging in Chapter 7).

# Water and Erosion Damage

Water rushing down a slope can quickly damage the lawn and erode the soil. Your best bet is to tackle the cause, such as by modifying the grade of the lawn, installing a drainage system, or building terraces (more on these in Chapter 7).

Another option is to create a dry creek bed, which is essentially a gully or swale filled with large stones (called riprap) that slow the flow of water and direct it to a desired location, such as a rain garden.

The design can be purely functional, or it can be a creative element for your landscape. For example, you can use attractive stones in a variety of sizes to create the appearance of a natural creek bed and plant the edges with ground covers.

Just be sure that the water is directed to a safe, appropriate spot in your landscape — not to the street or your neighbor's lawn.

# Moss

When sections of your lawn are being overtaken by moss, it usually means the soil fertility and pH are low and the overall environment is shady and wet. Those are the conditions in which moss thrives and grass struggles. Moss doesn't kill existing grass, even though it may seem so. Like any plant, all moss does is take advantage of bare or thin areas of turf.

**TIP**

If moss is prevalent in your lawn, have your soil tested. You may need to apply limestone to raise the soil pH. Learn more about soil testing and how to raise soil pH in Chapter 6.

To replace moss with grass you need to do two things: Change conditions sufficiently so that moss is discouraged from growing and grass is encouraged — raise pH level, add fertilizer, improve air circulation and light penetration (thinning existing trees may be necessary). Then, remove existing moss and plant new grass. See Chapter 14 for information about renovating a lawn.

**TIP**

The other option is to tolerate areas of moss. After all, people spend a lot of time and money trying to get moss to grow between paving stones and on rock walls and flowerpots. Moss is a natural alternative to the challenge of growing grass under trees, for example. Why fight Mother Nature when she's offering you an easy solution?

Mosses are a diverse and fascinating group of plants. Plus, they don't need mowing or fertilizing, and some even have air-purifying qualities.

# 5

# Cultivating Sustainable Lawns and Landscapes

**IN THIS PART . . .**

Discover the many attractive, environmentally friendly lawn alternatives that are easy to care for and are inviting to birds, butterflies, and other wildlife.

Find low-maintenance ground cover options for the parts of your landscape where growing a lawn doesn't make sense.

Find out which trees adapt well to lawn life and be introduced to tips for planting and caring for them.

Get step-by-step instructions for planting a wildflower meadow.

# Chapter **19**

# Considering Lawn Alternatives

Growing a lawn may not be the best option for all areas of your landscape. An expanse of green grass, as wonderful as it looks, often requires lots of water and other natural resources. To keep it looking its best you also invest a lot of your time and physical labor. Fortunately, there are many alternatives and good reasons to consider them.

In dry climates, such as the desert Southwest, providing the irrigation required by a large lawn comes at a big cost to you as well as to the environment. And even if you live in a region with reliable rainfall, lawns still gobble up resources. Fortunately, there are many attractive, low-maintenance options for the parts of your landscape where growing a lawn doesn't make sense. Some of these have further benefits, such as supporting pollinators. In this chapter, you'll find lots of lawn alternatives to consider.

# Growing Ground Covers

Ground covers are usually low-growing, spreading plants that form a uniform layer of foliage. Plants used for ground covers range from very low-growing types that are just a few inches high to more shrubby plants that are a foot or more high. Some ground covers knit together to create an even carpet of foliage that, from a landscape design perspective, has an overall impact that's similar to a lawn. Others add landscape interest with their attractive foliage and colorful flowers.

## The pros and cons of ground covers

The upsides of ground covers are impressive:

>> **Most ground covers need less water than lawns.** Once established, many ground covers can get by on just the water supplied by rainfall, and they'll withstand periods of drought. If some supplemental water is needed, you can install water-thrifty drip irrigation.

>> **Ground covers offer diverse beauty.** In contrast to a lawn that's just flat and green, ground covers come in a variety of leaf textures and colors, some with flowers, berries, and attractive fall foliage.

>> **Ground covers are ideal for sloping ground.** Steep hillsides and slopes spell trouble for lawns. Irrigation water washes away and gets wasted before it can soak into the soil, sometimes taking fertilizer with it. In addition, mowing lawns on slopes can be dangerous. Instead, consider planting ground covers that will stabilize the soil. If needed, you can use drip irrigation, which applies water very slowly without runoff. Best of all, you can skip the harrowing task of weekly mowing that steep slope.

>> **Ground covers need less care.** If the prospect of no mowing and less fertilizing sounds appealing, consider a ground cover. Many types will fill in an area so thickly that you don't even have to weed.

>> **Ground covers are perfect for small spaces.** Ideal locations for ground covers include narrow areas along the side of the house, that strip between the sidewalk and street, and other spots that are impossible to water properly and a pain to mow.

>> **Ground covers can fill in less-used areas of your landscape.** You can still have the big, expansive look of a large lawn by planting ground covers around the perimeter of it. You decide how much lawn you want for a play surface, recreation space, and tidy look around your entryway, without the big commitment of time and resources required by an entire landscape covered in turfgrass.

>> **Ground covers can increase biodiversity and support pollinators.** By planting a variety of low-growing plants, including some that offer the benefit of flowers, you'll invite pollinators and other beneficial insects.

>> **Ground covers can grow in shade.** Many ground covers grow better in heavy shade than most lawn grasses. Some even adapt well to growing under trees, where thirsty tree roots compete for moisture.

Like most plants, ground covers have their own requirements for sun, shade, soil, water, and so on, so you need to do some research before you make a final selection.

There are a few downsides to ground covers.

>> **You can't walk or play on them like a lawn.** Most aren't as tolerant of foot traffic, and they aren't conducive to games of croquet.

>> **They don't provide instant gratification.** Lawns grown from seed or sod are ready to enjoy in weeks or months. Most ground covers take longer to fill in.

>> **Flowering ground covers invite bees.** To keep stinging insects at bay, plant flowering ground covers in out-of-the way areas or at the edges of the lawn, where there's less foot traffic.

**WARNING**

>> **Some ground covers are invasive.** The qualities that make ground covers desirable can also lead to problems. Many ground covers are, by their very nature, aggressive spreaders, and some of the worst offenders are still readily available at garden centers and home improvement stores. See the "Ground covers with a high potential to become invasive" section later in this chapter.

## Planting ground covers

Proper plant spacing and thorough soil preparation are keys to success in planting ground covers.

### Plant spacing

Plant tags and variety descriptions for ground covers usually offer recommendations on how far apart to space the plants. Measure the square footage of the area (see Chapter 6) to determine how many plants you'll need to buy. Here are some guidelines for plant spacing:

>> **Mature size:** For plants that grow in clumps or mounds, space plants based on their width at maturity. If a plant grows 1 foot wide at maturity, you'll want to give each plant 1 square foot of garden space. In other words, space the

plants so the centers of the plants are 1 foot apart. You can space plants closer together (about 9 inches apart) to encourage them to fill in faster and form a solid cover. If you're planting ground covers that spread through vines or horizontal stems, a spacing of 8 to 12 inches is usually best.

>> **Speed of growth:** Vigorous, fast-growing plants will fill in more quickly than slower-growing plants, so you can space them further apart.

>> **Mulching:** Applying a layer of organic mulch, such as shredded bark or pine straw, between widely spaced plants will help keep weeds in check and conserve soil moisture. If you don't plan to mulch, then consider spacing plants closer together so they'll fill in more quickly.

## Soil preparation and planting

1. **Start by getting rid of any weeds and grass in the planting area.**

   (Learn all about preparing a planting site in Chapter 7.)

2. **Perform a soil test so you know the soil's nutrient levels and pH.**

   For example, if you find out your soil is naturally acidic, you can look for plants that prefer that condition. Alternatively, you can amend the soil with limestone to raise the pH to match your ground cover's preference. (Learn about soil tests and adjusting pH in Chapter 7.)

3. **Add organic matter, such as compost, prior to planting.**

   This will improve the overall soil health. (Learn about compost in Chapter 7.)

4. **Water purchased ground cover plants thoroughly prior to planting.**

   If the roots feel dry, place the pots in a tray or shallow bin filled with water so the roots and soil can slowly absorb the water.

5. **Water the planting area, ensuring that the soil is moistened to a depth of 6 to 8 inches.**

6. **Set the pots in the planting area in staggered rows according to the spacing you determined.**

   If the area is roughly square or rectangular, pound in two stakes on either side and run a string between them to ensure a straight row. (Move the stakes and strings for each subsequent row.)

   **TIP**

   Use a ruler or yardstick to measure the space between plants as you place them in the planting area. Evenly spaced plants will fill in better and the area will look much more visually appealing as the plants fill in to create a solid cover.

**7.** **Dig the planting holes.**

If you prepared the planting area by tilling, you should be able to use a trowel to dig the planting holes. For larger holes or to dig in undisturbed soil, you may need to use a shovel. Dig the holes so that, when planted, the top of the growing mix in the container is at the same height as the surrounding soil. You don't want to bury the plants too deeply, nor do you want any of the roots sitting above the soil line. Set the excavated soil next to the plants; you'll be using it to backfill.

**8.** **Set the plants, in their pots, in the planting holes.**

Then step back and check the layout and spacing, adjusting if necessary.

**9.** **Plant your ground cover.**

One by one, remove each plant from its pot, set it in the hole, and backfill around the roots with the soil you excavated. Gently firm the soil around the roots. Water the area with a dilute fertilizer solution to settle the soil and help the plants get off to a good start.

WARNING

Don't backfill with compost or purchased topsoil; doing so can encourage the roots to remain confined to this area rather than expanding into the surrounding soil, especially in clay soils.

**10.** **Keep the area weed-free.**

It's helpful to apply an organic mulch, such as shredded bark or pine straw, between plants, especially if there are large gaps of bare soil. Mulch helps control weeds and helps keep soil moist. If you don't plan to mulch, then be prepared to pull weeds that sprout.

**11.** **Water regularly.**

Keep the soil consistently moist until the plants are well-established (learn more about watering in Chapter 11). Then, water as needed. In general, ground covers will need less-frequent irrigation than lawn grasses. However, you'll still need to provide water according to the needs of the particular ground cover you planted. Fertilize the plants again after a few weeks to promote rapid growth and help them fill in faster.

**12.** **Replace plants as needed.**

Keep an eye on your ground cover planting and replace plants as needed or add plants to fill in gaps. Be patient; your ground cover may take a few years to fill in.

# Choosing ground covers

Before you dive in and purchase dozens of the first pretty plant you see, take some time to consider the following attributes to help you choose the best ground cover.

>> **Cold hardiness:** Is the plant hardy in your region? In an ideal world, garden centers and home improvement stores would only sell plants that are suitably hardy for their locale, but this isn't always the case. And if you're buying plants from an online store, it'll be totally up to you to make sure they're hardy enough to withstand your coldest winter temperatures.

You can find your hardiness zone on the USDA Plant Hardiness Zone Map at `https://planthardiness.ars.usda.gov`. The map divides the country into zones based on one statistic: the average minimum winter temperature. Hardiness zones are most useful in cold-winter areas; they don't take into account any of the many other factors that determine whether a plant will thrive in your region.

>> **Heat tolerance:** In many parts of the country, summer heat plays a bigger role than winter cold in whether a plant will grow well. In regions where soaring summer temperatures can really take a toll on plants, look to the American Horticultural Society's Heat Zone Map for guidance: `www.usbg.gov/sites/default/files/2024-06/AHS-heat-zone-map.pdf`. The map is made up of 12 zones based on the average number of "heat days" an area experiences in a year. A heat day is defined as a day in which the temperature climbs to over 86°F. (The map is based on National Weather Service statistics from 1974 through 1995.) Note that most plants can survive short bursts of high temperature, especially if they receive adequate water. Drought-stressed plants, on the other hand, may succumb to short periods of intense heat.

>> **Tolerance to high humidity:** The adage, "It's not the heat, it's the humidity," has some bearing on plants, too. Prolonged periods of high humidity can lead to fungal diseases, especially in plants that are better adapted to arid conditions.

>> **Sunlight needs:** It should go without saying, but here it is: Choose shade-tolerant plants for shady conditions, and sun-loving plants for sunny sites.

>> **Soil preference:** Some ground covers are widely adaptable, whereas others require particular soils conditions (for example, consistently moist, very well drained, rich in organic matter, high or low pH, and so on).

>> **Resistance to deer, rabbit, and other hungry herbivores:** Plants that have strong aromas or have fuzzy foliage tend to be unbothered by deer.

Because of their nature to grow quickly and spread aggressively, some of the plants commonly used as ground covers are considered invasive in some regions. Before buying and planting a particular ground cover, check local laws and contact your state's native plant society or department of natural resources to determine if the plant is considered invasive in your region. This website by the Center for Invasive Species and Ecosystem Health lets you search by plant species and has links to state invasive species lists: www.invasive.org/species.cfm.

## Low- to medium-height ground covers

Many of these ground huggers can withstand light foot traffic; you can walk on them periodically, and they're ideal for planting around steppingstones or in the narrow planting strip between the sidewalk and street. Others are taller and best planted where there's little to no foot traffic. This list is by no means complete; however, it will give you a sampling of the many low-growing plant options available.

Some listings start with a warning about the plant's tendency to become invasive. Keep in mind that a plant can invasive in one area or habitat, while its spread is kept in check in another, perhaps by winter cold. Even so-called native plants can be invasive outside their actual native range. Take the time to look into your local laws and guidelines.

>> **Wooly yarrow (*Achillea tomentosa*):** This tough, hardy ground cover reaches about 6 to 9 inches high and can take foot traffic. In the summer, yellow flowers complement the ferny, gray-green foliage. The leaves are also aromatic, a fragrant bonus when you walk on it. Evergreen. Full sun. USDA Hardiness Zones 3–9.

>> **Japanese ardisia (*Ardisia japonica*):** *Note: This plant is considered invasive in parts of Florida.* The glossy, dark-green foliage reaches 6 to 12 inches high and spreads by runners to form a dense mat. Clusters of small, pale-pink, star-shaped flowers appear in summer, followed by red berries. Also called marlberry, the plant prefers moist, slightly acidic soils. Evergreen, though cold temperatures may cause foliage to turn brown. Part shade to shade. USDA Hardiness Zones 6–9.

>> **Wild ginger (*Asarum canadense*):** With heart-shaped foliage and a dense root system, this plant forms an attractive ground cover. Native to woodlands in the eastern half of the United States, it prefers moist, acidic soils and will not tolerate drought. Deer tend to avoid this plant. Not related to culinary ginger. Deciduous. Part shade to shade. USDA Hardiness Zones 3–8.

**WARNING**

» **Asparagus fern (*Asparagus densiflorus*):** *Note: This plant is considered invasive in some regions.* This plant, which isn't a true fern, is related to asparagus and grows 8 to 24 inches tall, depending on the variety. Grouping plants together creates the effect of a tall, graceful ground cover. The variety 'Sprengeri' has a bushy appearance and can be sheared to keep it compact. 'Myers' grows in more upright plumes. Evergreen, though the tops of the plants may die back in winter in the colder areas of its range. Full sun to part shade. USDA Hardiness Zones 9–10.

» **Horseherb or straggler daisy (*Calyptocarpus vialis*):** This tough, drought-tolerant plant grows 8 to 10 inches tall and blooms with tiny yellow flowers from spring to fall. It prefers well-drained soils, tolerates dry shade, and can be mowed to maintain an even height. Native to the southeast coastal areas of the United States. It's evergreen in regions with mild winters. Sun to part shade. USDA Hardiness Zones 8–10.

» **Foothill sedge or Berkeley sedge (*Carex tumulicola*):** This clump-forming plant grows 12 to 20 inches tall with arching, dark-green leaves. It spreads slowly by underground rhizomes, and mass plantings create a graceful, meadowlike groundcover. Native to western North America. Evergreen. Full sun to part shade. USDA Hardiness Zones 8–10.

» **Chamomile (*Chamaemelum nobile*):** This plant's fine-textured, aromatic foliage reaches about 6 inches high. Chamomile has white, daisylike flowers with yellow centers (herbal tea is made from the dried flowers). It is relatively drought tolerant and can withstand light foot traffic. Evergreen. Full sun. USDA Hardiness Zones 4–9.

» **Hardy ice plant (*Delosperma cooperi*):** This fast-growing plant has succulent, needlelike leaves and is covered with pinkish-purple, asterlike blooms in summer. Tolerant of hot, dry locations, it requires excellent soil drainage. Although this species readily spreads, it isn't considered invasive. However, there are other plants with the common name "ice plant" that are listed as invasive in some regions. Evergreen in regions with mild winters. Full sun. USDA Hardiness Zones 6–10.

» **Silver ponysfoot (*Dichondra argentea*):** Two-inch high, sprawling vines have silver-gray foliage with tiny white flowers that are barely visible. (The plant is frequently used as a trailing element in hanging baskets.) This heat-tolerant plant prefers moist, well-drained soil. Native to desert regions of the United States, including western Texas, New Mexico, and southeastern Arizona. Evergreen. Full sun. USDA Hardiness Zones 9–10.

» **Snake herb (*Dyschoriste linearis*):** This plant, which is similar in appearance to rosemary, grows 6 to 12 inches tall and sports lavender-to-purple flowers in spring, with occasional reblooming in late summer. It's drought tolerant and can withstand moderately wet conditions. Native to Oklahoma and Texas. Deciduous. Full sun to part shade. Zones 7–10.

» **Sweet woodruff (*Galium odoratum*):** Growing 8 to 12 inches tall, this plant has attractive whorls of glossy green leaves and blooms with small white flowers in spring and early summer. Also called sweet-scented bedstraw, the plant's foliage gives off the scent of freshly mown hay when cut or crushed. It prefers rich, moist soils and will go dormant in summer if allowed to dry out. Deer tend to avoid this plant. Deciduous. Part shade to shade. USDA Hardiness Zones 4–8.

WARNING

» **Aaron's beard or creeping St. John's wort (*Hypericum calycinum*):** *Note: this plant is considered invasive in some regions.* Sunny yellow flowers highlight this hardy plant, which grows 12 inches high. The plant spreads rapidly via underground stems and can be difficult to control once established. Deciduous. Full sun to part shade. USDA Hardiness Zones 5–9.

WARNING

» **Trailing lantana (*Lantana montevidensis*):** *Note: This plant is considered invasive in some regions.* This sprawling, semi-woody plant grows 12 to 18 inches tall and bears clusters of lavender-to-purple flowers in summer. (A white-flowered variety is also available.) Contact with the foliage may irritate the skin. Evergreen. Full sun. USDA Hardiness Zones 8–10.

» **Blue star creeper (*Laurentia fluviatilis*):** This plant spreads by runners to form a dense mat of foliage that grows just a few inches tall. In late spring and summer, tiny, star-shaped, pale blue or white flowers appear. It prefers evenly moist, sandy soil. Once established, it can tolerate light foot traffic and brief periods of drought. Evergreen in regions with mild winters. Full sun to part shade. USDA Hardiness Zones 5–9.

» **Lily turf (*Liriope muscari*):** This grasslike perennial grows in clumps about 12 inches high with arching, dark green leaves and spikes of flowers in summer. Varieties with variegated foliage are available. Set plants closely together and they'll grow to form a continuous ground cover. To keep plants looking tidy, shear them back to 3 to 4 inches in late winter, just prior to the appearance of new growth. A taller type, called "giant liriope," grows 18 to 24 inches tall. (Note that creeping lily turf, *Liriope spicata*, is considered invasive in some regions.) Evergreen in regions with mild winters. Part shade to shade. USDA Hardiness Zones 6–10.

» **Corsican mint (*Mentha requienii*):** This durable plant tolerates foot traffic, and it releases a refreshing minty scent when trod upon. Adaptable to a wide range of growing conditions, the plant grows well in full sun to part shade and prefers moist soil. Also called creeping mint, it's covered with pale lilac flowers in summer. Evergreen. USDA Hardiness Zones 6–9.

WARNING

» **Mexican feather grass (*Nassella tenuissima*):** *Note: This plant reseeds readily and is considered invasive in some parts of the country.* Mass plantings of this fine-textured, clumping grass create a tall, graceful groundcover growing 14 to 20 inches tall. The plant tolerates drought by going dormant and turning brown in hot, dry weather; it does not tolerate wet soil. Native to rocky scrublands and arid regions of Texas and New Mexico. Full sun. USDA Hardiness Zones 6–10.

» **Mondo grass or monkey grass (*Ophiopogon japonicus*):** This clump-forming, grasslike plant grows 6 to 8 inches tall, with dark-green arching foliage. A variety with very dark, almost black foliage is available, as is a dwarf form that grows just 3 to 4 inches tall. Valued for its tolerance to shady sites, it forms an attractive ground cover. Space plants closely and mulch around them to prevent weeds and keep soil moist as the clumps slowly fill in. Mow periodically if needed to keep tidy. Evergreen. Part shade to shade. USDA Hardiness Zones 6–10.

» **Mountain pea (*Orbexilum pedunculatum*):** This fast-spreading groundcover grows 8 to 12 inches tall with clusters of small purple flowers from late spring to midsummer. This deep-rooted legume is useful for erosion control. Shear it periodically to keep it compact. Also called Sampson's snakeroot. Native to the southern and southeastern United States. Full sun to part shade. Mostly evergreen. Zones 6–8.

» **Oregano (*Origanum vulgare*):** Although it naturally grows 10 to 24 inches tall, the plants can be kept shorter by shearing in late winter, cutting them back to a few inches high. Repeat the shearing as needed to remove upright shoots to promote horizontal growth. Also called wild marjoram. Deciduous. Full sun. USDA Hardiness Zones 6–10.

» **Allegheny pachysandra (*Pachysandra procumbens*):** Also called Allegheny spurge, this attractive foliage plant grows about 10 inches tall with whorls of dark green foliage. Prized for its adaptability, it grows best in moist, well-drained soil. Native to the central-southern United States, this species spreads more slowly than its close relative, Japanese spurge *(Pachysandra terminalis)*, which spreads by rhizomes to form large colonies and is considered invasive in some regions. Deer tend to avoid this plant. Evergreen in regions with mild winters. Part shade to shade. USDA Hardiness Zones 5–9.

» **Frogfruit (*Phyla nodiflora*):** Growing just 2 to 3 inches tall, frogfruit is becoming a popular lawn alternative. Sporting small, white blossoms on upright stalks, it tolerates brief drought periods but does best with moderate soil moisture. Other common names include turkey tangle frogfruit, sawtooth frogfruit, matchweed, and common lippia. Native to the southern half of the United States. Evergreen in regions with mild winters. Full sun to part shade. USDA Hardiness Zones 6–10.

» **Spring cinquefoil (*Potentilla neumanniana*):** Spring cinquefoil is a mat-forming plant with neatly lobed leaves and yellow flowers. Growing 3 to 6 inches tall, it prefers moist, well-drained soils and can withstand some foot traffic. It doesn't do well in areas with hot, humid summers. Evergreen in regions with mild winters. Full sun to part shade. USDA Hardiness Zones 4–8.

>> **Lungwort (*Pulmonaria* spp.):** There are several species of these low-growing ground covers. The foliage has interesting speckles, and the tiny, bell-shaped flowers turn from pink to violet as they mature. Deer tend to avoid this plant due to its fuzzy leaves. Evergreen in regions with mild winters. Part shade to shade. USDA Hardiness Zones 3–8.

>> **Sedum or stonecrop (*Sedum* spp.):** There are many species and varieties that offer a range of plant heights, foliage size and color, and blooms. Sedums require excellent drainage. The most common sedums used as groundcovers grow 4 to 6 inches tall. Several species are native to the United States. Some types are evergreen; others are deciduous. Full sun. USDA Hardiness Zones 6–10.

**WARNING**

>> **Wedelia (*Sphagneticola trilobata*):** *Note: This very vigorous spreader is considered invasive in Florida. Elsewhere, it's best planted in beds where building or sidewalk edges make it easier to contain its spread.* This plant grows 8 to 12 inches tall and bears 1-inch wide yellow flowers, especially in sunny locations. Shear back freeze-damaged foliage in early spring. Evergreen. Full sun to part shade. USDA Hardiness Zones 9–10.

>> **Woolly stemodia (*Stemodia lanata*):** This plant grows just 3 to 5 inches tall and spreads to form a mat of fuzzy, silvery-gray foliage with light purple flowers in summer. Requires a very well-drained site. Native to coastal and southern Texas. Evergreen in regions with mild winters. Full sun. USDA Hardiness Zones 9–10.

>> **Creeping germander (*Teucrium cossonii*):** Sporting silvery or dark green foliage, depending on the type, creeping germander grows about 6 to 10 inches tall with pink-lavender flowers in summer. Relatively drought tolerant, it also adapts to wet conditions better than most drought-tolerant ground covers. Evergreen. Full sun. USDA Hardiness Zones 6–10.

>> **Creeping thyme (*Thymus praecox*):** This spreading herb with aromatic foliage grows 3 to 6 inches high and features tiny, fuzzy, blue-green leaves. Creeping thyme is hardy and can withstand foot traffic, and the white to pink flowers are magnets for bees and other pollinators. The plant requires well-drained soils and is drought tolerant once established. Deer tend to avoid it. Evergreen. Full sun. USDA Hardiness Zones 4–9.

>> **Asian star jasmine (*Trachelospermum asiaticum*):** Slender, wiry stems grow 10 to 15 inches tall, sprawling to form a dense ground cover. Blooming with fragrant white flowers, the plant can tolerate brief periods of drought but grows best with consistently moist soil. Shear it back as needed to maintain a uniform height and appearance. Evergreen. Part shade to shade. USDA Hardiness Zones 7–10.

>> **Harebell speedwell or prostrate speedwell (*Veronica prostrata*):** This low-growing, mat-forming ground cover reaches 6 to 8 inches tall and spreads by horizontal stems. In late spring to early summer, the plants are covered with tiny, pale-to-deep blue flowers, with occasional rebloom in late summer. Shear plants after flowering to promote new growth. Other names include rock speedwell and *Veronica rupestris*. Evergreen in regions with mild winters. Full sun to part shade. USDA Hardiness Zones 5–8.

## Ground covers with a high potential to become invasive

**WARNING**

These popular ground cover plants are readily available, despite their tendency to become invasive in many regions and climates. Before choosing any of these plants, be sure to check your local laws and consider planting less aggressive options.

>> **Carpet bugle or bugleweed (*Ajuga reptans*):** *Note: The plant spreads aggressively via runners and is considered invasive in some parts of the United States.* Carpet bugle grows 4 to 6 inches high with glossy, deep green or purplish leaves. This hardy plant sports 8-inch spikes of blue flowers in spring and early summer. It prefers slightly acidic, moist soil. Evergreen. Part shade to full shade; can tolerate full sun in cool-summer regions. USDA Hardiness Zones 3–10.

>> **Lamium (*Lamium* spp.):** *Note: Lamiums are vigorous spreaders, and some types are considered invasive in some regions.* This group of mat-forming ground covers typically grow 5 to 8 inches tall and produce yellow or pink flowers. Spotted deadnettles (*Lamium maculatum*), especially the named varieties such as "White Nancy," appear to be a bit less aggressive than other lamiums. Yellow archangel (*Lamium galeobdolon*) is a particularly aggressive spreader and should be avoided or carefully contained. Most lamiums are evergreen in mild climates and deciduous in regions with cold winters. Lamiums prefer moist, well-drained soil and part shade to full shade. Most grow well in USDA Hardiness Zones 4–8.

>> **Aurea Creeping Jenny (*Lysimachia nummularia* "Aurea"):** *Note: This plant is considered invasive in many areas.* This plant forms a 2- to 4-inch-tall mat of foliage and readily spreads by creeping stems that root wherever they touch the ground. Bright yellow flowers appear in early summer. Other names include moneywort and creeping yellow loosestrife. The foliage of the variety "Aurea" ranges from bright lime green to soft chartreuse and the plant is generally not as aggressive as the darker-leaved species. Deciduous. Full sun to part shade. USDA Hardiness Zones 3–9.

» **Bigleaf periwinkle or greater periwinkle (*Vinca major*):** *Note: This aggressive plant is considered invasive in some regions.* Growing 6 to 8 inches tall, this vining plant has dark green leaves. It blooms in spring and occasionally throughout the summer, with phloxlike, violet flowers. It roots at the nodes along the vines and can spread quickly under favorable growing conditions. Evergreen. Full sun to part shade. USDA Hardiness Zones 6–9.

» **Dwarf periwinkle or lesser periwinkle (*Vinca minor*):** *Note: This vigorous spreader is considered invasive in some regions.* Growing 6 to 8 inches tall, this hardy and adaptable vining ground cover features dark green leaves and violet blue flowers in spring and sporadically throughout the summer. (A white-flowered form is also available.) It tends to be somewhat less invasive than *Vinca major*. Evergreen. Full sun to part shade. USDA Hardiness Zones 6–9.

**WARNING**

Avoid planting the following, which are nearly impossible to control once they become established:

» Goutweed (*Aegopodium podagraria*), also called bishop's weed or ground elder), including "Variegatum," a variety with variegated foliage that is sometimes called snow-on-the-mountain

» English ivy (*Hedera helix*)

» Chameleon plant (*Houttuynia cordata*, also known as rainbow plant)

## Shrubby ground covers

Shrubby ground covers include plants that have woody stems and are usually taller than the ones described in the preceding section.

» **Kinnikinnick or bearberry (*Arctostaphylos uva-ursi*):** This hardy shrub grows to about 12 inches high and sports small white flowers and red berries. It prefers acidic, well-drained, sandy soils and is tolerant of drought once established. Does not do well in regions with high humidity. Evergreen. Full sun to part shade. USDA Hardiness Zones 2–7.

» **Cotoneasters (*Cotoneaster* spp.):** This large group of deciduous and evergreen plants includes many excellent ground covers. Cotoneasters boast white flowers and red berries, and some deciduous types have beautiful fall color. Most prefer well-drained soil and full sun to part shade. Hardiness varies by species, but most do well in USDA Hardiness Zones 5–8.

>> **Junipers (*Juniperus* spp.):** These hardy evergreen plants have needlelike foliage that is rough to the touch. Tough and versatile, junipers come in many heights and some interesting foliage colors. Deer tend to avoid these plants. Hardiness varies widely by species. Creeping juniper (*Juniperus horizontalis*) grows 1 to 3 feet tall and is hardy in USDA Hardiness Zones 3–9.

# Growing Ferns

You'll find ferns in a wide range of shapes and sizes, with additional variation in the color and shape of the fronds. Because most ferns prefer part shade to full shade, they are good options for shady spots where turfgrasses struggle. (A few types of ferns will tolerate sunnier conditions.)

In addition to being good ground covers, ferns also make agreeable companions for shade perennials. Some ferns stay in tidy clumps, while others spread to form large colonies. Given the right conditions, most ferns are easy to grow and are relatively untroubled by diseases and pests. There are many types of ferns; here is a selection of popular species.

>> **Lady fern (*Athyrium filix-femina*):** Growing 2 to 3 feet tall, this fern has lacy, light green fronds. It prefers moist, well-drained soil, though it will tolerate drier soil than some ferns. It does best in part shade to full shade, though in northern areas the plants will tolerate some sun as long as the soil stays consistently moist. Rarely damaged by deer. The 'Lady in Red' variety has showy red stems and is slightly smaller than the species. Native to the Northeast and North-Central United States. Deciduous. USDA Hardiness Zones 3–8.

>> **Hay-scented fern (*Dennstaedtia punctilobula*):** The name of this compact fern refers to the fragrance of freshly mown hay that is released by the fronds when they're brushed with a hand or crushed. Growing about 2 feet tall, this plant is native to the Eastern and Midwestern United States. The lacy fronds turn yellow in fall. Deciduous. Part shade to shade. USDA Hardiness Zones 3–7.

>> **Marginal shield fern (*Dryopteris marginalis*):** Featuring dark gray-green fronds with a leathery texture, this fern grows in tidy, vase-shaped clumps up to 2 feet tall and doesn't readily spread. Native to the eastern United States, it's rarely damaged by deer. Other common names include marginal wood fern, marginal fern, and leatherwood fern. Evergreen in regions with mild winters. Part shade to shade. USDA Hardiness Zones 4–9.

» **Ostrich fern (*Matteuccia struthiopteris*):** This impressive fern can reach up to 6 feet tall in moist, cool conditions, though the plants often stay smaller in the landscape. Tolerant of a range of soil types, it grows best in rich soil that stays consistently moist and will spread by underground rhizomes to form dense colonies. The name likely refers to the fronds' resemblance to ostrich plumes. Native to the Northeast and North-Central United States. Deciduous. Part shade to shade. USDA Hardiness Zones 3–7.

» **Christmas fern (*Polystichum acrostichoides*):** With narrow, dark green fronds, this fern grows 1 to 2 feet high and prefers most, well-drained, acidic soil. Though individual plants will increase in size, the plants don't readily spread to form large colonies. The common name refers to the plant's tendency to remain green through the winter holidays in mild-winter regions. Part shade to shade. USDA Hardiness Zones 3–9.

» **Wood fern or river fern (*Thelypteris kunthii*):** This fern grows 2 to 4 feet tall with bright green, arching fronds. It prefers moist, humus-rich soil but will tolerate both wet soils and drought. It spreads by rhizomes to form large colonies and is ideal for wetland plantings. Rarely damaged by deer. Native to the Southeastern United States, the plant's other names include southern shield fern and southern maiden fern. Deciduous. Dappled sun to shade. USDA Hardiness Zones 7–10.

# Planting a Bee Lawn

If you're looking for a way to reduce lawn maintenance chores and support pollinators, a "bee lawn" might fit the bill. Bee lawns (sometimes called pollinator lawns) are areas planted with flowering ground covers, sometimes mixed with turfgrasses.

You can plant your entire yard in a bee lawn or just one section. If you're concerned about bee stings, site your bee lawn in an out-of-the-way place that gets little foot traffic. The perimeter of the yard and/or along a fence line are two good locations. (Consider planting a bee lawn in that hard-to-mow, impossible-to-irrigate strip between the road and sidewalk, too.)

If your neighbors or homeowners association would look askance at a full-on meadow in your front yard, they might be willing to accept — and even appreciate! — this colorful, low-growing alternative to a traditional lawn.

**TIP**

To support pollinators, you mow a bee lawn higher, and less often, than you do a traditional lawn. This allows flowers to bloom and provide pollen and nectar to pollinators. You must also refrain from using herbicides, insecticides, and fungicides on your bee lawn. You'll need to fertilize your bee lawn less often than a traditional lawn, and avoid excess nitrogen, which stimulates leafy growth at the expense of flowers.

## Choosing bee lawn plants

Although turfgrasses are especially suited to tolerate frequent mowing, there are also some flowers that adapt well to "lawn life." Here are some traits to look for in your bee lawn flowers:

>> Naturally low-growing

>> Tolerant of mowing

>> Produce flowers at low heights

>> Provide abundant nectar and pollen

>> Withstand foot traffic

>> Vigorous, so it won't get crowded out by grasses

>> Perennial, so they don't need to be replanted each year, or they readily self-seed

Here are some plants to consider for your bee lawn.

>> **Yaak Yarrow (*Achillea millefolium* var. 'Yaak'):** Rugged and adaptable, this plant grows well in a remarkable range of conditions. A compact form of a native western yarrow, it spreads by rhizomes. Like all yarrows, the flowers support a wide range of pollinators. It's especially adaptable to sandy soils and shows good tolerance to drought. Full sun to part shade. USDA Hardiness Zones 3–9.

>> **Lanceleaf self-heal (*Prunella vulgaris* ssp. *lanceolata*):** A member of the mint family, self-heal is a hardy, low-growing plant that, like other mints, spreads vigorously. The spikes of purple flowers are magnets for pollinators. Lanceleaf self-heal is native to the United States. (Another subspecies, *Prunella vulgaris* subsp. *vulgaris*, is native to Eurasia and is sometimes considered a lawn weed.) The plant grows best in soil that stays consistently moist and prefers full sun to part shade. USDA Hardiness Zones 4–9.

- » **Narrowleaf blue-eyed grass (*Sisyrinchium angustifolium*):** Although the foliage resembles grass, this plant sports small blue to blue-violet flowers on branching stems, in early to mid-spring. It prefers moist, well-drained soil and spreads by both seed and rhizomes. Native to the Eastern North America, it will grow in full sun to part shade, though it will flower most profusely in full sun. USDA Hardiness Zones 4–9.

- » **Creeping thyme (*Thymus praecox* subspecies *arcticus*):** This low-growing, adaptable plant is often planted between steppingstones, but it's just as at home in a bee lawn. Like its culinary cousin, this thyme has tiny, dark green leaves that release their signature fragrance when crushed (or walked on). It prefers well-drained soil and tolerates dry conditions, and it's commonly featured in xerlscapes (a type of landscaping that reduces or eliminates the need for irrigation). Creeping thyme grows 3 to 6 inches high, readily spreads to form a dense mat, and produces abundant, pinkish purple flowers that attract a variety of pollinators. The variety 'Coccineus' is especially showy. Full sun. USDA Hardiness Zones 4–9.

- » **Violets (*Viola* spp.):** Growing to a height of 4 to 6 inches, violets have heart-shaped leaves, and their purple flowers attract a variety of pollinators. They are also host plants for several types of fritillary butterfly larvae. Although they prefer moist soil, they are adaptable to a wide range of conditions and spread vigorously by both rhizomes and seeds. The common blue violet (*Viola sororia*) and sweet white violet (*Viola blanda*) are native to Eastern and Central North America and are good choices for bee lawns. Hardiness varies by species but most grow well in zones 3 to 7 or 8.

- » **Early-blooming bulbs:** Bulbs that flower in early spring are good additions to bee lawns, adding beauty and a supply of pollen and nectar when little else is in bloom. Many of these bulbs will readily multiply and spread to form a carpet of blooms. Good choices include crocuses (*Crocus* spp.), grape hyacinth (*Muscari* spp.), squill (*Scilla* spp.), snowdrops (*Galanthus* spp.), winter aconite (*Eranthus hyemalis*), dwarf iris (*Iris reticulata*), and glory-of-the-snow (*Chinodoxa* spp.). Other good options are dwarf varieties of daffodils and species tulips. Hardiness varies.

- » **Clovers, including microclover and Dutch white clover:** These legumes fix nitrogen, reducing fertilizer needs (learn about clovers in the "Considering Clovers" section later in this chapter).

- » **Turfgrasses:** The best cool-season grasses to include in a bee lawn include creeping red fescue, chewings fescue, and hard fescue, as well as Kentucky bluegrass. The best warm-season grass option is centipedegrass.

## Establishing a bee lawn

If your lawn is relatively healthy and weed free, and it consists of mostly bee-lawn-friendly grasses (see the preceding section), you may be able to over-seed the area with the desired flower seeds. The seeds need to contact the soil to germinate, so before sowing, mow the area very short to help expose the soil surface. Core aerating prior to planting is also helpful.

**TIP**

If your lawn is struggling and has lots of weeds, consider a full renovation by getting rid of existing vegetation prior to planting (refer to Chapter 7).

Sow seeds for your bee lawn in late fall or early spring. Water the seeds in well to ensure good contact with the soil. Once your bee lawn is up and growing strong, you can mow every two or three weeks, adjusting your mower deck to the highest setting.

# Considering Clovers

Prior to the introduction of broadleaf herbicides in the 1950s, many grass seed mixes included clover. (Most broadleaf herbicides and "weed-and-feed" products will kill clover.) Likely due the rise in popularity of these herbicides and their frequent use on lawns, many of today's grass mixes no longer contain clover, and many people now consider clover a weed. That's unfortunate, because adding clover to your lawn, or creating an entire lawn out of clover, confers many benefits.

>> Clovers are hardy, adaptable, resistant to pests and diseases, and thrive in full sun to medium shade.

>> They reduce the need for synthetic nitrogen fertilizers because, like all legumes, clovers form a mutually beneficial relationship with certain soil bacteria, allowing them to "fix" nitrogen — that is, to convert nitrogen in the air into a form that plants can use. That nitrogen helps feed nearby grasses.

>> The nectar-rich blooms attract pollinators like butterflies and bees, adding biodiversity to your landscape.

>> Clovers tend to need less frequent irrigation and are more drought tolerant compared to lawn grasses.

Note that, on its own, clover doesn't tolerate heavy foot traffic as well as lawn grasses. In areas of your lawn that get lots of use, use clover in combination with turfgrasses. There are numerous types of clover that can be added to turfgrasses or grown on their own:

>> **Strawberry clover (*Trifolium fragiferum*):** This clover adapts well to alkaline soils and grows in a range of sunlight conditions, from full sun to shade. USDA Hardiness Zones 4–8.

>> **Red clover (*Trifolium pratense*):** Featuring deep roots that make it particularly drought tolerant, red clover has pink to purple flowers. It grows 12 to 18 inches high but responds well to regular mowing. USDA Hardiness Zones 4–8.

>> **Dutch white clover (*Trifolium repens*):** Left unmowed, this clover will grow to a height of 8 to 10 inches but can be kept shorter with regular mowing. It prefers moist soils and full sun to part shade. USDA Hardiness Zones 3–10.

>> **Microclover (*Trifolium repens* var. 'Pirouette' and 'Pipolina'):** This relative newcomer is lower growing and has smaller leaves than the white clover from which it was developed. Growing just 4 to 6 inches tall, it stands up to foot traffic better than other clovers and tends to form fewer flowers. USDA Hardiness Zones 3–10.

# Going Wild with Wildflowers

If you want to bring a wild, natural beauty to your landscape, wildflower meadows are an attractive, long-blooming alternative to a traditional grass lawn. The show starts in spring with the earliest blooming flowers and continues nonstop until late fall. In winter, seed heads offer additional interest and attract birds.

Taking their cues from natural meadows, wildflower meadows incorporate a diversity of species that together support an abundance of butterflies, bees, and other wildlife. They require minimal maintenance, nurture soil health, help manage stormwater, and provide endless opportunities for enjoyment. Find out how to plant a wildflower meadow in Chapter 21.

# The Deck or Patio Solution

A deck or patio can be a useful and low-maintenance alternative to a lawn. Granted, this alternative can be quite a bit more expensive than turf, but the beauty and style that decks and patios add to a landscape are usually worth it.

Even in the front yard, many people find that a deck or patio — especially when combined with a fence or wall for privacy — can add character and utility to a house.

>> Decks are naturals wherever the ground is sloping or hilly. These structures can turn a rolling backyard of impossible-to-water-or-mow grass into very usable space. Decks are also very useful around old trees that cast too much shade for grass to grow well. Decks can be stained to match the house, covered and/or enclosed, or multitiered for even more interest.

>> You can create patios from many different materials, from exposed aggregate to brick to flagstone. Even just a plain concrete or decomposed-granite patio in the middle of a yard draws people out into the landscape. Tables and chairs set on a patio don't need to be moved for mowing.

IN THIS CHAPTER

» **Exploring the benefits of lawn trees**

» **Choosing trees for your landscape**

» **Caring for trees in lawns**

» **Caring for lawns growing under trees**

» **Looking at twelve lawn-friendly trees**

Chapter **20**

# Choosing and Caring for Trees in Your Lawn

awns and trees are a classic combination, but they don't always make good landscape partners. Some trees cast such heavy shade that no grass can grow underneath them. Other trees have thirsty roots that suck water out of the ground so fast that the grass is lucky to get a drop. Lawn grasses also can outcompete trees, especially young ones. The grass can hog all the water and nutrients, causing the tree to grow poorly.

Trees also can suffer from damage by lawn equipment. Improperly used, a lawn mower or string trimmer repeatedly striking the tree can damage the bark and girdle the trunk. This impedes the movement of water and nutrients, weakening and possibly killing the tree.

A tree can be an expensive addition to your landscape, so it makes sense to choose the species wisely. When you're planting the tree in your lawn, there are some additional considerations. This chapter shows you how to choose the right lawn tree and then care for it properly.

**WARNING**

Before you plant any trees, it's always a good idea to research the laws and regulations regarding trees in your area. If there's a homeowners association where you live, check the rules regarding which trees you can and can't plant in your yard.

# Exploring the Benefits of Trees

Trees offer many benefits. They provide habitat for wildlife, connect communities, and support our health. Neighborhood trees make an enormous contribution to air and water quality. Here are a few ways trees contribute to our well-being.

## In our landscape

Trees help define our property by providing visual interest and focal points. They can be used to frame desirable features and serve as screens to hide less appealing ones. Trees and shrubs increase privacy so we can more fully enjoy our yards. They also shield us from street noise and lights and intercept dust and other pollutants.

Trees help keep our homes more comfortable by casting cooling shade onto our houses, which can reduce summer air conditioning needs by up to 50 percent. Planted in strategic locations, trees and shrubs can also create windbreaks in the winter.

## In our communities

Trees provide shade, and they cool our cities by up to 10 degrees on a hot summer day. Studies have shown that neighborhood trees reduce residents' stress, improve overall health in children, and encourage physical activity. Big trees provide neighborhood gathering places that can foster a sense of connection and belonging. A healthy, community-wide tree canopy also boosts property values and increases civic pride among residents.

Trees help manage stormwater by absorbing rainfall, filtering pollutants, and reducing erosion, leading to safer, healthier neighborhood ecosystems.

According to the Arbor Day Foundation's 2024 Canopy Report, 91 percent of Americans believe trees help make neighborhoods more livable. However, 56 percent must drive to their nearest park or green space to experience the benefits of trees. Planting trees in our yards is a gift to our neighbors.

## In the larger ecosystem

Trees support an array of plants, insects, and animals. They offer food, shelter, and support birds during migration. Trees support aquatic life by providing habitat, shading streams to keep water cooler, and filtering pollutants. Native species in particular support native pollinators, birds, and other wildlife. As soon as you plant a tree, all sorts of animals begin to benefit from it.

## PLANTING TREES TO CONSERVE ENERGY

In bygone days, before people could flip a switch to turn on heat or air conditioning, landscaping played an important role in maintaining a comfortable home. Trees and shrubs were planted in certain spots so that they shielded the house from hot summer sun and cold winter winds. Trees were selected and sited to allow summer breezes to cool the house and winter sunshine to warm it.

According to a study published by the U.S. Environmental Protection Agency, trees planted strategically alongside buildings can decrease indoor temperatures by more than 15 degrees on hot, sunny days and allow window air-conditioning units to operate up to 10 percent more efficiently. A similar study conducted in California concluded that energy savings from reduced cooling needs ranged between 7 and 40 percent when container-grown trees were located in different positions around a house.

You might find old homesteads where tall deciduous trees on the southeast and southwest sides of a house shade it from morning and late-afternoon summer sun. Once leafless in autumn, these trees allow the winter sun to reach the house. Sometimes, the area on the south side of the house was left treeless. That's because in summer, the midday sun is so high in the sky that trees on the south side wouldn't provide much shade unless their branches overhung the roof. So it made sense to leave the south side of the house treeless to allow the midwinter sun, which is low in the sky, to warm the house unimpeded. Evergreen trees and shrubs were planted on the northwest (often the windiest) side of the house to block the wind.

# Choosing Trees for Your Landscape

You can grow almost any tree successfully in a lawn, provided you properly take care of the tree *and* the lawn. For example, you might need to prune densely growing tree branches to let more light through so that grass can grow underneath. You must also find ways to protect young trees from the damage from lawn mowers and trimmers.

The trees you plant now will impact your landscape for many years. The small oak sapling will provide generations to come with a shady retreat and the perfect spot for a treehouse or tire swing. Trees are an investment in time, money, and effort. It's comparatively simple to redo a perennial garden or even a lawn; removing a large tree is expensive, and replanting it with a different type will require patience as the tree grows to maturity. That's why it's so important to choose your trees wisely.

# Identifying your goals

Start by reviewing the benefits trees provide described earlier in this chapter and deciding on your goals for your tree planting efforts. Ponder these questions:

>> Are you looking for trees that offer shade to help cool your home in the summer? Provide a shady spot for your picnic table?

>> Do you want to add privacy to your yard? If so, are you looking for year-round privacy or just in summer, when you spend the most time in your yard?

>> Is your goal to beautify your landscape? Offer visual appeal and a focal point? Are you looking for a tree that blooms?

>> Are you hoping to harvest fruits or nuts?

# Incorporating trees into your landscape plan

Start by making a list of all the existing features in your landscape, such as patios, fences, arbors, walkways, and sheds. Then make a wish list of features you hope to add in the future. You'll want to keep all these in mind as you consider where one or more trees might fit in. You don't want to plant a tree that will shade a future vegetable garden.

Start putting your ideas down on paper. It's helpful to sketch a landscape map that shows a bird's-eye view of your property, including rough measurements. Draw in the location of the house, garage, driveway, walkways, gardens, and other existing features. Draw circles to indicate existing trees and shrubs. Sketch in planned additions, such as a future patio or deck. (See Chapter 1 for information on how to draw a landscape map.)

If your yard has low spots that collect water, note the locations of these. Few trees will thrive in soil where water puddles for more than a few hours after a rainstorm. You can improve drainage by regrading your yard, which is a big job but might be necessary to realize your dream landscape. (Learn about regrading in Chapter 7.) Or use that low-lying spot for a rain garden planted with moisture-loving plants.

Once you've completed your map, step back and take a realistic view. Are there open areas suitable for trees? How big are the spaces? Make a note of the dimensions; this will help you narrow down your options. For example, if space is at a premium, you'll probably want to stick with tree species that stay small or have an upright growth habit. As much as you might want a big ol' oak tree or weeping willow, they may not be wise choices and ones that you'll come to regret later.

**TIP**

If your landscape is large or has lots of elements, or if you're just unsure of where to start, you may want to hire a professional to help you decide what types of trees to plant and where. Although there's an upfront cost, getting professional advice can save you time, money, and aggravation in the long run. Learn about hiring landscape designers and landscape architects in Chapter 1.

# Understanding the Characteristics of Different Trees

To help you narrow down the many options you have for landscape trees, here are some important considerations.

## Height and spread at maturity

The height and the spread of a tree at maturity are fundamental dimensions worth thinking carefully about. Be realistic about how much space is available when researching different tree types for your yard. Even the best trees for small yards need room for healthy root development and canopy growth. Saplings at the nursery may look small and perfectly suitable for the space right now, so read plant labels and do your homework.

**WARNING**

The roots of certain trees spread wide, and if planted in the wrong place, the roots can damage sidewalks, underground drainage, septic lines, and foundations. Trees can block that window view that you love. Overhanging branches can loom over your roof, requiring frequent pruning and shedding leaves that clog your gutters.

**WARNING**

It's a common mistake to plant trees too close to overhead utility lines. If you're planning to plant a tree anywhere near overhead lines, consider very carefully the tree's mature size. If a tree you plant encroaches on power lines, you may be responsible for paying a certified line clearance arborist, who is trained to work near power lines, to remove the problem limbs. It's a big expense and can lead to disfigured trees with big gaps for the lines, or even complete removal of the tree.

**WARNING**

Don't plant a tree that gets too large for the space with the intention of cutting the top back to keep it to size. "Topping" trees results in an overgrowth of weak sprouts and creates wounds that are places for wood decay fungi to take hold.

Make sure you select trees that are appropriately sized for each specific planting site, with adequate room to grow to their full, mature glory.

# Overall shape of tree

Consider the size and shape of the tree. There are tall, narrow trees with a cone-shaped canopy; broad, spreading trees with canopies wider than the tree is tall, and everything in between. Consider how the shape of the tree will complement your home and other landscape plants. A line of narrow trees might be appropriate to define the edge of your property line but could look odd if just one of them is plopped into the middle of your front yard. If you're looking for tall, narrow trees, look for varieties described as "columnar."

Weeping forms of trees have branches that droop downward; the weeping willow is a familiar example. With graceful branches that sway in the breeze, weeping trees are often planted as "specimen" trees that are intended as a focal point in the landscape. Other than the weeping willow, most weeping trees have been introduced by plant breeders. Many are grafted, with a weeping portion grafted to a hardy trunk or rootstock. Because these trees require extra labor to produce (including grafting, frequent pruning, and careful staking for several years of their young lives), they are usually a more expensive option than standard trees. Weeping trees also require some extra care. For example, if the tree is grafted, the region of the graft can be weak and susceptible to insect pests and diseases, and any shoots that sprout below the graft must be removed regularly.

# Degree of shade they cast

The density of the branches and foliage will affect the amount of shade a tree casts. Some types of trees, such as aspens, birches, Japanese maples, and service-berries, have open, airy canopies that cast light, dappled shade. Sugar maples and oak trees, on the other hand, have dense canopies that create deep shade. If you hope to grow lawn or gardens beneath the tree, you'll likely want a tree that allows some sunlight to filter through.

TIP

If your landscape is mostly in full sun, planting a tree or two will greatly expand the palette of perennials and other plants you can grow. The dappled shade provided by a small tree is perfect for plants that need some, but not too much, sun. Many plants' flowers retain their color best if they receive some respite from the hot afternoon sun.

# Amount of sun or shade they need

Just like grasses and other garden plants, trees differ in the amount of sun they need. Most large trees, as well as fruit and nut trees, grow best in full sun. Some smaller-stature trees, like dogwoods, are adapted to grow in the understory beneath taller trees or at the edges of woodlands.

## Soil preferences

Different kinds of trees require different soil conditions, so knowing your soil type is important for choosing the best trees. Some trees require loose, well-drained soil, while others tolerate heavier clay. Some tolerate dry conditions once they're established, while others need consistently moist soil. Some prefer acidic soil, and others do best in neutral or alkaline soil. You get the picture.

Ideally, you'll choose trees that are adapted to your soil type and conditions, rather than trying to change your soil. Learn more about soil types in Chapter 6.

## Cold hardiness

Most garden centers only sell plants that are hardy enough to withstand the coldest winter temperatures in your region, but it's up to you to confirm this. And if you're buying plants from an online store, it will be totally up to you to make sure the species are suitably hardy. You can find your hardiness zone on the USDA Plant Hardiness Zone Map (`https://planthardiness.ars.usda.gov/`).

## Heat tolerance

In many parts of the country, summer heat plays a bigger role than cold hardiness in determining whether a plant will survive. In regions where soaring summer temperatures can really take a toll on plants, look to the American Horticultural Society's Heat Zone Map for guidance: `https://www.usbg.gov/sites/default/files/2024-06/AHS-heat-zone-map.pdf`.

## Evergreen or deciduous

Deciduous trees drop their leaves each autumn and grow new ones in spring. Examples include beech, elm, maple, oak, and willow trees. Fully leafed out, deciduous trees offer welcome shade in summer. When leaves drop in fall, winter sunlight can filter through the bare branches to warm you and your home.

Evergreens keep their foliage year-round. They're ideal for adding winter interest to your landscape and make good windbreaks to shield your home from cold winds. Evergreens increase privacy and block unsightly views throughout the year, and they provide a buffer from street noise and headlights. Many evergreens are conifers, meaning they bear cones, and many have needle-shaped leaves, including pines, firs, and spruces. There are also broad-leaf evergreens, such as camellia, holly, and sweet bay magnolia. Birds and other wildlife make abundant use of evergreens, especially during the winter, to protect them from the harsh weather.

## LOOK TO VARIETIES FOR SPECIFIC ATTRIBUTES

Plant breeders have given us an astonishing array of tree choices. They've introduced and created compact and dwarf varieties of tree species that would normally tower over our landscapes. They've developed varieties with wide-ranging attributes that set them apart from the parent species, such as unusual foliage and flower colors, different shapes and growth habits, and superior resistance to pests and diseases, among others.

For example, red maples (*Acer rubrum*) generally grow 40 to 70 feet tall with a spread of 30 to 50 feet. A variety called Armstrong (*Acer rubrum* 'Armstrong') reaches about 40 feet tall and just 12 feet wide at maturity, making it much narrower than the species. Another example is a variety of paper birch called Renaissance Reflection (*Betula papyrifera* 'Renci'); it's resistant to bronze birch borer, a major pest of paper birches.

Named varieties are often more expensive, but if they have qualities you want, or offer resistance to pests that are common in your region, they're probably worth the added cost.

Keep in mind that planting tall evergreens on the south side of your house can block winter sunlight from warming and brightening your home.

## Growth rate

A tree's growth rate depends on many factors, most importantly the species. Other factors include sun exposure, climate, and soil moisture and fertility. Note that dwarf and compact varieties of trees will grow more slowly than the species.

**WARNING**

Although it's tempting to look for fast-growing trees that will quickly reach an impressive size, this quality often comes with problems. Many trees touted for their speedy growth rates also have less desirable qualities, such as weak wood, short lifespans, aggressive root systems, and susceptibility to diseases. Consider the silver maple (*Acer saccharinum*). Native to the Eastern and Central United States, these trees grow quite large, and the wood is quite brittle. This combination leads to large limbs that can break off during strong winds and ice storms. Also, the thirsty roots are notorious for invading leaky underground pipes. If you have a large landscape and can plant this tree far from anything that could be damaged by falling limbs and invading roots, by all means go ahead and plant one. Otherwise, avoid it.

## FAST-GROWING TREES TO STEER CLEAR OF

These trees have negative qualities that outweigh the benefit of their fast growth. Some are also on many state and regional "please don't plant these" lists.

- **Leyland cypress (x *Cupressocyparis leylandii*):** Often planted as hedges, this tree can quickly grow to unmanageable heights, has a relatively short lifespan, and is susceptible to numerous insect pests and diseases.

- **Bradford pear (*Pyrus calleryana* 'Bradford'):** This tree's beautiful spring blooms and fast growth are more than offset by its weak wood and poor structure that leads to large branches splitting from the trunk, as well as its short lifespan and tendency to become invasive.

- **Lombardy poplar (*Populus nigra*):** This tree's fast growth and desirable columnar shape are offset by its weak branches that readily break, as well as its short life expectancy and tendency for its roots to damage sidewalks and invade sewer lines.

- **Norway maple (*Acer platanoides*):** Native to eastern and central Europe and western Asia, this adaptable tree quickly grows to an impressive size. However, the tree's shallow and extensive root system deprives nearby plants of moisture and nutrients, so much so that it outcompetes native species and is considered an invasive plant in some regions.

- **Empress tree (*Paulownia tomentosa*):** Native to Central and Western China, this wildly fast-growing species (growing up to 15 feet per year!) is sometimes called the "royal empress tree." It boasts huge leaves and showy, fragrant flowers. Unfortunately, its wood is weak and subject to breaking, and it freely self-sows via winged seeds, leading to its designation as an invasive plant in much of the eastern half of the United States.

# Habitat for wildlife

Birds love trees for resting, sheltering from storms, building nests, and raising their young. As anyone who has tried to grow fruit-producing trees like elderberries knows, birds will flock to berry-laden branches and gobble up the fruit (usually the day before you plan to harvest). Pollinators are drawn to flowering trees, and while they're nearby they might just pollinate some of the plants in your vegetable garden. Squirrels love trees and will entertain you with their antics and agility; chipmunks rely on trees to escape from predators. Countless types of wildlife nest in tree cavities.

According to some estimates, a single mature oak tree can support up to 2,300 species of insects, birds, mammals, fungi, and other organisms. This remarkable diversity of species relies on the tree for food, shelter, and breeding sites, both above and below-ground. As you consider what types of trees to plant, keep in mind your nonhuman neighbors and what types of trees might best support their well-being.

## Bloom season and color

What is more breathtaking than a cherry tree in full bloom or a crape myrtle bursting with summer color when few other trees are in bloom? No wonder flowering trees are such popular choices for home landscapes. With some careful planning (and depending on your climate), you may be able to plant a variety of trees that will offer color from spring to late summer (or even year-round — for fall and winter blooms, look to the witch hazels, *Hamamelis* spp.).

Some trees bloom in spring before the branches leaf out; redbud (*Cercis canadensis*) and star magnolia (*Magnolia stellata*) are two in this category. Keep in mind that, for some trees, blooms are followed by fruits and nuts. This characteristic can be a bonus, or a cleanup hassle.

## Production of fruit and nuts

If you love the idea of making crabapple jelly or harvesting pecans in your yard, fruit and nut trees might make sense for you. There are dozens of types to consider, and within each type there may be handful of varieties or, in the case of apples, about 7,500 varieties to choose from! Your local cooperative extension office is a good source of information on the best fruit and nut varieties for your region.

**WARNING**

To bloom and set fruit, most deciduous fruit and nut trees require a certain amount of chilling; that is, a certain number of winter hours between about 32 and 45°F. This is often expressed as a variety's "chilling requirement." If the tree doesn't receive adequate chilling, it may produce little or no fruit. Different types of fruit have different chilling requirements. And even different varieties of the same fruit often have different chilling requirements.

**WARNING**

Some fruits and nuts are self-pollinating, meaning that you can plant one tree and expect to get fruit. Peaches and most citrus are good examples. Plants like these are sometimes called "self-fruitful." Other types of fruits require cross-pollination from a different but compatible variety to produce the best crop; examples include apples and sweet cherries.

If you plant fruit and nut trees, be prepared to clean up after them, if necessary. Some create hazards to passersby (think ankle-twisting walnuts, the spiky balls of sweet gums, or the slippery mess created by crabapples). Some can create offensive odors, such as fruits dropped by female gingko trees.

## TREE POLLEN AND ALLERGIES

Some trees' flowers are pollinated by insects; others rely on the wind to carry their pollen. It's the latter that are the cause of so much allergy misery. Today's urban and suburban landscapes are packed with high-allergy trees and shrubs.

Some tree species bear separate male and female flowers on the same plant; others ("dioecious") bear male and female flowers on separate plants. Mulberries, for example, are widely planted dioecious trees in the United States. Because the female trees produce "messy" fruit, the landscape industry has for years promoted planting fruitless male trees as shade trees. The result is that copious amounts of pollen get released into the wind each spring, ready to torment those afflicted with allergies. Some cities have even banned the planting of male mulberry trees.

The Ogren Plant Allergy Scale (OPALS) measures the allergy potential of garden and landscape plants, including trees. As you consider what types of trees to plant in your yard, consider looking their OPALS rating (keeping in mind that pollen can travel great distances on the wind, so your neighborhood trees can still pose problems).

## Susceptibility to pests

Trees vary widely in their susceptibility to insect pests and diseases. For some species, plant breeders have introduced varieties that exhibit resistance to common pests. A local arborist or your cooperative extension office can provide guidance on pests and diseases that are common in your region, so you can look for trees that will resist them.

## Maintenance requirements

Another consideration is ongoing maintenance. Some types of trees require annual pruning, routine pest management, and extensive fall cleanup. Others are notorious for regularly shedding lots of twigs and sticks or big seed pods. Fruit trees, in particular, can be labor-intensive if you hope to get a decent crop. Newly planted trees require regular watering for the first few years to ensure they develop deep, extensive root systems. All trees benefit from some regular maintenance; see the section "Caring for Trees and the Lawns under and around Them," later in this chapter.

## Other considerations

Here are a few additional things to keep in mind.

>> Some trees produce low, horizontal branches that making mowing underneath them a challenge.

>> Some trees, such as hawthorns and some types of citrus, have sharp thorns along their branches; plant these well away from foot traffic.

>> Some trees are notorious for roots that invade leaky water and sewer lines.

>> Trees with large, shallow roots can crack and lift sidewalks.

WARNING

>> Be mindful of planting trees and shrubs that could grow in such a way as to obstruct traffic signals, stop signs, streetlights, and visibility of oncoming traffic.

WARNING

>> Watch out for poisonous trees and shrubs. For example, one or more parts of these common plants are toxic: oleander (*Nerium oleander*), black locust (*Robinia pseudoacacia*), chinaberry tree (*Melia azedarach*), and English yew (*Taxus baccata*).

# Buying Lawn Trees

Trees are generally sold in one of three forms:

>> **Growing in pots (sometimes called "containerized" or container-grown trees):** Young trees are often sold in 5-gallon black nursery pots, though saplings are sometimes sold in smaller containers. A 5-gallon nursery pot is about 12 inches in diameter and 12 inches tall and, oddly, it holds about 4 gallons. Larger trees are sold in larger pots, and these can get very heavy — a tree in a 25-gallon nursery pot can weight several hundred pounds. Trees growing in pots can get root-bound, a situation in which the roots completely fill the container and start circling the pot and wrapping around the perimeter. Avoid buying root-bound trees; they will struggle to get established in your landscape.

>> **Balled and burlapped (B&B) trees:** Trees are sometimes sold with the roots wrapped in burlap. These trees are dug from the ground, and the root balls are wrapped in burlap and sometimes placed in a wire cage to keep soil and roots contained. This technique is usually reserved for larger trees. They are often so heavy that they require professional help to deliver them, dig the planting holes, and set them in place.

>> **Bareroot:** These trees are generally small saplings that have been dug and stored without any soil around their roots. They are often shipped in boxes with the roots wrapped in moist sawdust or peat moss. The availability of bareroot trees is usually limited to late winter or early spring because they're shipped and should be planted while the trees are still dormant. That said, quality bareroot trees have healthy root systems that grow quickly after planting. Fruit trees are often sold in bareroot form.

**WARNING**

Although it's tempting to buy the biggest tree possible, so you get the biggest immediate impact in your landscape, this isn't always the best idea. For starters, the bigger the tree, the more expensive it will be. Additionally, you may need to have it delivered and hire professionals to dig the planting hole and set the tree in place. Also, large trees often struggle to get established after planting. If you want to plant large trees, it's best to work with an established nursery and/or landscaping company that offers the full scope of services, from selling high-quality trees to delivering and planting them to backing them up with a guarantee.

Small trees are less impressive when newly planted, but with proper care, they'll settle in more readily than large trees. Once their roots get established, they'll grow surprisingly quickly.

# Planting Lawn Trees

When planting a tree, you want to place it so that the root flare (the area at the base of the trunk that flares out slightly from the trunk above it) is several inches above ground level. Never bury the flare; this can quickly lead to rot.

**WARNING**

**1.** **Dig a hole just deep enough to accommodate the depth of the root ball and at least twice the diameter of the root ball.**

Don't dig the hole any deeper; this risks the tree settling into the loose soil. This can create a depressed area around the trunk that's prone to collecting water, which can lead to rot. Planting too deep is the top reason that trees and shrubs die.

**2.** **If the tree is in a nursery pot, check the root ball for circling roots when you remove it from the container.**

If you find any, loosen them from the rest of the root ball. If you can't loosen them, cut them off with pruners. If the tree is wrapped in burlap, remove the wire cage, if any, and the burlap.

**WARNING**

Although most burlap is made from jute or hemp and is biodegradable, some types are made from synthetic materials that won't biodegrade. And even biodegradable burlap can inhibit root growth. It's usually best to remove it to be on the safe side.

**3.** **Gently place the tree in the hole.**

Begin backfilling with the soil you removed from the hole, watering the soil as you go to settle it. Continue backfilling until the hole is filled.

**WARNING**

Don't amend the soil you use for backfilling with compost or other soil amendments. Doing so will encourage the roots to remain within that fortified area rather than venturing out into the native soil. You want the roots to reach as far and wide as possible.

**4.** **Grade the soil to create a slight slope away from the tree's trunk.**

This ensures water drains away from the trunk, rather than pooling there where it can cause rot.

**TIP**

Using some of the leftover soil, create a 3- to 4-inch-high ridge of soil around the outer edge of the planting hole to create a temporary berm. This berm will create a basin to hold irrigation water so it can soak into the area around the roots rather than running off. After one growing season, you can knock down the berm, because by then the roots should have ventured into the surrounding soil.

5. **Apply an organic mulch, such as shredded bark or pine straw, over the soil.**

   Keep the mulch a few inches from the trunk to prevent rot.

Your local nursery or cooperative extension service will have additional helpful resources to further guide you on tree planting.

# Caring for Trees and the Lawns Under and Around Them

Trees growing in lawns need special care and protection. Here are some guidelines on how to keep both your trees and lawn healthy.

## Plant shade-tolerant grasses under trees

St. Augustinegrass, zoysiagrass, and many of the fescue grasses are more tolerant of low light than sun-loving turfgrasses, such as bermudagrass and Kentucky bluegrass. If you already have trees, or if you plan to have trees, plant a lawn grass with a known tolerance of shade. For more about selecting a lawn grass for shade, see Chapters 4 and 5.

TIP

Note that even "shade-tolerant" grasses won't grow in deep shade. In these areas consider growing shade-tolerant ground covers (see Chapter 19) or look at other alternatives (see "Other options for deep shade under trees," later in this chapter).

## Prune lower branches

You can do selective pruning on mature trees with dense canopies to allow more light to reach the lawn. Prune out some of the interior branches to allow more light to pass through to the lawn. Simply removing a branch here and there can make a significant difference in the amount of light available to the grasses. You can also "limb up" trees by removing some of the lowest limbs.

WARNING

If you're unsure about pruning, have an arborist do it for you. Pruning mistakes on mature trees can be unsightly, cause structural problems, and invite pest and disease problems. Pruning errors on young trees can lead to unstable and unsightly growth later on, as the tree matures.

## Mow high

Raise the cutting height of your mower for grass in shady areas. Longer grass blades have more surface area to capture whatever sunlight makes it through the tree canopy and down to the grass. Although it can't completely make up for the scarcity of sunlight, it will help.

# Water trees differently from the lawn

Using a sprinkler to apply water to your lawn to a depth of 6 to 8 inches is the standard to support healthy grass with deep roots (see Chapter 11 for details on watering lawns), but it's not the best way to water trees. Soaker hoses, drip irrigation, or a hose with a hose-end bubbler attachment are better options. These allow you to better target where the water goes.

**WARNING**

Adjust lawn sprinklers so that the water wets the area near the trunk but not the trunk itself. Keeping bark continuously wet invites rot and problems with insects and diseases.

## Watering newly planted trees

Water newly planted trees regularly, focusing your efforts on the root ball right around the trunk as well as the area around it, moistening the soil to the depth of the original root ball. This will encourage the roots to expand out into the surrounding soil, rather than staying within the original area of the root ball. Note that the soil in the root ball can dry out faster than the surrounding soil, so check both the root ball and surrounding soil frequently — at least twice a week in hot, dry weather. See the tip on creating a temporary berm to hold the water in the "Planting Lawn Trees," earlier in this chapter.

Keep a close eye on watering for the first two or three years, especially during hot, dry spells. These first few years are critical ones for your new trees.

## Watering established trees

Water established trees — those that are three years old and older — so that soil is moistened to a depth of at least 12 inches. Start by noting the tree's drip line (draw an imaginary line on the ground where drips from the outermost leaves of the canopy would fall). Because a tree's root zone can extend well outside the widest branches, you need to water the area both under the tree and several feet beyond the drip line. The larger the tree, the larger the tree's root zone. There's no need to apply water right up against the trunk; there are few water-absorbing roots there, and any water that pools there can promote rot.

**TIP**

You can't tell how deeply water has penetrated by looking at the soil, you have to check. One simple way is to probe the ground with a stiff metal rod or long screwdriver. The rod moves easily through wet soil and then stops, or becomes difficult to push, when it reaches dry soil. You can also buy a soil probe at a local nursery or irrigation supply store. The probe removes small cores of soil that you can feel to see how wet they are.

**WARNING**

Frequent shallow watering results in shallow surface roots in trees — you don't want those. Shallow surface roots are prone to drying out, and over time, they also create bumps that make mowing difficult. In contrast, deep, extensive root systems helps trees stay anchored and allows them to withstand periodic dry spells.

# Fertilize lawns less in shade

Grass that's growing under trees must compete with tree roots for moisture and nutrients. And because most turfgrasses prefer sunny conditions, lawn growing in shade leads a more stressed, trouble-prone existence. Improper fertilizing adds to those troubles. Overdo the fertilizing and the grass becomes overly lush and disease prone. Too little fertilizer and the grass loses out to the roots of the tree, becomes thin, and dies.

How to feed lawn under trees "just right"? Calculate the proper amount of fertilizer for the whole lawn and then give the area in the shade about 20 percent less. It's also best to choose slow-release or organic fertilizers that provide a slow, steady supply of nutrients.

# Fertilizing trees sparingly

An annual application of compost under your trees and to the area surrounding them benefits both the trees and the lawn. Organic mulches, such as shredded bark, also provide nutrients as the material decomposes. Other than that, trees adapted to your soil conditions generally need little to no additional fertilizer.

That said, trees that show signs of struggling, such as pale green foliage and undersized leaves, may need addition fertilization to stimulate more robust growth. However, it's often best to consult an arborist if trees are struggling because there are many possible causes.

# Be wary of "weed-and-feed" products

**WARNING**

Some fertilizers include an herbicide, fungicide, and/or insecticide in their formulations. "Weed-and-feed" products, for example, contain fertilizer to supply nutrients and herbicide to control weeds. Although popular, combination fertilizers pose problems. Applying them to lawn areas under trees and near shrubs and gardens can result in root damage from the herbicide.

When working with weed-and-feed products, read the labels carefully. Weed-and-feed products can contain some herbicides that harm trees if you apply the product over a tree's root zone, an area that can extend well outside the widest branches. If you have any trees or shrubs in your lawn and are the least bit unsure if a weed-and-feed product is safe to use around them, don't use it. (Learn more about weed-and-feed products, including the problems they pose, in Chapter 12.)

# Mulch under trees

Keep a grass-free zone around the trunks of trees (especially young ones). Mulching this area helps soil retain moisture and keeps it cool. Mulching also creates a buffer between the trunk and mowers and trimmers (more on that below). Make the mulched area at least 3 feet in diameter (larger for bigger trees) and cover it with a 2- to 3-inch-deep layer of organic mulch, such as shredded bark or pine straw. Keep the mulch a few inches away from the trunk to minimize the risk of rot. As the mulch breaks down, it adds organic matter to the soil. You can refresh the mulch every year or as needed, but make sure the depth of the mulch never exceeds 3 or 4 inches. Mulch that's too deep causes roots to grow upward into the mulch, and it can prevent water and air from reaching roots.

**WARNING**

Never apply mulch "volcano-style" around trees! Piling mulch against tree trunks traps moisture against the bark, which can lead to rot, fungal diseases, and insect infestations.

# Protect the trunks

A grass-free zone is the best way to protect tree trunks from damage by mowers and trimmers. Although a variety of tree wraps are sold to serve this purpose, they generally aren't a good idea. Tree wraps hold moisture against the bark, which creates an ideal environment for diseases and pest insects.

Tree wraps are useful for protecting trees in winter from damage by sunscald, temperature fluctuations, and gnawing rodents. Most wraps should be removed during the growing season.

# Lawn Alternatives for Deep Shade Under Trees

Rather than struggling to get grass to grow in a spot that's too shady for it to thrive, consider other options.

>> Numerous ground covers adapt well to the shady spots under trees; see Chapter 19 for suggestions.

>> Plant shade-tolerant perennials or shrubs, such as hostas, astilbes, and azaleas.

>> Mulch the area under the tree (see the "Mulch under trees" section earlier in this chapter) and place a bench, hammock, bistro set, or picnic table there. Add some containers planted with shade-tolerant annuals, such as impatiens to create an inviting shady retreat.

>> Install some fun garden art in the mulch or ground cover, such as a wind spinner or sculpture. You won't have to mow around it.

# Thirteen Lawn Trees to Consider

There are so many options for lawn trees, and the best choices for you depend on many factors. Just to get the wheels turning, here are some common deciduous trees that get along with lawns. Most adapt well to a variety of growing conditions and climates.

Wherever you live, consult with your favorite tree nursery or local cooperative extension office to get their recommendations prior to purchase.

## Serviceberry (*Amelanchier* spp.)

Showy white flowers in early spring are followed by edible, dark red fruits much loved by birds. These trees are easily grown in full sun to part shade, and they're tolerant of a wide range of soils. Mature height is 15 to 25 feet. There are numerous species of *Amelanchier*, most of them native to North America. The trees have attractive silvery bark and, in fall, colorful foliage. The various species go by numerous common names, including juneberry, saskatoon, shadblow, and shadbush. Most are hardy in USDA Hardiness Zones 4–9.

# Japanese maple (*Acer palmatum*)

Delicately lobed leaves and brilliant orange, red, or yellow fall color are the Japanese maple tree's claims to fame. Many varieties are available that offer foliage other than green (usually purplish or red); tree shapes (some are very small and weeping); and leaf patterns (some are very finely cut, almost feathery). Japanese maples prefer well-drained soil and ample water. In hot, arid climates, Japanese maples need a location with afternoon shade, such as the east side of the house, and protection from wind. The most common unnamed varieties grow to about 20 feet high. USDA Hardiness Zones 5–8.

# Birch (*Betula* spp.)

Loved for their striking bark and bright yellow fall color, birches make fine lawn trees — that is, if you live in an area with summer rainfall and relatively cold winters. In the dry-summer West and mild-winter deep South, birches are pest-prone and usually short-lived. But in other regions, they usually do just fine as long as the soil stays consistently moist. Some types are available as either single-trunk or multitrunk trees. Most are hardy in USDA Zones 5–8.

The paper birch or canoe birch, *B. papyarifera,* is native to the northern United States. It has white bark that peels off to reveal the orange-brown inner bark and needs consistently moist soils. The European white birch, *B. pendula,* is similar but is native to Europe and Asia. The river birch, *B. nigra,* has peeling pink to dark-brown bark and is more tolerant of heat.

# Eastern redbud (*Cercis canadensis*)

The Eastern redbud has lovely red flowers in early spring and lobed leaves. It grows about 25 to 35 feet high and does best in areas with some winter chill. In warm climates, it grows best in part shade; elsewhere it likes full sun. Native to eastern and central North America, this tree is relatively tough and adaptable. Some named varieties have purplish red leaves. USDA Hardiness Zones 4–8.

# White fringetree (*Chionanthus virginicus*)

Often multistemmed and somewhat shrubby with a mature height of 12 to 20 feet, this tree bears abundant, creamy white, fragrant flowers in late spring, followed by dark blue fruit that's attractive to birds. It prefers full sun to part shade and adapts well to urban settings, but it won't tolerate prolonged dry conditions. Native to the eastern United States, it's relatively low maintenance and seldom needs pruning. USDA Hardiness Zones 3–9.

# Flowering dogwood (*Cornus florida*)

One of the most beloved spring-flowering trees, flowering dogwood is native to the eastern United States, which is where it really does best. That said, in some regions, a disease called dogwood anthracnose has taken hold, making it inadvisable to plant this tree (check with your cooperative extension office). If the disease is a problem in your area, Kousa dogwood (*Cornus kousa*) is a good alternative. In dry heat, dogwoods do better in partial shade. Be especially careful to keep the lawn mower and string trimmer away from the trunks of dogwoods because wounds to the bark invite borer infestations. Dogwoods usually grow about 20 to 30 feet high. USDA Hardiness Zones 4–8.

# Franklin tree (*Franklinia alatamaha*)

This tree, which produces camellialike, fragrant white flowers with yellow centers in late summer to early fall, reaches 15 to 30 feet tall at maturity, with an open, airy form. Foliage begins turning showy red in autumn, even as the tree continues to bloom. All trees in cultivation descend from cuttings taken from a tree in Georgia in the late 1700s; it's extinct in the wild. The tree prefers full sun to part shade and organically rich soil that is moist yet well-drained. USDA Hardiness Zones 6–8.

# Ginkgo (*Ginkgo biloba*)

Grow the ginkgo for its stunning yellow fall color and neat-looking fan-shaped leaves. Sometimes called maidenhair tree, ginkgos grow slowly but can eventually get huge — upward of 80 feet high. Leaves drop all at once, making for easy, one-time cleanup. Make sure that you get a male variety such as 'Autumn Gold.' If the tree isn't labeled as being fruitless, ask your nursery expert. Female trees drop fruit that is so messy and smelly that another common name is stinkbomb tree. USDA Hardiness Zones 3–8.

# Carolina silverbell (*Halesia carolina*)

Named for the dainty, white, bell-shaped flowers that hang from its branches in early spring, this tree prefers well-drained but moist soils, preferably acidic. Sometimes called mountain silverbell, it generally grows to a height of 30 feet but can grow taller in ideal growing conditions. The wood is relatively brittle and prone to breaking, so plant it in a place protected from wind. USDA Hardiness Zones 4 - 8.

### Golden rain tree (*Koelreuteria paniculata*)

Leaves emerge pinkish bronze to purplish in spring, mature to a bright green in summer, and turn yellow in fall. Brilliant yellow flowers bloom in midsummer, followed by unusual, papery, Japanese–lanternlike fruit. This tree is tough once it gets established (three to four years after planting), reaching 35 to 40 feet high at maturity. USDA Hardiness Zones 5–9.

### Sweetbay magnolia (*Magnolia virginiana*)

The fragrant, creamy white blossoms that appear in late spring to early summer are similar to, but smaller than, southern magnolia blossoms. The unusual seed-pods contain bright red fruits that are attractive to birds. A host plant for swallowtail butterflies, sweetbay prefers consistently moist soils; Mature height is around 30 feet. USDA Hardiness Zones 6–9.

### Palo verde (*Parkinsonia* spp.)

Native to the deserts of the Southwestern United States, the palo verde tree has bright green bark and small leaves that it sheds during drought conditions. In spring it produces abundant yellow flowers that attract pollinators. The tree casts light shade and thrives in the searing desert heat. The 'Desert Museum' variety is a popular choice because it's thornless. Mature height is 20 to 30 feet. USDA Hardiness Zones 8–11.

### Chinese pistache (*Pistachia chinensis*)

Glorious red, yellow, or orange fall color and finely cut leaves that cast wonderful shade make this an attractive lawn tree. Widely adapted to all but the coldest climates, Chinese pistache has a spreading habit, reaching at least 50 feet high and nearly as wide. It grows best in full sun but will tolerate light shade. There are separate male and female trees. Planting male trees eliminates the mess of fallen fruits. USDA Hardiness Zones 6–9.

# Trees and Shrubs to Avoid

**WARNING**

Avoid planting these trees and shrubs, due to their tendency to become invasive. Although they may be well-behaved in your yard, when birds and other wildlife inadvertently spread these species through their fruit or seeds, the plants can take hold in new areas and crowd out native species. Consult your state's department of natural resources and/or native plant society to learn about invasive species in your area.

- » Amur maple (*Acer ginnala*)
- » Boxelder (*Acer negundo*)
- » Norway maple (*Acer platanoides*)
- » Tree-of-heaven (*Ailanthus altissima*)
- » Japanese barberry (*Berberis thunbergii*)
- » Autumn-olive (*Elaeagnus umbellata*)
- » Burning bush (*Euonymus alatus*)
- » Chinese lespedeza (*Lespedeza cuneata*)
- » European privet (*Ligustrum vulgare*)
- » Japanese honeysuckle (*Lonicera japonica*)
- » Amur honeysuckle (*Lonicera maackii*)
- » Morrow's honeysuckle (*Lonicera morrowii*)
- » Tatarian honeysuckle (*Lonicera tatarica*)
- » Chinaberry tree (*Melia azedarach*)
- » White mulberry (*Morus alba*)
- » Heavenly bamboo (*Nandina domestica*)
- » Amur corktree (*Phellodendron amurense*)
- » Callery pear (*Pyrus calleryana*)
- » Common buckthorn (*Rhamnus cathartica*)
- » Glossy buckthorn (*Rhamnus frangula*)
- » Black locust (*Robinia pseudoacacia*)
- » Siberian elm (*Ulmus pumila*)

Chapter **21**

# Planting a Wildflower Meadow

Wildflower meadows are an attractive, long-blooming alternative to a traditional grass lawn. When you plant a meadow with a wide variety of species, the flower show starts in spring with the earliest bloomers, and it continues nonstop until late fall. In winter, seed heads offer additional interest and attract birds. Meadows change with the seasons, and that's part of their appeal and charm. One week, you might be enjoying swaths of yellow blooms and then the next week, blues and purples might take center stage. A meadow is like a symphony that plays all summer long, with peaks of high-volume color and valleys of subtle hues.

Meadows soften the transition between cultivated landscapes and the natural areas that surround them. They also support an abundance of butterflies, bees, and other wildlife. Planting a meadow doesn't have to be an all-or-nothing proposition. Adding even a small area of wildflowers and native grasses to your property supports your local ecosystem by providing food and habitat for resident and migratory pollinators, birds, and animals.

Compared to a manicured lawn, wildflower meadows require minimal maintenance. They need little supplemental water and fertilizer and infrequent mowing
(or none at all). This chapter is all about bringing a meadow's wild, natural beauty
to your landscape.

# Choosing Meadow Plants

There are different types of meadow plantings, so it pays to define your goals and
make a plan. Start by considering the overall look of your landscape, including
your home's architectural style. You'll want your new meadow to complement
your home, and, if it will be visible from the front yard, you may also want to take
into consideration the styles of homes and landscapes in your neighborhood.

For example, if you live on a large lot in a windswept prairie, a meadow that combines native grasses with tough, drought-tolerant wildflower species might fit the
bill. If you live in a cottage-style house on a modestly sized lot, planting wildflowers (without any grasses) would add loads of color in a compact space. If you're
concerned about a tall meadow overwhelming your landscape (or raising concerns
among your neighbors) you can create a low-profile meadow by choosing low-
growing species.

## Native grasses

Native grasses are superbly adapted to their native ranges and often well-adapted
to other areas, too. Grassland-style meadows have a strong component of native
grasses that are accented by flowers and sometimes shrubs, mimicking the native
prairie grasslands of the Midwestern and Central United States.

Native grasses that are good choices for meadows include blue grama (*Bouteloua
gracilis*) and buffalograss (*Bouteloua dactyloides*), which are both warm-season
grasses native to the Great Plains. Red fescue (*Festuca rubra*) is a cool-season grass
native to much of the United States.

Most natural meadows contain abundant grasses, which provide nesting habitat
for wildlife and offer structural support to prevent tall flowers from flopping.
Grasses act as a living mulch, covering the soil between flowering plants to prevent weeds from taking over. However, avoid mixing traditional turf-type grasses
with your wildflowers; most are aggressive growers that will outcompete the
flowers and take over. Stick to native and bunch-type grasses.

**WARNING**

# BEWARE THE "MEADOW-IN-A-CAN" PROMISE

Don't be fooled into believing you can get an instant meadow because the product label shows a field of lush and colorful flowers. You can't just open a shaker can, sprinkle seeds over a weedy patch, and expect a miraculous transformation.

While it's true that wildflower meadows require less irrigation, fertilizing, and mowing than traditional lawns, they aren't maintenance-free. In particular, it takes time and effort to prepare the planting site properly to ensure the meadow plants have a chance to get established without competing against turfgrasses and weeds.

Be sure to read wildflower seed packages carefully; some contain less than 10 percent seeds, with the remaining 90 percent or more made up of fillers (sometimes called "inert matter" on the label). Although the inert matter can help you disperse the seeds evenly, it's usually best to buy seed mixes that contain 100 percent seed, so you know what you're paying for. You can then mix the seeds with sand to help you spread them evenly.

## Wildflowers

Wildflowers are most often planted from seed; it's the easiest and most economical method. Small meadows can be started from small plants or plugs. Here are a few ways that wildflower seed is typically sold:

» **Regional mixes:** Some seed companies combine seeds for wildflowers that are well adapted to specific regions. Although there will be some overlap of the most adaptable species, the mixes often include some regionally adapted flowers. For example, you might find seeds for Canadian columbine (also called eastern red columbine) in a northeast wildflower seed mix but not in a mix designed for the arid Southwest.

» **Annual mixes:** Annual plants have a one-year life cycle; they grow, bloom, and set seed in one growing season, and then die. Some annuals readily self-sow, meaning the seeds they drop will sprout and grow the following season. Others must be reseeded each year. Annuals are quick to bloom and offer some of the most exuberant color. They're ideal for temporary plantings, for areas you plan to replant each year, and for overseeding an existing wildflower meadow.

» **Perennial mixes:** Perennial plants live for three or more years, returning each season from the overwintering root system. Some perennial wildflowers take a year or two to get established before they begin to bloom. (Perennial mixes may also include biennials, which have a two-year lifecycle.) Perennial wildflowers are the workhorses of a wildflower meadow. The plants grow stronger and bloom more with each passing year.

>> **Annual/perennial mixes:** Combining the benefits of both, these blends offer abundant color from the annuals in the first season, and the staying power of the perennials in subsequent years.

>> **Single-species seeds:** If you have a particular color scheme in mind or relish in the creativity of designing your own meadow, consider buying seeds for individual species and combining them yourself. Be sure to include flowers with a variety of bloom times for season-long color.

>> **Sun or shade mixes:** Most wildflowers prefer full sun (at least six hours of direct sun each day). Some species will grow well in part shade (at least four hours per day) and in the dappled shade cast by trees with thin canopies. Although some wildflowers will grow in shade, blooming is usually diminished. (If you're looking for lawn alternatives for shady spots, see Chapters 19 and 20.)

>> **Native species:** Many people are passionate about choosing native species for their landscapes, and with good reason. A plant in its natural habitat is well adapted to the climate, fills an ecological niche, and is less likely to spread rampantly and become a problematic invader. Native wildflowers are particularly important in supporting native pollinators, including serving as host plants for butterfly and moth larvae.

>> **Pollinator mixes:** Although most wildflowers offer nectar, pollen, and habitat for pollinators, some flower species are particularly generous in this regard. Most pollinator mixes will include some native species.

>> **Low-growing mixes:** Most of the plants in these mixes grow to heights of 6 to 12 inches, making them ideal for areas where taller plants would be overwhelming or impede visibility. They're particularly good options for hard-to-mow areas, hillsides, and the strip between the sidewalk and the street. A low-growing meadow might cause less of a stir with neighbors who are used to manicured lawns, too.

## SUPPORT POLLINATORS WITH BEE CITY USA

According to Bee City USA, the United States is home to about 3,600 types of native (wild) bees, including species of bumble bees, leafcutter bees, sweat bees, mason bees, longhorn bees, and mining bees. Native pollinators evolved alongside native plants and, in many cases, they are the plants' most effective pollinators.

# Ten Steps to Planting a Meadow

The more care you take in preparing the area and planting your meadow, the greater the chance you'll get the results you're hoping for.

## Choose a site

Look for a spot in full sun (at least six hours per day) with well-drained soil. If your chosen spot is in part shade (four to six hours of sun) or the soil is on the wet side (low-lying areas that drain poorly), you'll want to choose plants adapted to those conditions.

## Decide what to plant

Browse the many options you have for flowers and grasses. Decide what plants you want to grow and how you'll plant them (seeds, plants, plugs). You can order seeds ahead of time but wait to purchase plants until the planting area is ready (see the "Prepare the planting area" section later in this chapter).

## Decide when to plant

If you live in a warm-winter climate, early to mid-fall planting is ideal. The soil is warm enough to ensure good germination. The cooler air temperatures and winter rains give plants a chance to get established before things heat up the following spring. You can also sow seeds of annual wildflowers in early spring.

In cold-winter climates, plant wildflower seeds after your last frost date when soil has warmed to 55°F. If you want to sow seeds in fall, wait until you've had a few hard frosts and soil temperatures have dropped into the 40s. This will prevent seeds from germinating and growing, only to freeze with the next cold snap. The seeds will lay dormant and sprout in spring.

## Prepare the planting area

Prepare the soil in much the same way you would if you were planting a lawn by seed. You'll need to get rid of any existing lawn grasses and weeds. Don't skimp on this step! Nonchemical options include tilling, renting a sod cutter, and smothering the sod. Chemical options include herbicides. (Find detailed instructions on preparing a planting area in Chapter 7.)

## Mix the wildflower seeds with sand

Most wildflower seeds are tiny (very tiny — think poppy seeds). To make it easier to sow them evenly, you'll want to mix the seeds with clean, dry sand. Aim for a ratio of about six parts sand to one part seed. Mix the sand and seeds thoroughly in a large bucket. The sand, which is lighter in color than soil, will help you see where you've sown the seed. Note that some wildflower seed mixes already contain filler or inert matter that helps you sow the seeds evenly. See the "Beware the meadow-in-a-can promise" sidebar earlier in this chapter.

## Sow the seeds

You'll get the most even coverage with a hand-held seed spreader. Put half the seed/sand mixture in the spreader. Spread the first half of the seed by walking in one direction and then spread the second half crisscross to the first direction. This pattern ensures even coverage. Learn more about sowing seeds in Chapter 8.

## Press the seeds into the soil

This step ensures the seeds make good contact with the soil, so they don't blow away and they have good access to soil moisture. The easiest way to press the seeds into the soil is with a water-filled lawn roller, which is a big, empty cylinder that you fill with water for added weight. You can buy one or rent one at a rental center. Many species of wildflowers need light to germinate, so you there's no need to apply mulch, or just apply a very thin (⅛ inch) scattering of straw or compost.

## Water the planting area

After sowing the seeds, give the entire area a gentle soaking with a sprinkler, applying water slowly so you don't wash away the seeds, erode the soil, or create puddles. (If you're sowing seeds in fall in a cold-winter region, you don't need to water the seeds after planting, because the seeds will stay dormant and won't begin to grow until spring.)

Water as needed to keep the top inch or so of the seedbed moist until seeds germinate (in hot, windy weather, you may need to lightly water the seedbed daily). Continue to water regularly until the seedlings are about 8 inches high. After that, depending on your climate and weather, your wildflowers may only need watering during extended dry spells.

## Keep the area weeded

If you removed all existing weeds and grasses prior to sowing, your weeding chores should be minimal. Because meadow seed mixes usually contain a dozen or more species, it's difficult to distinguish sprouting weeds from flowers, and walking on the area can crush delicate seedlings. That's why preparing the area thoroughly prior to planting is so important.

## Watch your meadow grow

Depending on the species you've sown, you will likely start to see flowers in as little as eight weeks after sowing. Fast-growing annual flowers will be the first to fill in and bloom. Some perennials will bloom in their first season, but they'll really take off in the second and subsequent seasons.

# 6

# The Part of Tens

**IN THIS PART . . .**

Get an overview of some of the most environmentally friendly ways to design and maintain lawns and landscapes.

Discover sustainable landscape features that might find the perfect home in your yard.

Explore ways to reduce water usage, collect rainwater, and nurture pollinators and wildlife.

Chapter **22**

# Ten Eco-Friendly Lawn Care Practices

Lawns offers numerous environmental benefits. Like all plants, grass absorbs carbon dioxide from the air and gives back fresh oxygen. Lawns allow rain-water to permeate the soil rather than running off into storm drains, like it does when it lands on pavement. Grass plants have deep, fibrous root systems that hold soil in place and decrease erosion.

That said, lawns that are manicured to perfection are significant consumers of limited resources, such as water and fertilizers. In addition, improper application and overuse of the insecticides, herbicides, and fungicides can cause significant harm to the environment.

The way we design and care for our landscape has a direct effect on the health of the surrounding ecosystem. This chapter covers ten ways to make your lawn and landscape more eco-friendly.

# Choose the Right Turfgrass

One of the biggest factors in choosing a type of lawn grass is its adaptability to cold and heat. Lawn grasses can be divided into two types: cool-season and warm-season. Plant the wrong kind and your lawn will struggle, if it survives at all.

Generally, cool-season grasses are best suited for moist, northern climates, where summers, although warm, are relatively short, and winters are cold. If you plant cool-season grasses in a hot, dry climate, you'll need to irrigate them frequently just to keep them alive. In contrast, warm-season grasses are the grasses of southern climates, where summers are long and hot (consistently over 85°F), and winters are relatively mild. They're more able to withstand the heat, and some can go dormant during periods of drought, resuming growth when the rain returns. Learn more about lawn climates in Chapter 2. Cool-season grasses are covered in Chapter 4, and warm-season grasses in Chapter 5.

Another factor to consider is the level of sunlight. Most turfgrasses prefer full sun; some tolerate light shade. No lawn grass thrives in full shade. For shady spots, consider alternatives, such as ground covers (see Chapter 19). Many ground covers require little to no irrigation, minimal fertilizing, and watering can be done with water-thrifty drip irrigation.

# Nurture Soil Health

Just like the plants in your flower or vegetable garden, your lawn needs healthy soil to flourish. The way you treat your soil has a huge effect on how well it can support a lush, green lawn. Healthy soil supports an astonishing array of subterranean organisms that together form a dynamic soil ecosystem that supports plant growth. You can nurture that ecosystem by using slow-release fertilizers, avoiding or minimizing synthetic pesticides and herbicides, and topdressing your lawn with organic matter, such as compost. Visit Chapter 6 to learn about soil tests, adjusting soil pH with limestone or sulfur, and other ways to boost the health of your soil.

# Use Slow-Release Fertilizers

Fertilizing properly helps your lawn grow into a healthy, lush carpet of green. But there are more benefits to fertilizing than just keeping a lawn looking good. Proper fertilizing makes it more resistant to insects and disease, helps keep weeds at bay, and makes it more resilient.

**WARNING**

Quick-release forms of nitrogen provide fast green-up, but that lush growth can be susceptible to insect and disease problems. Also, quick-release fertilizers can disrupt the soil ecosystem.

Slow-release fertilizers don't act as quickly, but provide more consistent, sustained growth, and they are friendlier to soil life. Most organic fertilizers require the presence of soil microbes to break them down into forms plants can use. This provides a slow, sustained release of nutrients and contributes to the overall health of the soil ecosystem. In essence, you feed the soil, and the soil feeds the plants. Organic fertilizers usually contain a wide range of nutrients, including micronutrients. Learn more about slow-release fertilizers in Chapter 12.

# Irrigate Properly to Conserve Water

Ensuring your lawn has enough water — but not too much — is the most important aspect of caring for your lawn. However, watering your lawn is more than just making sure that the grass gets enough moisture. Water is a precious resource. Lawns and landscaping account for up to half of the average household's water use, especially in dry summer areas, such as the Southwest.

Building soil health, aerating, dethatching (for some types of turf), and mowing high are good ways to create a water-thrifty lawn. When you do need to irrigate, water deeply but infrequently to encourage deep roots. Water in early morning, applying water slowly to ensure it soaks in rather than running off. Make sure your sprinklers are adjusted to water the lawn, not the sidewalk or road. Check that your irrigation system is in good shape and use a programmable controller, or, better yet, a smart controller that factors in weather and other variables. Learn more about watering in Chapter 11.

# Mow High

Proper mowing is one of the most important practices in keeping your lawn healthy. Specifics, such as how high and how often you mow, and what you do with the clippings, influence the amount of water and fertilizer your lawn will need and how serious insect, disease, and weed problems become.

For the healthiest, most water-thrifty lawn, mow at the upper end of the appropriate mowing height range for your species of turfgrass (see Chapter 13). By allowing grasses to grow to the high end of the range, they'll have more leaf surface (and therefore more capacity for photosynthesis) and they'll develop deeper roots. These create a thicker, denser turf that helps keep weeds at bay. Taller grass also shades the soil, keeping it cooler and conserving moisture, both of which reduce irrigation needs.

# Leave Clippings on the Lawn

As long as you mow often enough to remove no more than one third of the grass blade, the easiest thing to do is just to leave the grass clippings on the lawn. The pieces break down quickly, and the nutrients they release reduce the amount of fertilizer you have to use by as much as 25 percent. Leaving clippings on the lawn doesn't cause thatch to build up. A mulching mower chops the grass into small pieces that scatter evenly and decompose quickly. Learn more about lawn clippings in Chapter 13.

# Use Integrated Pest Management Techniques

Spraying pesticides at the first sign of a pest might be satisfying in the moment, but the long-term effects of this approach can be harmful. Overuse of pesticides not only wastes money, but it can also hurt beneficial organisms like butterflies and bees, pollute water resources, and expose you, your family, and your pets to unnecessary toxins. Integrated pest management (IPM) describes a commonsense approach to keeping plants healthy. IPM outlines logical steps with a focus on long-term pest and disease prevention, but it also offers options for dealing with infestations. Learn about IPM and eco-friendly pest and disease controls in Chapters 16 and 17.

# Aerate and Dethatch

Years of walking on a lawn or driving heavy equipment on it during construction can compact soil, smashing the particles tightly together, forcing all the air out, and causing water to puddle on the surface. Eventually, the grass declines because the roots don't get the air and water they need. You can loosen compacted and clay soils by aerating them, which is a process of removing small plugs of soil all over your lawn. This opens up pathways for air, water, compost, and fertilizer to get into the soil where roots can access them.

Aerating your lawn also helps control thatch, which is a layer of stems and surface roots that can form between grass blades and the soil line. (A thick layer of thatch prevents water from reaching the soil and can inhibit root formation on warm-season grasses.) Aerating improves the habitat for the soil microorganisms that break down organic matter, including thatch. Aerating thatch-prone grasses annually is one of the best things you can do to both prevent thatch buildup and control it when it starts to build up. If you have thatch buildup that's thicker than 1/2 inch, you need to address it. Dethatching involves using a machine that rakes through the thatch with knife-like blades. For warm-season turfgrasses such as St. Augustinegrass and centipedegrass, a verticutting machine is preferable to a dethatching machine. Learn more in Chapter 14.

## Make the Most of Fall Leaves

Fallen leaves are a source of organic matter and plant nutrients. If the leaves are dry and not too thick or heavy, a mulching mower should be able to chop them into fine enough pieces so that they filter down harmlessly into the lawn, where they'll quickly decompose (find more on this in Chapter 13).

That said, a thick layer of leaves can smother a lawn, preventing light from reaching the grass. You might be able to mow over them and collect them in the grass collector of your lawn mower. Empty the grass collector into your compost pile. Or you can rake the leaves and pile them near your compost bin and use them as the dry/brown layer (see Chapter 6 for composting tips).

Wet leaves are especially problematic because they can form a slimy cover that limits air movement to the turf. In this case, you'll probably need to rake them up and collect them. Pile them in an out-of-the-way place to decompose.

## Replace Unused Lawn Areas with Alternatives

How much lawn do you need and want? Lawns are usually one of the most labor-intensive parts of a landscape. You need to mow, water, fertilize, and more. The average size lot in the United States is about 14,000 square feet, or 1/3 acre. For most homes, much of that lot is in lawn, and that's far more than the average family will use. What activities do you realistically need lawn space for?

According to the National Wildlife Federation, lawns consume a mindboggling 9 billion gallons of water per day. In return, most lawns offer little in the way of food or habitat for birds, pollinators, and other wildlife. Creating a landscape that serves all life forms — human and wild — starts by envisioning your yard as part of the larger ecosystem.

Consider converting some of your lawn to a rain garden, pollinator garden, or wildflower meadow. This doesn't require sacrificing your patch of green lawn. Instead, it invites you to consider how you define your ideal landscape. Find lawn alternatives in Chapter 19 and consider incorporating some of the sustainable landscape features described in Chapter 23.

Chapter **23**

# Ten Sustainable Landscape Features

ncorporating sustainable landscape features benefits you as well as the environment. Sustainable features are designed to reduce the impact your yard has on the ecosystem. Some features do so by reducing inputs, such as water and fertilizer. Others prevent pollution or reduce waste. And still others create a welcoming habitat for wildlife. Here are ten landscape features that will increase the sustainability of your landscape.

## Rain Gardens

Water that runs off landscapes and into streets ends up traveling down storm drains, where is it not only wasted, but it can also overwhelm sewer systems. Water that washes from lawn areas often contains fertilizers and pesticides that pollute waterways, too. Rain gardens are a good way to conserve water and reduce pollution. They're planted in low-lying areas where water naturally collects, so the soil can slowly absorb it and recharge the groundwater. As water passes through the soil, it gets filtered and many of the pollutants are removed.

If you have a low spot where water collects after a rainstorm, it might be the ideal location for a rain garden. Or, if you have a sloped areas where water runs off into the street or into storm drains, you might be able to modify the grade of your land to direct water to a low spot you create. Then, you can plant the area with water-tolerant plants, including those native to your region that will provide food and habitat for pollinators and other wildlife.

This University of Massachusetts Cooperative Extension website has additional information about designing and installing a rain garden:

www.umass.edu/agriculture-food-environment/landscape/fact-sheets/rain-gardens-way-to-improve-water-quality

# Xeriscapes

*Xeriscaping* (pronounced ZARE-eh-scape-ing or ZEER-eh-scape-ing) refers to a style of landscaping that is focused on water conservation and reducing the need for irrigation while still maintaining an attractive landscape. The term was coined in 1981 by the Denver Water Department, Denver, Colorado, like many arid and semiarid areas of the western United States, doesn't receive enough natural rainfall to support lush lawns.

Xeriscaping offers alternatives, such as replacing thirsty turfgrass with drought-tolerant plants — especially native plants that are well-adapted to the local climate and support your region's wildlife. Some municipalities even offer rebates and other incentive for replacing lawns with less water-intensive landscape options.

The Denver Water website has more information on xeriscaping:

www.denverwater.org/residential/rebates-and-conservation-tips/remodel-your-yard/xeriscape-plans

# Pollinator Gardens

The plight of pollinators continues to make headlines, with good reason. About one out of every three bites of the food we eat depends on pollinators, so protecting them is of utmost importance. Pollinators are critical to the ecosystem, too. Many plants rely on pollinators to move pollen between flowers, facilitating fertilization so the plants can produce the seeds that will grow into the next generation of plants.

When choosing plants for your pollinator garden, look for plants that are native to your region. Choose flowers in a range of shapes and colors that bloom over the entire growing season. Be sure to include host plants for the larval stages, such as milkweed for monarch caterpillars. Include flowering trees and shrubs to provide additional food sources and habitat.

Other ways to support pollinators include replacing some of your lawn with wildflowers and reducing your use of lawn chemicals. Learn more about these in Part 4 and Chapter 20.

These organizations have information about creating pollinator-friendly gardens:

>> Pollinator Partnership: www.pollinator.org/learning-center/gardens

>> Xerces Society: https://xerces.org/pollinator-conservation/pollinator-friendly-plant-lists

# Permeable Surfaces

Some materials used for paving walkways and patios, such as asphalt and concrete, are impermeable; water runs off them into streets and storm drains, leading to erosion and polluting waterways. Where it's feasible, using permeable surfaces, such as those made from crushed stone or decomposed granite, is an eco-friendly alternative because they allow water to soak in. Flagstones set into a bed of these materials also allow water to infiltrate.

# Rainwater-Harvesting Systems

By collecting and storing rainwater for later use in your landscape, you'll make good use of this precious natural resource and reduce your water bill. Rain barrels that collect roof runoff are a simple way to get started. You can also create swales in your landscape that direct water toward garden areas. More complex systems collect water in underground cisterns. Some states, especially in arid regions, regulate how rainwater can be collected, so check local regulations before incorporating any rainwater-harvesting features in your landscape.

# Permaculture Plantings

Permaculture is a design philosophy that focuses on sustainable ways of living. In the home landscape, it often takes the form of edible landscaping. By replacing some or all of a conventional landscape with carefully designed gardens of food plants, you can have a beautiful landscape that's bountiful, too. Permaculture plantings often include not only vegetable and herb gardens, but also woody plants like fruit trees and berry bushes.

# Outdoor Lighting That Minimizes Light Pollution

Many animals depend on the daily cycle of light and dark to regulate their activities, including feeding, hunting, sleeping, and migration. The bright, artificial lights we use in our landscapes can disrupt these activities. We can reduce the harmful effects of this light pollution by reducing the amount of landscape lighting we use, directing light so it falls only where it's needed, and choosing "dark sky-friendly" lighting. Learn more at DarkSky International: https://darksky.org.

# Terraced Gardens

Steeply sloped areas are prone to erosion because rainwater rushes off, often taking topsoil with it. Terraces break up slopes into smaller, flatter, steplike sections that catch water, allowing it to soak the ground rather than running off. You can use concrete blocks, lumber, rocks, or similar materials to create the barriers that hold soil in place. Terraced areas can be planted with ground covers, annual and perennial flowers, or vegetables and herbs. As an added benefit, you'll no longer need to mow the grass on that steep slope.

# Native Plant Gardens

Native plants are plants that grow naturally in a region in which they evolved. Not only are they well-suited to thrive in the climate and soil conditions, but they also support native insects, birds, and other wildlife. Many native plants also need less maintenance than nonnative plants that might, for example, need protection from winter's chill. Native plants are less likely to become invasive and overrun natural areas. Your state's department of natural resources and local native plant society are good sources of information about plants that are native to your region.

# Leaving Some Areas Wild

In contrast to highly manicured, intensively maintained landscapes, areas left "untidy" offer food and habitat for native wildlife. A pile of branches and twigs provides a place for insects, birds, and small mammals to find shelter from inclement weather and protection from predators. Leaving flower stalks and seedheads on perennials, rather than cutting them back in fall, provides winter food for birds and overwintering sites for beneficial insects. Leaf litter left on the ground decomposes, enriching soil.

A beetle bank is a mound of soil planted with bunching grasses and/or perennial plants that provides habitat for beneficial insects which can, in turn, help keep pest insects in check and reduce the need for insecticide sprays.

# Index

battery-powered core aerators, 193

battery-powered electric mowers, 173

  area mowed, 176

  capacity, 176

  cutting swath, 177

  run time, 176

  versatility, 176

  voltage, 176

bearberry (*Arctostaphylos uva-ursi*), 291

*Beauveria bassiana*, 243

Bee City USA, 326–327

bee lawn, 293–294

  establishment of, 296

  plants, 294–295

beetle bank, 343

bentgrasses, 40–41

berkeley sedge (*Carex tumulicola*), 286

bermudagrass, 20, 23, 30, 31, 33, 49–50, 117, 119, 132, 209, 219–220

*Betula* spp.

  *nigra*, 318

  *papyrifera*, 306, 318

  *pendula*, 318

big diggers, in lawn, 264

  armadillos, 265

  raccoons, 265–266

  skunks, 265

bigleaf periwinkle/greater periwinkle (*Vinca major*), 291

billbugs, 241–242

biological controls, of insect, 236

birch (*Betula* spp.), 318

black gold, 67

black locust (*Robinia pseudoacacia*), 310

blue grama, 324

  warm-season native grasses, 52

blue star creeper (*Laurentia fluviatilis*), 287

board or piece of plywood, 109, 111, *112*

Bobcat, 78

botanical insecticides, 237

*Bouteloua* spp.

  *dactyloides*, 324

  *gracilis*, 52, 324

Bradford pear (*Pyrus calleryana*), 307

broadcast

  spreaders, 100, 164, 168

  sprigging (*see* stolonizing)

broadleaf

  herbicides, 296

  plantain (*Plantago major*), 210, 220

  weeds, 207–208

broad-spectrum herbicides, 79, 214

brown

  materials, 69

  patch, 254–255

*Buchloe dactyloides*, 52

buffalograss, 30, 33, 324

  warm-season native grasses, 52–53

bugleweed (*Ajuga reptans*), 290

bulk compost, 67

bulldozing, 78

bunching grasses, 30

burclover, 220–221

bygone days, 301

# C

*Calyptocarpus vialis*, 286

"can test" method, 142–143

capric and caprylic acid, 80

  in organic herbicides, 217

*Carex tumulicola*, 286

Carolina silverbell (*Halesia carolina*), 319

carpet bugle/bugleweed (*Ajuga reptans*), 290

centipedegrass, 23, 50–51

Central Southeast zone, 22–23

*Cercis canadensis*, 308, 318

*Chamaemelum nobile*, 286

chamomile (*Chamaemelum nobile*), 286

chewings fescue, 37, 38

chinaberry tree (*Melia azedarach*), 310

chinch bugs, 242–243

Chinese pistache (*Pistachia chinensis*), 320

*Chionanthus virginicus*, 318

chlorophyll, 149

christmas fern (*Polystichum acrostichoides*), 293

# About the Author

**Suzanne DeJohn** delights in spending time in her gardens and in the surrounding woods at her home in Williston, Vermont. Her fascination with plants combines a curiosity about the natural world with a passion for the science that explains what she sees. Suzanne believes that, as gardeners, we are most successful when we take our cues from nature and follow the principles that govern healthy ecosystems. Her background includes a B.S. in geology from Tufts and university coursework in botany, soils, and plant pathology.

Suzanne has been writing about botany and gardening for more than 25 years for a variety of horticulture-related publications, companies, nonprofits, and educational organizations, and she has revised and updated *Organic Gardening For Dummies*, *Herb Gardening For Dummies*, and *Container Gardening For Dummies*.

# Author's Acknowledgment

Suzanne would like to thank Lance Walheim for his incredible work on the first edition of this book. It was an honor and pleasure to update a book that was so filled with useful information. A big thank you goes to technical editor Skip Richter for scrutinizing the content and offering his expertise on ways to improve it. Skip served as a county horticulturist with Texas AgriLife Extension for 34 years, advising home gardeners and commercial producers on research-based horticultural practices. His *Gardening with Skip* website includes resources for growing gardens and lawns in Texas. A round of applause goes to Charlotte Kughen, the project editor at Wiley whose insights greatly improved the organization, clarity, and usability of the book.

Appreciation also goes to the following for their input on various chapters: Mike Hills, technical agronomist at DLF North America; Ken Johnson, DPM, horticulture educator, University of Illinois Extension; Edward Nangle, PhD, associate professor of Turfgrass Science, Ohio State University ATI; and Douglas S. Richmond, PhD, professor and extension specialist, Department of Entomology, Purdue University. Additional thanks go to Giovanni Daniels and Logan Lanfear from United Ag and Turf for help with the section on mowers.

A big thank you to Dave Whitinger and the National Gardening Association for the opportunity to work on another gardening-related Dummies book. And, last but not least, this book wouldn't have been possible without the loving support of my partner, Michael Casarico, whose wisdom, patience, and generosity inspire me every day.

## Publisher's Acknowledgments

**Executive Editor:** Steve Hayes

**Senior Managing Editor:** Kristie Pyles

**Project Editor:** Charlotte Kughen

**Technical Editor:** Skip Richter

**Production Editor:** Tamilmani Varadharaj

**Cover Image:** © komuna photo/Shutterstock